The Evolution of the United Nations System

The Evolution of the United Nations System

Third Edition

Amos Yoder
Research Associate
Mershon Center
Ohio State University
Columbus, Ohio

Taylor & Francis
Publishers since 1798

Taylor & Francis
1101 Vermont Avenue, NW, Suite 200
Washington, DC 20005-3521
Tel: (202) 289-2174
Fax: (202) 289-3665

Distribution Center:

Taylor & Francis
1900 Frost Road, Suite 101
Bristol, PA 19007-1598
Tel: (215) 785-5800
Fax: (215) 785-5515

UK

Taylor & Francis Ltd.
1 Gunpowder Square
London EC4A 3DE
Tel: 0171 583 0490
Fax: 0171 583 0581

THE EVOLUTION OF THE UNITED NATIONS SYSTEM, Third Edition

1 2 3 4 5 6 7 8 9 0   B R B R   9 8 7 6

This book was set in Times Roman by Sandra F. Watts. The editors were Christine Williams and Christine Winter. Cover design by Michelle Fleitz. Printing and binding by Braun-Brumfield, Inc.

A CIP catalog record for this book is available from the British Library.
∞ The paper in this publication meets the requirements of the ANSI Standard Z39.48-1984 (Permanence of Paper)

Library of Congress Cataloging-in-Publication Data

Yoder, Amos.
    The evolution of the United Nations system / Amos Yoder. —3rd ed.
        p. cm.
    Includes bibliographical references and index.

    1. United Nations. 2. International agencies. 3. Security, International. I. Title.
    JX1977.Y6 1996
    341.23—dc20   96-25063
                                                                    CIP

ISBN 1-56032-545-3 (case)
ISBN 1-56032-546-1 (paper)

To Janet, in recognition of her editorial help
and other support that made this edition possible.

Contents

Preface xi

I. Introduction 1

II. The League of Nations Experiment 7
    The Birth of the League 7
    The League Covenant 10
    The League in Action 13
    The League in Retreat 15
        The Manchurian Incident 16
        Italy Attacks Ethiopia 18
    Who Were at Fault? 21

III. The Birth of the United Nations 25
    Drafting the Charter 25
    Major Provisions 29
        Purposes and Principles 29
        The General Assembly 31
        The Security Council 31
    Membership Issues 34

IV. Collective Security Before Detente 39
    The Iranian Confrontation 39
    The Greek Crisis 40
    The Korean War 41
    The Arab-Israeli Wars 48
        The First Arab-Israeli War 49
        The 1956 War 52

The 1967 War 56
The 1973 War 60
War in Lebanon 62
The Congo Operation 64
The Cuban Missile Crisis 66
The India-Pakistan Conflicts 68
Soviet Control of Eastern Europe 72
The Cyprus Wars 73
The Vietnam War 75
Conclusions 79

V. **UN Collective Security in the New Era** 81
The War in Afghanistan 81
The Iran-Iraq War 82
Iraq Attacks Kuwait 83
The War in Yugoslavia 86
Somalia 88
Other African Conflicts 90
Angola 90
Western Sahara 90
Rwandan Civil War 90
Mozambique 92
Cambodia 93
Nicaragua and El Salvador 93
Haiti 94
Georgia 95
Conclusions 96

VI. **Agreements on Limiting Nuclear and Other Arms** 99
Early Efforts at Limiting Arms 100
Agreements to Limit Nuclear Arms 102
Control of Nonnuclear Weapons 114
Conclusions 114

VII. **The United Nations and International Law** 117
The Sources of International Law 119
War and Intervention Under International Law 120
The World Court 124
The Law of the Sea, Genocide, and Other Agreements 127

UN Attempts to Stop International Terrorism 129
    UN Resolutions 130
    ICAO Conventions 131
    Crimes Against Diplomats 132
    Convention on the Taking of Hostages 132
    International Cooperation to Recover Nuclear Materials 133
UN Human Rights 135
Conclusions 138

VIII. Economic and Social Activities of the United Nations 141
    The Economic and Social Council 141
    The Regional Economic Commissions 143
    The UN Development Program (UNDP) 145
    The UN Children's Environment Fund (UNICEF) 149
    Refugee Relief 149
    The UN Environment Program (UNEP) 150
    Population Activities 151
    Drug Abuse Control 152
    UN Conference on Trade and Development (UNCTAD) 153
    UN Monitoring of Transnational Corporations 155
    UN World Conferences 159

IX. The International Monetary Fund, the World Bank,
and Other Specialized Agencies 163
    The International Monetary Fund 163
    The World Bank 167
    The World Debt Crisis 168
    Food and Agricultural Organization 171
    International Fund for Agricultural Development 171
    World Health Organization 172
    International Civil Aviation Organization 172
    Universal Postal Union 173
    International Telecommunications Union 173
    World Meteorological Organization 173
    International Marine Organization 174
    General Agreement on Tariffs and Trade 174
    World Intellectual Property Organization 175
    UN Economic, Social, and Cultural Organization 175
    International Labor Organization 175

UN Industrial Development Organization 176
Nongovernmental Organizations 177
Conclusions 177

X. **Managing the UN System** 179
The Secretary General 179
The UN Debt Crisis 186
The Secretariat 188
The Permanent Missions 190
Conclusion 191

XI. **Achievements, Criticisms, and Prospects**
for the United Nations 195
Peacemaking Achievements Before the New Era 195
The Mideast Wars 196
The Korean War 199
The Congo War 200
The India-Pakistan Wars 201
Other Conflicts 202
Achievements 202
Peacekeeping Achievements in the New Era 203
Soviet Aggression in Afghanistan 203
Iraq's Attacks Against Iran and Kuwait 204
The War in Yugoslavia 206
Somalia 208
Other African Conflicts 209
Economic, Social, and Other Achievements 212
Sources of Criticism of the United Nations 215
Prospects 216

Appendices
A. The Covenant of the League of Nations 221
B. The Charter of the United Nations 233
C. Resolution 242 263
D. A UN Security Council Exercise—Bosnia 265
E. U.S. Contributions to the United Nations
and Specialized Agencies 271
References 275
Index 281

Preface

This book aims to bridge the gap between democratic internationalists and advocates of power politics. Democratic internationalists have used power politics with UN approval and advocates of power politics have used the United Nations to achieve foreign policy goals. The advocates of power politics as well as isolationists have been attacking the United Nations as it has addressed international crises, so it is important to evaluate how the United Nations has used power to support international law and order.

Before World War II democratic internationalists tended to rely on international agreements to deter aggression. This helped to create the impression they were appeasers in the worst sense of the word. We will examine the Axis aggression of the 1930s, which indicates that diplomats as well as the democratic internationalists were appeasers.

After World War II many democratic internationalists had unrealistic hopes of what the United Nations could accomplish, and many were disillusioned when it failed to prevent major wars. Nevertheless, leaders after World War II did use military strength and other coercion within a framework of UN approval and international law to support collective security. The advocates of power politics have failed to recognize those UN successes in addressing world crises.

Until recent years American leaders had avoided requesting approval from the UN Security Council to use force. The United States pledged to support such limits when it ratified the UN Charter as a treaty, but leaders have since lost their vision on how nations can work together to achieve a peaceful world order.

There also has been too little recognition of the work of the UN System in the economic and social realm. As the world grows more interdependent, the UN network of Specialized Agencies has increased the scope of its activities. Their work is seldom reported in the news media, and I hope to provide perspective on their accomplishments.

Since the late 1980s there have been dramatic, positive changes in the attitudes of the two superpowers toward supporting the United Nations. Many observers are hoping this will enable the United Nations to operate more effectively, in the way its founders envisaged.

I would like to call attention to the Security Council exercise described in Appendix D. This type of exercise encourages students to address real problems and shows how difficult it is to get an agreement on a resolution and action, if students accurately represent the position of their country. Students often get hooked on such an exercise and will debate and argue over issues as their counterparts do in the United Nations.

United Nations Headquarters, New York, New York, 1985. (*Courtesy*: UN Photo 165070/Louis Conner)

Chapter I

INTRODUCTION

As the United Nations celebrated its fiftieth anniversary in 1995, the U.S. Congress was mounting the most serious attack on it in the history of the United Nations. Although the United Nations continued to enjoy 70 percent or more support in U.S. public opinion polls, Congress slashed UN appropriations and placed onerous conditions on payments for dues and voluntary contributions. In 1995 the United States was more than $1 billion delinquent in dues for the regular UN budget and the peacekeeping budget. This was about 25 percent of these total budgets.

At the beginning of the 1990s the United Nations had enjoyed a revival of prestige, particularly in the United States. The UN secretary general and his representative had mediated a withdrawal of Soviet forces from Afghanistan, UN mediators had brought about an end to the Iran-Iraq war, and UN peacekeepers had guided Namibia to independence. The UN Security Council in 1990 and 1991 issued ultimatums to Iraq to end its aggression in Kuwait, and when these were ignored, the Security Council authorized the United States to lead a UN coalition to force Iraq to withdraw. Iraq was defeated by this coalition in a short, decisive war. Later, UN inspectors under the Security Council forced Iraq to destroy tens of thousands of chemical weapons and major nuclear facilities. Pundits commented that the United Nations was functioning then as its founders had intended. Yet U.S. support was not firm, and the United Nations did not regain the prestige that it had at the close of World War II.

Critics and supporters of the United Nations had divided along two lines of arguments. Before 1988 the power brokers derided the United Nations for its weakness. Criticisms in the U.S. news media were widespread. The United States had ignored the condemnation of the International Court of Justice for supporting attacks against the government of Nicaragua. The Soviet Union had violated the UN Charter and ignored its resolutions by suppressing dissent in Eastern Europe and by invading Afghanistan.

Academics who supported the United Nations noted that the world is becoming interdependent and that countries are relying more and more on international organizations for economic and social services. David Mitrany called this "functionalism." This theory implies that as the world becomes more interdependent and people depend more on organizations involving other countries, this will spill over into the political field and increase the activities and influence of international organizations such as the United Nations. This would act as a self-reinforcing process. Internationalist supporters of this view asserted that if the world is to avoid wars and a nuclear holocaust, governments should promote respect for the United Nations and international law. However, they seldom cited in their arguments the effectiveness of the United Nations in addressing crises of the 1980s, but instead blamed the superpowers for failing to support it.

Because the UN Charter was based on the League of Nations Covenant, we review the League's successes and failures. The review of its history notes the contests between internationalist delegates at the League and the power brokers outside the League, who undermined its initial actions against aggressors. This helps us understand the Soviets' and the United States' support after World War II to strengthen the UN Charter as a system for collective security. However, in the decades that followed U.S. government support for the United Nations weakened, only to be revived in the 1990s. We will follow the ups and downs and then peer into the future.

A major focus of the book is on the importance of the United Nations and the relevance of international law in addressing problems of war and peace. This includes analyzing the network of nuclear arms agreements, many of which were sponsored by the United Nations. The book also reviews economic and social activities of the UN System, emphasizing the operations of the International Monetary Fund and the International Bank, also known as the World Bank.

The long sentences of the preamble of the League of Nations Covenant and of the UN Charter state that their founders are determined to prevent war and respect international law. It is revealing briefly also to examine the sources of international law. The UN Charter also added an affirmation of a belief in human rights, which are also addressed in international law.

One of the most influential writers on such matters was Hugo Grotius, whom many point to as the father of international law. Grotius was a lawyer, diplomat, and theologian of the 17th century, who wrote the classic treatise concerning the law of war and peace. He wrote it in jail after he was imprisoned for trying to mediate in the Thirty Years War. In this work he tried to set forth the rules by which states should be governed, deriving these rules from natural law and reason and the consent of nations as set forth by philosophers and other writers.

The fundamental principle of his writings was that the sovereignty of states should be respected. His aim was to mitigate the horrors of war by international law, whether it was derived from nature, divine command, or custom and compact.[1]

Subsequent international lawyers built on these foundations, and many scholars followed with their learned works. Their writings have been of practical importance, not only in settling disputes between individuals in domestic courts but also in settling disputes among nations. It is estimated that between 1816 and 1900 about 200 disputes and differences between states were submitted to arbitration, and in the vast majority of these cases the awards of the arbitrator were accepted.[2]

This idea of settling disputes by international law was further developed in world conferences before World War I. The First Hague Conference in 1899 was called by the tsar of Russia with the aim of establishing peace and ending the arms race. This world conference failed to limit armaments, but with the help of the Interparliamentary Union and the International Law Association the conference adopted a convention committing signatories to use mediation in international disputes "as far as circumstances allow" and to establish the Permanent Court of Arbitration at the Hague. This institution was neither permanent nor a court, but it consisted of panels of arbitrators from states who would be called on to settle disputes.

The tsar called the Second Hague Conference eight years later in 1907 with 44 nations attending. Ominously, the major efforts of the delegates were to elaborate the laws of war. This conference made no further progress in getting a permanent international court or getting states to make a permanent commitment to arbitration, but it did call for another conference in eight years with a preparatory committee to be established two years in advance to prepare proposals for settling international disputes. World War I, of course, intervened to prevent the third conference.

The above moves toward establishing an international system to prevent war had been reinforced during the previous century by a growth of international organizations in the economic and social fields, which Mitrany would call functionalism. The revolutionary growth of technology in commerce brought about by the industrial revolution stimulated the growth of these organizations. By 1914 there were more than 30 including the Danube Commission (1856), the International Telegraphic Union (1865), the Universal Postal Union (1874), the International Health Office in Paris (1907), and others. Along with these were a number of influential nongovernmental organizations such as the International Law Association and the Interparliamentary Union mentioned above.

Although the Hague Conference and these organizations were devoted to the

idea of promoting international organization and international peace, they failed
to prevent the catastrophic first world war. Out of this catastrophe came a determination of world leaders to create a stronger international institution devoted to
preventing war. By the close of the war there was overwhelming popular support for the League of Nations.

Some writers have suggested that the Concert of Europe of a previous century was an ancestor of the League of Nations. The Concert was a meeting of
the great powers to divide up colonies, territories, and spheres of interest on the
basis of power factors rather than on the basis of international law and democratic procedures as reflected in the League Covenant and the UN Charter.
During the 19th century the great powers in the Concert meetings partitioned
Asia and Africa, while Chancellor Bismarck acted to prevent the building of
alliances that would threaten the new German nation. Bismarck was so skillful
in the use of power politics, including three international wars to unify Germany
from a group of more than 200 small states, that many diplomats tried to follow
his example rather than be guided by international law. Many internationalists
would say that the Concert of Europe—which lacked a secretariat and rules of
conduct—was the opposite of an international organization trying to work within
the limits of international law.[3]

The Concert of Europe was so weak by 1914 that Lord Edward Grey, the
British foreign minister, was not able to convene it to try to head off World War
I. It was this failure that led to his determination and the determination of others
to establish the League of Nations as a permanent institution that at least could
call a meeting of major powers on short notice to try to prevent war. We will
see in the next chapter how the power brokers and the democratic internationalists came together to agree on the League of Nations Covenant.

The Soviet Union at first was excluded from the League of Nations. Later,
the Soviet Union was admitted, but after a decade it became disillusioned. The
Soviets' historic suspicion of the United Nations is relatively easy to understand. Its Marxist-Leninist philosophy, growing out of its materialistic revolutionary origin, held that international politics reflect attempts of capitalist states
to dominate the world. The doctrine supported revolution and the use of military
and political means to oppose capitalist imperialism. In this view, the League of
Nations and the United Nations would be useful only as they contributed to the
defense of the Soviet Union and to communism's historic struggles. This suspicion was reinforced by the historic failure of the League of Nations to oppose
Hitler's aggression and the Soviet belief that the West tried to turn Hitler against
the Soviet Union before World War II.

During World War II Stalin decided to support the idea of the United
Nations, with the aim of maintaining the wartime alliance to prevent a resur-

gence of Germany and to prevent the capitalist nations from ganging up on the Soviets.[4] However, the Western nations tended to dominate the United Nations, and until 1988 the Soviets contributed a minimum to it because it was of little use in achieving the aims of Soviet foreign policy.

The split in U.S. views is harder to understand. After World War I there was a strong isolationist faction opposing the League. Much of the original support for the League of Nations had come from President Woodrow Wilson. Later, much of the support for the United Nations came from democratic internationalists like U.S. Secretary of State Cordell Hull and President Harry Truman.[5] After World War II there was consistently strong support in public opinion polls for the United Nations, but isolationist and unilateralist opposition to it reached a peak in the Republican Congress during the Clinton Administration, although the polls continued to support the United Nations.

The underlying hypotheses that I will examine in trying to explain the various fortunes of the UN System are the following: (1) Strong leaders such as President Truman and President Eisenhower had a vision of creating a world order based on respect for international law and the UN Charter. These democratic internationalists were able successfully to work with other nations in the United Nations on important world crises. (2) The United Nations, as was the League, is not an independent power that can be blamed or praised for actions in international affairs. At the present state of international development, nationalism commands the actions of states. The United Nations is mainly a forum and an instrument that depends on the support of its members, particularly the powerful United States. (3) Reporting on the United Nations has been unfavorably distorted, particularly in the United States. There is a natural bias of the news media to report the dramatic, bad news rather than the relatively dull news of constructive action in the UN System. Power politics always gets the headlines. The day-to-day constructive operation of the UN's family of agencies in the fields of international finance, development, health, and many other fields receives virtually no attention in the news media. This book will assess these activities with a more balanced perspective. (4) The current view of the lack of importance of the United Nations has been transferred back in history as if the United Nations never was of much importance. Yet, following World War II, the United Nations was regarded by many as man's best hope for peace, and it was used to settle important conflicts. The distortions of looking backward from a current perspective have also created negative perceptions of the League of Nations in the 1920s, and those observers remember only that nations in the 1930s under the League failed to rally against the fascist aggressors.

First, I examine how the United Nations evolved from the experience of the League of Nations. I will then analyze how the United Nations moved from center stage in preserving peace after World War II to a less important role in international crises. Next is a look at the important but underestimated network of agreements to control nuclear weapons, many of which originated in the United Nations. I will also look at the recent revival of the United Nations in security matters and its growing importance in economic and social affairs. The book concludes with an evaluation of the potential for the UN System to help solve the many problems of a troubled world.

Notes to Chapter 1

1. A. Campbell, *The Rights of War and Peace* (Washington, DC: M. Walter Dunne, 1981). Chapter 1.

2. F. P. Walters, *A History of the League of Nations* (London: Oxford University Press, 1952). Vol. I, p. 9.

3. F. S. Northedge, *The League of Nations* (New York: Holms and Meier, 1986), pp. 9–10.

4. J. Stalin, *The Great Patriotic War* (Moscow: Novosty Press Agency Publishing House, 1945).

5. The term "democratic internationalist" is used for those who want to promote a world order under the United Nations and international law. It also implies support for human rights as set forth in UN covenants and conventions. There are other "internationalists" who would use the United Nations to achieve foreign policy goals, but who would not want to be bound by having to get the approval of the UN Security Council for forceful actions. This type of internationalism exists in the U.S. Congress, which has cut the budgets and tried to limit activities of the United Nations.

Chapter II

THE LEAGUE OF NATIONS EXPERIMENT

THE BIRTH OF THE LEAGUE

After World War I, the democratic internationalists favoring international coop-eration and the power brokers of Europe cooperated to form the League of Nations. President Woodrow Wilson took the lead in proposing a framework for collective security, arbitration of disputes, and limitation of armaments—ideas that had been expressed in the Hague conferences. The victims of the war, who wanted to ensure that Germany would not again threaten the peace, joined in support of the League of Nations. The French, particularly, were determined to use the League to exact reparations from Germany and disarm the foe that had warred against them twice in the lifetime of many French leaders. Support-ers included members of many international organizations that were cooperating in the fields of mail, electronic communications, health, and other areas. Finally, many diplomats supported the idea of a league to maintain peace. Lord Grey, the British foreign minister who had vainly tried to call the leaders of Europe together to prevent World War I in 1914, was determined that after the war there should be a system where such a conference could readily be called.

Lord Grey, Prime Minister Lloyd George, and some of the leading dip-lomats, as well as historians who later examined the records of World War I, were convinced that the war could have been avoided by a conference of the powers.[1] The Serbian government did not support the assassination by Serb nationalists that triggered the war. Austria-Hungary, however, attacked Serbia in order to punish it to prevent that kind of terrorism from happening again—Austria-Hungary was not trying to conquer Serbia. Germany gave a "blank check" of support to Austria-Hungary mainly to reinforce Austria-Hungary as its only reliable ally. Germany did not have aggressive designs on Europe then as Hitler did 30 years later. Russia then stumbled into a mobilization to support

Serbia—this mobilization threatened Germany and triggered its attack against France, the major ally of Russia. Russia did not realize how its mobilization appeared to Germany as a threat from both Russia and France. Although during World War I and after, observers accused Germany of aggressive intent, in reality mistakes and poor communication were mostly to blame.[2]

Lord Grey, Sir Robert Cecil, and Woodrow Wilson, strong supporters of the League of Nations, realized how a world organization might have prevented the war. Others such as Clemenceau, the bulldog leader of France, and Lloyd George, the British prime minister, wanted to use the League of Nations to prevent Germany from becoming a threat again. Finally, there was a widespread yearning for peace and for an end to war from the many millions who had lost family and friends in the fight. This idea of a world organization was promoted by the many peace organizations. During the war lawyers and others in the United States and Britain had drafted plans for a world organization that incorporated features that later were incorporated in the League Covenant.

The League to Enforce Peace held its first meeting in Washington, DC, in 1916. Its main speakers were President Wilson, head of the Democrats, and Henry Cabot Lodge, leader of the Republicans in the Senate. Both men that day called for a new international system to maintain peace under a rule of international law. They stated that if necessary the armed forces of the major powers, including those of the United States, should be a full partner in a future league of nations.[3] (By this time the idea of a league of nations had become prevalent.) At this point Wilson was still hoping that the United States would be able to stay out of the war and use its strength and influence to mediate and help bring about a peace.

Ironically, the United States was drawn into World War I by insisting on its rights under international law—that is, the right to supply England with peaceful commerce as long as Germany did not mount an effective blockade by surface ships. The Hague conferences had helped work out these principles. When Germany sank U.S. merchant ships without warning, it triggered outrage in the United States and contributed to the decision by Wilson to ask Congress to declare war on Germany.

This was an agonizing decision for Wilson. He reasoned that he could use the war to "make the world safe for democracy" and establish a system to maintain peace. In his April 2, 1917, address to Congress calling for war against Germany, he said, "We shall fight for the things which we have always carried near our hearts—for democracy . . . for a universal dominion of rights by such a concert of free peoples that shall bring peace and safety to all nations and make the world at last free. To such a task we can dedicate our lives and our fortunes." Wilson spelled out American war aims in the famous Fourteen Points in his address to Congress on January 9, 1918. The following relate to the League of Nations: (1) open covenants, openly arrived at, (2) absolute freedom of navigation of the seas, (3) removal of trade barriers, (4) reduction of armaments, (5) free, open-minded, and impartial adjustment of all colonial claims, and (6) "a general association of nations must be formed . . . for the purpose of affording mutual guarantees of political independence to territories of great and small states alike." After the war Wilson went to the Versailles Peace Conference determined to establish a league of nations to enforce peace.

Wilson was welcomed with enthusiastic parades in Europe, where his Fourteen Points had struck a chord of public approval. He used this public support effectively to press for his views at the peace settlement. He was determined that the League of Nations would be an integral part of the peace settlement, and to his surprise he found no opposition. Wilson's proposal that the League be the first business of the peace conference was adopted, and a commission was appointed to draft the covenant. The president was made chairman of the committee, which included Bourgeois, a French internationalist; Ian Christian Smuts of South Africa; and Sir Robert Cecil of Britain, all supporters of the League idea. The committee included the major powers plus five minor powers—Belgium, Brazil, China, Portugal, and Serbia. The minor powers insisted on additional representation, so Greece, Poland, Czechoslovakia, and Romania were added. An Anglo-American draft worked out by Colonel House and Lord Cecil and incorporating basic ideas of Smuts was used as the basis for drafting the League Covenant. In 11 days the committee came up with the first draft.

What then happened to Wilson's beautiful dream? Why was it rejected by the U.S. Senate, including senators such as Senator Lodge who originally supported the idea? Most historians blame Wilson's bad political tactics. He made the League the major issue of the Democratic congressional campaign in 1918, asking the voters to give the Democrats a strong majority to enable him to speak with authority at the forthcoming peace negotiations. This aroused the violent resentment of the Republican opponents, and Senator Lodge, a former supporter of a league, led the opposition. Wilson's appeal was counterproductive, with the Republicans winning control of both houses. Moreover, Wilson kept his draft of the proposed league secret and only produced it officially at the Peace Conference itself. Wilson did not consult with the Republicans, and at no stage did the draft have the "benefit of criticisms of a clear-headed opposition."[4] As we see later, when President Truman was in a similar position, he consulted fully with Republican congressmen on the UN Charter.

Wilson returned to the United States after a few weeks at the Versailles Conference to defend the Covenant against growing criticism. After returning to

Paris and incorporating in the new draft suggestions by some opponents, he returned again to the United States to sell the idea to the American people. By this time, the strain of the war and the negotiations at Versailles had taken their toll, and Wilson was very ill. During the campaign to sell the League, he had a stroke and returned to Washington a broken man. Colonel House himself was also ill, too ill to testify before the Senate. In November 1919 the treaty was rejected by the Senate and then again in March 1920 by a vote of 49 in favor and 35 against. With the two-thirds constitutional requirement, a vote of 56 would have been required. Actually, by this time the Senate opponents had made such drastic amendments to the treaty that Wilson himself asked supporters to vote against it.

Wilson's last public words on November 11, 1923, were prophetic. He said: "I cannot refrain from saying it: I am not one of those who have the least anxiety about the triumph of the principles I stood for. I've seen fools resist providence before and I've seen their destruction, as will come upon these again—utter destruction. That we shall prevail is as sure as that God reigns."

If he had lived, Wilson would have blamed Hitler's rise to power before World War II on the failure of the United States to support collective security under the League of Nations, and he would have pointed to the formation of the United Nations as a fulfillment of his dream. Critics of Wilson would blame weakness and a reliance on international law instead of strength as the cause of World War II. There is truth in both sets of criticisms.[5]

THE LEAGUE COVENANT

The League of Nations Covenant was put in effect by the other major powers without the United States (see Appendix A). Its major provisions were the following:

1. The preamble emphasizes the aim to achieve international peace, not to resort to war, and to establish international law as a rule of conduct among governments.
2. Major organs of the League were an assembly, council, and permanent Secretariat. The Assembly consisted of representatives of all members of the League; the Council consisted of representatives of members of the principal powers together with nine representatives of other members of the League. The Assembly and the Council had overlapping authority, and a clear line was never drawn on their respective functions.[6]
3. The Assembly decided how the expenses of the League would be shared.

4. The secretary general was appointed by the Council with the approval of a majority of the Assembly.
5. A 1926 amendment to the Covenant called for a vote of two-thirds of the Assembly to elect new members to the League.
6. Article 8 called for the reduction of national armaments and designated the Council to formulate plans for reducing armaments.
7. Article 10 called for members of the League to "respect and preserve as against external aggression the territorial integrity and the existing political independence of all members of the League." It added an escape clause for the Council to advise the means by which this obligation should be fulfilled.
8. Article 18 called on the members of the League to register treaties and international agreements with the League of Nations.
9. Article 24 called for the international bureau to be placed under the direction of the League. (When the United Nations was founded, these international agencies were called Specialized Agencies. They are coordinated by the General Assembly.)

The aims and structure of the League of Nations were used as a model for the United Nations, with modifications by the drafters of the UN Charter to correct the weaknesses of the League Covenant. The Covenant and the Charter share the same stated aim—to achieve international peace and support international law as the rule of conduct among governments. Both the League and the United Nations have an assembly, a council, and a Secretariat. Both the League and the UN Council are primarily concerned with crises and give the big powers a major voice. The assemblies are like a legislature, with every member nation having one vote. The Secretariats arrange the meetings and provide all the services including interpreters and reports in many languages.

The International Court of Justice, established by the League of Nations shortly after it was formed, is an integral part of the UN Charter. Another major UN organ, the Trusteeship Council, corresponds to the Mandates Commission under the League of Nations. Just before World War II, a League committee considered creating a major body for economic and social affairs. This idea was picked up and used in establishing the UN Economic and Social Council, which is the other major organ of the United Nations.

There are, however, important differences between the League and the United Nations. The League of Nations worked by unanimity on all but procedural matters. The politicians of the League managed to get around this by making approval of reports with recommendations a procedural matter, so that the views of the League could not be vetoed by one member. This, of course, did not bind those who disagreed. Another major difference was that the mandates system in Article 22 of the League Covenant called for the well-being and development of colonies and territories as being a "sacred trust." The UN Charter went beyond this in Article 1 calling for friendly relations among nations based on "self-determination" of peoples. Moreover, the UN articles under the chapter on the trusteeships plainly call for the United Nations to promote "progressive development towards self-government or independence." Since World War II these aims have been dramatically carried out by the achievement of independence by over 100 nations. Moreover, paragraph three of Article 1 of the UN Charter calls for promoting and encouraging respect for human rights and for fundamental freedoms without distinction as to race, sex, language, or religion. This was not included in the League Covenant, and the United Nations has been much more of an activist in this regard than the League was.

The League, like the United Nations, coordinated the activities of the "bureaux," which today are called the Specialized Agencies. Some of the major activities of the League of Nations were carried out by special committees and commissions that later became international organizations in their own right, such as the World Health Organization.

Probably the most important difference between the League and the United Nations is that the League Covenant was less flexible than the UN Charter for settling disputes or containing a war. The United Nations is more of a political institution. Articles 15 and 16 of the League Covenant stated that disputes not submitted to arbitration or judicial settlement should be submitted to the Council. If the Council could not settle the dispute, it unanimously or by majority vote should make and publish a report. If there was unanimous agreement on the report, other than the votes of the parties to the dispute, the members of the League would not go to war with any party to the dispute that complied with the recommendations. They then reserved to themselves the right to take such action as they considered necessary for the maintenance of right and justice. If any member of the League resorted to war in disregard of its agreements under this procedure, it should be deemed to have committed an act of war against all other members of the League, which then were required to sever economic and financial relations and other contacts with the guilty state. It was the Council's duty, then, to recommend what armed forces should be used to protect the covenants of the League. The members of the League also agreed to cooperate in the financial and economic measures taken under this article. Under the Covenant these acts would be automatic; under the UN Charter there are almost an infinite number of options for ways to settle disputes. We now look at how the League applied the above provisions.

THE LEAGUE IN ACTION

For 10 years the League of Nations was the center of action for cleaning up the mess left by World War I, but it was not called upon to settle major disputes between the great powers. It helped reconcile Germany and France in the late 1920s, but by the 1930s it did not obtain the support necessary to handle the world economic crises of that decade or to meet the challenges of powerful fascist aggressors.

Let us first list the important successes of the League in the 1920s and then turn to two major crises of the 1930s—Manchuria and Ethiopia—where major powers failed to use the League or other instruments to stop the Axis powers on their way to World War II.

The accomplishments of the League listed below have received little attention from historians, who naturally focus on the tragic events of the 1930s. The first group of important activities arose out of the destruction and disorder of World War I, and the League set up and supported the following activities to alleviate the distress:

1. Fridtjof Nansen of the Red Cross under the authority of the League restored more than 425,000 prisoners of 27 nationalities to their home countries from Russia; these people were without means of subsistence. The League then conferred the title of High Commissioner for Refugees upon Nansen. Although it gave him little additional help, with assistance from private sources his organization helped resettle millions of Russians, Armenians, and Greeks, and alleviated famine.

2. Ludwik Rajchman, a Polish doctor and secretary of the Health Organization of the League, headed the League's Epidemic Commission, which in 1920 prevented the spread of typhus, cholera, and typhoid from Russia and Poland into the rest of Europe.

3. The Health Section of the League's Secretariat under Rajchman also did outstanding work in combating epidemics in the Middle East, Far East, and throughout the world, enlisting support of leading scientific experts. The organization was later transformed into the World Health Organization (WHO).

4. The League's finance committee worked out a plan for loans and reconstruction of Austria, a defeated country, and by 1925 it left Austria with a recovered economy. In 1923 and 1924 another League committee helped rehabilitate Hungarian finances.

The League Council also settled a number of difficult boundary disputes, some of which involved conflicts. It got off to an inauspicious start by allowing

Belgium to keep Eupen and Malmedy, areas disputed by Belgium and Germany, by refusing to challenge Belgium's plebiscite, which allowed its authorities to put pressure on the voters. The League then asserted its authority and settled the following territorial issues:

1. In 1921 League commissioners awarded the Aaland Islands to Finland with guarantees for the Swedish inhabitants.
2. The League Council in 1921 carried out a plebiscite in Silesia and drew a frontier line between Germany and Poland in the area. The Council then established a joint commission that managed relations along the border and settled grievances during the next 15 years.
3. In 1921 the Council with British support helped preserve Albania from being carved up by Yugoslavia, Italy, and Greece.
4. The League successfully administered the Saar until 1935, when it carried out a plebiscite that overwhelmingly indicated that the inhabitants of this rich coal-mining area wanted to return to Germany, and subsequently they were returned.
5. The League helped settle a major dispute between Greece and Italy over the murder of an Italian diplomat and Italy's occupation of the Greek island of Corfu. The Council was reluctant to confront Mussolini, but it eventually overcame the dictator's initial defiance of the League.
6. The Council settled the difficult problem of Memel, which had been turned over to Lithuania by Versailles, by protecting the right of German citizens there. League supervision lasted until Hitler took Memel in 1939.
7. The Locarno Pacts, which established normal international relations between Germany and France in 1925, were tied into the League as the ultimate authority. If the guarantees of those agreements had been honored by the major powers, the German aggression of the 1930s could have been contained.
8. The League Council during the 1920s also settled other frontier disputes, including those between Germany and Poland, Lithuania and Poland, Finland and Russia, Bulgaria and Greece, Bulgaria and Yugoslavia, Hungary and Romania, Hungary and Yugoslavia, Poland and Czechoslovakia, and Turkey and Iraq. In certain of the disputes, such as those between Bulgaria and Greece and between Poland and Lithuania, hostilities broke out and the Council was able to stop them by exerting pressure and offering mediation.

In the above disputes the League did not act like a policeman or judge imposing a solution. Rather it acted as a forum, an investigative body, and as a conciliator or arbitrator, allowing passions to cool and recommending solutions. Although neither side was happy about the solution, they were solutions that both sides could accept.

The League failed to give more than rhetorical support against repression by Turkey of the Armenians in 1920. It did not rewrite the Treaty of Versailles with its harsh territorial provisions that Hitler later exploited. It was saddled with administering entities created by this treaty such as imposing an international administration on the city of Danzig. Hitler demanded the return of Danzig and used this as a pretext for his invasion of Poland, which triggered World War II. The League failed to oppose France in 1922 when French troops occupied the Ruhr in demanding Germany meet reparations payments. The resulting disruption of the German economy laid the basis for the rise of the Nazi party, but it also resulted in a reparations settlement outside the League that permitted a temporary German economic revival until the Great Depression of the 1930s.

In acting as a political body, including avoiding some of the above major international issues, the League disappointed those who hoped it would assert more authority in its role.[7] At the end of the 1920s, however, the League's prestige was high and Geneva was a center of diplomatic action for solving issues other than the demands of radical German parties to again redraw the map of Europe. Prime ministers and heads of state regularly attended the League meetings to discuss major international issues. We now look at the crises of the following decade when the fascist aggressors led by Germany destroyed the League, and when the League's accomplishments were largely forgotten.

THE LEAGUE IN RETREAT

In the second decade of the League's existence, Germany, Japan, and Italy, the Axis powers, surged toward a world empire and World War II, and in the process destroyed the League. After the stock market crash in the fall of 1929, the malaise spread to Europe, and the cycle of debt repudiation, runs on banks, and financial crises grew until in 1931 the world was in the grip of the Great Depression. The economic chaos that followed gave Hitler and the aggressive leaders of Japan the opportunity to take control and lead their governments into World War II. Many economic observers believe that it was the burden of reparations and war debts that was a fundamental cause of the international economic crisis of the 1930s. If the United States had been an active participant in the League's activities, it would have been easier to address the world economic crisis, and action could have been taken more quickly. The world's leaders were not able to cope with the economic and political crises in Europe or with the events in Manchuria, where Japan began aggression that led it to direct confrontation with the United States and the attack on Pearl Harbor.

The Manchurian Incident

In 1928 the Japanese army blew up a train to kill a local Manchurian warlord who would not cooperate with it. The new emperor, the late Hirohito, demanded of Prime Minister General Tanaka that the officers be disciplined. The army refused because it would damage its prestige and its leaders would not take orders from the civil government. At that time, the army showed that it could defy the government, and the emperor was put in his place as a figurehead.

The Japanese military took control of Manchuria in 1931. At that time Manchuria was the industrial heart of China. Russia had dominated it at the beginning of the century, but Japan challenged it and by 1930 had achieved economic dominance. By 1931 Japan's investment in Manchuria of $1.1 billion represented over 80 percent of the total Japanese overseas investments.[8] Japan's colonial ambitions ran head-on into the desire of the new nationalist government of Chiang Kai-shek to reassert control over Chinese territory. His programs of boycotting Japanese goods and of building a railroad competitive to the Japanese rail line stimulated Japanese opposition, particularly among the military.

The boycott hurt because Japanese industry, like others, was suffering from the drop in trade from the Great Depression. There were numerous disputes concerning trade, rights of Japan to settle in China, and functions of Japanese administrators and teachers, but the Japanese military was determined to impose its will without stooping to negotiate these complex issues. The military brought the situation to a head in September 1931 by secretly blowing up a small section of railroad and blaming it on the Chinese. They then moved in to "restore order."

The Japanese prime minister, who opposed the action, was assassinated by a group of nationalistic naval officers on May 15, 1932. The Japanese then set up a puppet emperor ("The Last Emperor" of China) and took over control of what they called the new state of Manchukuo. This was open aggression in defiance of the League.

President Chiang Kai-shek called on the Chinese people to remain calm, and appealed to the League. On September 21, 1931, soon after the news of the attack arrived, the League was distracted by the European financial crisis of Britain going off the gold standard. The Japanese representative on the League Council assured it that Japan wanted to negotiate the issue with China and, backed by pressure from the United States to permit negotiation and not to weaken the position of the Japanese civilian prime minister against the military, the League merely called on both sides to contain the conflict. The Japanese army, however, pressed forward. Over a month later the United States changed its position and called on the League to assert pressure and announced that the American government, acting independently, would reinforce what the League did. On October 16, Prentiss Gilbert, the American consul in Geneva, took a seat at the Council table. Secretary of State Stimson, under attack by the isolationist press, however, withdrew Gilbert from the last meeting of the League sessions.

Meanwhile, Japan was in the grip of war fever with troop trains being surrounded by cheering crowds. The great powers were reluctant to challenge the other great power on the other side of the world. When the Council met again, the Japanese delegate, apparently stalling, proposed an investigation, which was in line with the regular procedures of Article 15 in such a crisis. This proposal was supported by the Chinese delegate.

On December 10 the Council adopted a unanimous resolution to send a League Commission of Inquiry to the Far East. On February 3, 1932, the commission, with Lord Lytton at its head, left for the Far East, but it did not arrive in Manchuria until April, traveling through Japan to Shanghai and then north to Manchuria.

Meanwhile, on January 7, 1932, the United States sent a note to China and Japan, later called the Stimson Doctrine, asserting that the United States would not recognize any situation that would impair American treaty rights or that was brought about by means contrary to the Kellogg Pact of 1929, in which nations had agreed to outlaw war. Stimson was concerned that the attack would cause "incalculable" damage to the structure of international societies provided by postwar treaties.[9] A few weeks later the Council adopted a statement similar to the Stimson Doctrine that refused to recognize Manchukuo. Severe fighting continued with the Chinese troops resisting the Japanese. In March 1932 an armistice was arranged.

At the end of February, Secretary of State Stimson published a letter to Senator Borah of Idaho, which was communicated to the League. Borah was a strong opponent of Japanese aggression in China. The letter suggested that the Assembly adopt the principle of nonrecognition as set forth in the January 7 note. The Assembly accepted the suggestion and also formed a committee, which participated along with the great powers, to arrange the truce between Japan and China. Meanwhile, Japan consolidated its hold on Manchuria.

In September 1932 one year after the Japanese attack, the Lytton Report was finally published. It vindicated the Chinese position. The Council passed the report to the Assembly, which debated it at length. It soon became apparent that the small powers of the Assembly were calling on the great powers to take an action that would involve them in the dispute with Japan. On February 24, 1933, the Assembly adopted the report of its Special Committee affirming that the members would not recognize the new state of Manchukno or do anything to prejudice a settlement consistent with the sovereignty and administrative integrity of China. The Japanese delegation dramatically left the Assembly, and a month later, on March 27, 1933, Japan formally withdrew from the League.

This was the end of "action" by the League on this issue. On May 31, 1933, Chiang Kai-shek accepted an armistice with Japan controlling Manchuria, and for the next four years there was relative peace.

The outcome was not all bad, considering that the major powers were reeling from the Great Depression. Although Japan had taken control of Manchuria, China gained time to prepare for the final showdown, beginning about five years later. Japan was condemned and forced to withdraw from the League. This was painful because it had been a useful and cooperative member before the military took control of policy. It is also noteworthy that the Assembly, which represented the small powers, took a more forthright stand against aggression than the Council, which was dominated by the major powers. But the members of the League had failed to maintain the territorial integrity of one of its members, or impose the sanctions called for in Articles 15 and 16.

China was so far away from Europe, where the League's center of power rested, and Japan's military strength was so dominant in Eastern Asia, that none of the League members seriously considered military or even economic confrontation with Japan.[10]

Italy Attacks Ethiopia

Benito Mussolini, the Italian dictator, made the next attack against the League with a drive to expand a colonial empire. Mussolini was the father of fascism, an extreme nationalistic, totalitarian philosophy that places the welfare of its own state above other values, and particularly above the values of international law that would try to protect the weaker nations. Hitler supported Mussolini until the end, rescuing Mussolini from Italian partisan forces in the final days of World War II.

At the end of the nineteenth century, Britain, France, and Italy had staked out claims around Abyssinia (Ethiopia), with Italy getting the poor and barren areas of Eritrea and Somalia on the northern and southeastern boundaries of Ethiopia. In 1935 all a weak Ethiopia could muster for defense were primitive weapons such as matchlock rifles. By 1933 Mussolini began to plan his attack with the aim of obtaining colonies like other major world powers.[11]

Italy worked out military and intelligence plans to create disorder in Ethiopia, and on December 5, 1934, the opportunity occurred with a clash between the forces of Ethiopia and Italy in a disputed area between Italian Somaliland and the Ogaden province of Ethiopia. Italy had occupied a border area since 1928 claimed by Ethiopia, and the clash occurred between troop units in the area. It was settled by the arrival of a few tanks and airplanes supporting the Italian garrison. The Italians widened the attack and positioned troops to threaten a major Ethiopian military post. Ethiopia brought the matter before the League Council in December 1934 and January 1935.

The Council and the Secretariat looked to London and Paris to take the lead. Although the two powers were bound by a 1906 treaty to maintain the independence of Ethiopia, the natural tendency of the foreign offices was to settle the dispute at the expense of the weak and relatively defenseless Ethiopia. This was a great temptation because Mussolini had originally opposed Hitler's attempt to take control of Austria in 1934, and Britain and France hoped to use Italy to offset the threat of German aggression in central Europe. There is a "painful doubt" that by this time France's foreign minister had promised Italy "a free hand for military action in Ethiopia."[12] The Council stalled while the Ethiopians pressed their case during the next nine months. Meanwhile, the League Assembly met and took up the case.

In June 1935 the results of a "Peace Ballot" of about 12 million British persons were published showing an overwhelming support for League membership and fulfillment of the Covenant's provisions for collective security by economic and military sanctions. This initially stiffened the British policy toward Italy.

During the crisis the Russian representative Litvinov spoke out strongly for the League to uphold the principle of collective security, pointing out that Italian claims that Ethiopia was backward and oppressive were not relevant. Pressures in the Assembly and by outside groups finally had an impact on the Council.

In October 1935, just as the Italian army mounted a major attack, the Council issued a report supporting the Ethiopian case. The report stated in the language of Article 15 of the Covenant that Italy had resorted to war in violation of its pledges under the Covenant. Council President Benes of Czechoslovakia then directed the Assembly's attention to the issue, and after a three-day debate, 50 of the 54 members accepted the report of the Council calling for a ban on exports of key commodities to Italy. Since Albania, Austria, and Hungary did not make the acceptance unanimous, Benes announced that sanctions were up to the decision of the individual members of the League. It then set up a Co-ordination Committee that drew up proposals that could be accepted or rejected by the individual states. It is significant that in this crisis the Assembly over-came the handicap of the unanimity requirement.

Anthony Eden, the British representative, led the debate with proposals to stop additional loans to Italy, already heavily in debt, and to stop imports from Italy. However, agreement could not be reached on stopping exports of oil and other essential commodities. Meanwhile, the conservative government of Britain had just been returned to power after an election in which it received support as a result of its pledges to support the League.

Under the threat of war from Italy, British Foreign Secretary Hoare met with French Foreign Secretary Laval secretly in December 1935 to propose the ces-sion to Italy of 60,000 square miles of Ethiopia and to mark off a further zone of 160,000 square miles for economic expansion exclusively for Italy. Ethiopia was to receive only about 3,000 square miles. The Hoare-Laval plan, which was leaked to the French press, was received with shock by League members, be-cause the French and British on the record had supported sanctions against Italy.[13] On December 16 Emperor Haile Selassie rejected the British and French plan in a historic speech, warning that the plan would encourage aggressors.

The uproar in Britain over the Hoare-Laval plan was so strong that the prime minister accepted Hoare's resignation after only six months in office. The issue was carried back to the League, but in January and February 1936 Mussolini's troops used the dread weapon of mustard gas and won important military victories.

At the beginning of March 1936, Hitler's troops marched into the Rhine-land, putting great pressure on Britain and France to liquidate the Ethiopian crisis so they could face the greater threat from Hitler, and possibly enlist Italy in the effort. The Council stalled and failed to intensify the sanctions against Italy. At the end of June it finally turned the matter over to the Assembly. Prime Minister Chamberlain expressed the view there that to continue sanctions would be madness. This effectively pulled the rug on sanctions, and despite an elo-quent plea from Emperor Haile Selassie, only two nations voted to continue the sanctions.

There has been confusion about the role of the United States, with some writers suggesting that it undermined the League effort to apply sanctions. The U.S. Congress was opposed to trade sanctions because it had been drawn into World War I on the principle of maintaining trade to England—freedom of the seas. U.S. neutrality legislation in 1936 prohibited trade with any belligerent country. However, in response to the League's October 1935 appeal, President Roosevelt said that the United States would issue moral appeals to American oil producers, and in response major oil suppliers said they would cooperate. However, the League committee stalled on implementing the oil sanctions for several months, and the Hoare-Laval plan and Hitler's invasion of the Rhineland destroyed the chances for implementing the oil embargo.[14]

The denouement of this tragedy occurred when Italy intervened on the side of Nazi Germany in the Spanish Civil War, joined Germany and Japan in the Axis, and did not oppose Germany's conquest of Austria in 1938. The Axis powers pictured their actions as crusades against communism and concluded the Anti-Comintern Pact of November 25, 1936. The Axis then mounted a major propaganda campaign against the League as an agent of communism, and continued along the path of aggression that led to World War II.

WHO WERE AT FAULT?

Professors and practitioners of the power politics school, like Professors Hans Morgenthau, George Kennan, and Zbigniew Brzezinski, blame supporters of the League for encouraging governments to rely on international law and the League of Nations to stop aggression in the 1930s, when actually the aggressors of that era would respect only power. The above account suggests that this is not a fair appraisal. The League institutions were actually taking a stronger stand against Mussolini and the Japanese aggressors than the power brokers in control of foreign policy, who were acting outside the League framework to muddle through and to appease Mussolini and the Japanese. Partly these diplomats realized their position was weak against these aggressors, partly they hoped to get Mussolini to help stop Hitler, and partly they wanted to protect their economic and military assets from attack by the aggressors. At the time, these appeared to them to be compelling reasons, although the diplomats' solution was not supported by the British people, at least those who demonstrated support for the League and collective security by a decisive majority in the 1935 Peace Ballot. In retrospect, the world would have been better off and World War II perhaps avoided if the power brokers had backed the instincts of the British people and the League's Assembly during this period, which was calling on the major powers to support the collective security provisions of the League Covenant.

The Axis and particularly Hitler, of course, were primarily to blame for the final demise of the League, which was incidental to the shattering of the Versailles Treaty system. Many also fault the United States for not joining the League and thereby weakening it from the beginning. F. P. Walters, former deputy secretary general of the League, stated the following:

> The immediate loss in power and influence of the Council and Assembly, due to the absence of the United States was great; it was destined to show itself in a hundred ways as the years went by. The indirect effects were no less calamitous.

Within each member-state anti-League elements were encouraged. . . . Again with the United States outside the League, any dissatisfied member could henceforth make effective use of the threat to withdraw. To leave the League was not to isolate oneself, but to follow an illustrious example.[15]

Walters could also have noted at this point the disastrous effect of the U.S. failure to cooperate in the world economic conference in 1933 that tried to address the causes of the Great Depression.

It is not the purpose here to make another judgment on that complicated question. Hopefully, this chapter puts the positive contributions of the League in clearer perspective and shows the record that helped shape the minds of those who gathered in San Francisco in 1945 to draft the charter of a more powerful international organization designed to prevent a third world war. Public opinion polls at the time confirmed that there was overwhelming support for the idea of establishing an organization like the United Nations after the war was over. In addition, it was clear that colonialism was dying and that new nations would be born to take part in the new world organization.

Ironically, Japan's attempts to control its enlarged empire acquired at the beginning of World War II led to a surge for independence in the closing months of the war by colonies formerly controlled by the West. Pearl Harbor had grown out of the Japanese drive for empire—the Greater East Asian Co-Prosperity Sphere—plus its slogan of Asia for the Asians. During the war, Japan proved to be a harsher colonial master than the Western powers. In the closing days of World War II, Japan attempted to rally support from its new possessions by granting them more independence. When the Western victors came back to their colonies, they found that the people had had a taste of independence and self-government and were demanding that the Western allies make good on their wartime pledges for democracy and self-government. The move of the colonies for independence strengthened the drive for a universal world organization based on collective security and self-determination.

Notes to Chapter 2

1. B. Scott, *The Rise and Fall of the United Nations* (New York: Macmillan, 1973), p. 33.

2. A. Yoder, *World Politics and the Causes of War* (Lanham, MD: University Press of America, 1983), Chapter III.

3. *New York Times*, May 28, 1916, pp. 1–2.

4. J. Bassett, *The League of Nations* (New York: Longmann, Green, 1930), p. 2.

5. R. Baker, *Woodrow Wilson: Life and Letters* (Doubleday: New York, 1927).

6. P. Walp, *Constitutional Development of the League of Nations* (Lexington: University of Kentucky, 1931), pp. 77–81.

7. F. P. Walters, *A History of the League of Nations* (London: Oxford University Press, 1952); League of Nations Secretariat, *Ten Years of World Cooperation Geneva: League of Nations* (1930); G. Scott, *The Rise and Fall of the United Nations* (New York: Macmillan, 1973); E. Berdiner, *A Time for Angels* (New York: Knopf, 1975); Bassett, *League of Nations*.

8. T. Takeuchi, *Amerasia*. July 1938.

9. H. Stimson and M. Bundy, *On Active Service in Peace and War* (New York: Harper, 1948), p. 227.

10. Walters, *League*, pp. 466–496; F. S. Northedge, *The League of Nations* (New York: Holms and Meier, 1986), pp. 137–164.

11. Walters, *League*, p. 624.

12. Ibid., p. 830.

13. F. Hardie, *The Abyssinian Crisis* (Hamdon, CT: Archon, 1976), pp. 164–200; G. W. Bair, *Test Case: Italy, Ethiopia and the League of Nations* (Stanford: Hoover Institution Press, 1976), pp. 95–155.

14. Northedge, *League*, pp. 224–225.

15. Walters, *League*, pp. 72–78.

Chapter III

THE BIRTH OF THE UNITED NATIONS

DRAFTING THE CHARTER

Cordell Hull, the American secretary of state, more than any other official, helped nurture the birth of the United Nations. In the mists of history, he is not regarded by Americans as a strong secretary of state, but he received the honor of a Nobel Prize for his efforts to create the United Nations. President Roosevelt supported the idea of the United Nations, but he was preoccupied with winning the war against the Axis, and in the early stages of the war Roosevelt was afraid that his obvious support might stir up isolationism, the type that had defeated President Wilson's League of Nations. A few months before Pearl Harbor, Roosevelt and Prime Minister Churchill of Britain met in the Atlantic Ocean to draft the Atlantic Charter, which set forth their goals for which the United States would provide material support to Britain against Nazi aggression. One of the points won in the negotiation by Roosevelt was Britain's pledge to respect the right of people to choose the form of government under which they live, which foreshadowed the end of the colonial system.

There was also a relatively weak statement about setting up a world organization. Churchill supported a stronger wording of this phrase of the Atlantic Charter than did Roosevelt. Originally the phrase read, "They (United States and Britain) seek a peace which will not only cast down forever the Nazi tyranny, but *by effective international organization* will afford to all states and people the means of dwelling in security." Roosevelt insisted on striking the italicized words because of the fear that it would stir up isolationist opposition in the United States. At that time Roosevelt said he would not favor creating a new assembly of the League of Nations after the war until "an international police force composed of the United States and Great Britain had had an opportunity to function."[1]

Soon after Pearl Harbor the Atlantic Charter became "the United Nations Declaration" that was subscribed by 26 "United Nations" fighting the Axis. Later, the name "United Nations Organization" or "United Nations" was adopted for the new world organization.

In a meeting in Moscow in November 1943, Secretary of State Hull got Soviet and British representatives to agree to establish "a general international organization based on the principles of the sovereign equality of all peace-loving states and open to membership by all such states, large and small, for the maintenance of international peace and security." This was the first wartime conference of the three foreign secretaries, Secretary of State Hull, Secretary Anthony Eden, and Foreign Minister V. M. Molotov.

Shortly after that, Senator Connally obtained the endorsement of the Senate of this wording by a vote of 85 to 5. This gave a green light to the executive branch for drafting a charter and the calling of the Dumbarton Oaks conference to approve a first draft of the UN Charter. Meanwhile, Secretary of State Hull set up a series of committees including members of Congress and public leaders to discuss and make proposals for a world organization.[2]

Cordell Hull, who was head of the Democratic party during World War I, had tried to get President Wilson to stay home and not go to Paris because Hull feared Senate opposition to the League would gain strength. As we have noted, Wilson ignored this advice, went to Paris, and failed to get the League of Nations Covenant ratified by the U.S. Senate. Secretary of State Hull's careful preparation by congressional and other conferences during World War II was instrumental in getting the UN Charter ratified by an overwhelming vote.

In August 1944 the United States convened "conversations" with the Soviet Union and Britain, and later China, at Dumbarton Oaks, a mansion in Washington, DC. The State Department was still afraid of stimulating isolationist sentiment in Congress, so it called the meeting "conversations" instead of a conference, which would have been more descriptive. The Soviets did not participate with China during the second part of the conference because China was at war with Japan, and the Soviet Union wanted to maintain its neutrality. There had been general agreement on the responsibilities of the Security Council, General Assembly, and Secretariat in the preconference consultations, so the conference was able to agree on a rough draft of the "charter." During the first part of the conference, the United States consulted with China, so that the second part with China and without the Soviets went smoothly. The draft charter was then circulated among the "United Nations," the name given to the alliance fighting the Axis. At Roosevelt's insistence, the name United Nations was also proposed for the new organization.

The major issue not settled at Dumbarton Oaks concerned voting, in particular the "veto" in the Security Council. The Soviet Union wanted a chance to veto all resolutions, whereas the United States wanted a provision that a party to a dispute could not vote on recommendations, but a permanent member of the Security Council could veto enforcement action. Also, the Soviets wanted a vote in the General Assembly for each of their 15 republics. These issues were resolved at the beginning of 1945 in the Yalta Conference in Russia when Roosevelt, Churchill, and Stalin agreed that any of the five permanent members of the Security Council (United States, Britain, USSR, France, and China) could veto action by the Security Council; however, a party to a dispute could not veto a discussion of an issue or attempts at peaceful settlement that did not involve action or measures to restore peace. In return for yielding on this issue, the Soviets insisted on three votes in the General Assembly. Although it had first insisted on 15 votes, after hard bargaining, including a counterproposal by President Roosevelt for the United States to have a vote for each of the then 48 states, the Russians settled for three votes—Russia, Byelorussia, and the Ukraine. President Roosevelt was convinced that membership of the Soviet Union was essential, so he agreed to the request, while refusing its offer that the United States also get three votes. The Soviet demand did not appear unreasonable to Churchill, who perceived England as getting a vote for each of its dominions. Until the revolutions of 1989 the Ukraine and Byelorussia automatically voted with the Russians on important issues. Ironically, their facade of independence then helped them achieve real independence as the Soviet Union broke apart.

Senator Vandenburg, the Republican Senate leader, in a letter suggested that congressional consent should be required if the Security Council used forces outside this hemisphere against aggression. He suggested that use of U.S. forces in a worldwide war should require a congressional declaration of war. Secretary Hull replied with a memorandum suggesting that the U.S. representative on the Security Council would be under instructions by the president and that our commitment was controlled by a U.S. veto. He added that the president had the authority to involve the United States in a war in any one of a number of ways. A limitation of a declaration of war by Congress would cause the safeguards under the United Nations to lose much of their force. Vandenburg dropped the issue. Six years later President Truman committed U.S. forces in a war to defend Korea under a Security Council request and without a declaration of war. This was not challenged by the Congress.[3]

After the voting formula and membership issues were resolved at Yalta, the three leaders of the Western alliance decided to call the United Nations Conference on April 25, 1945, and the United States, as host, selected San Francisco as the site.

Truman's first announcement as president after Franklin Roosevelt died was that the UN Conference in San Francisco would be held as planned. "It is of supreme importance" he said, "that we build an organization to help keep the future peace of the world." In his memoirs, Truman stated that it had always been his hope that independent nations would some time work out a world parliament set up along the lines of the Senate and House of Representatives of the United States.[4] He knew this was not possible at the current stage of national rivalry, so he wanted to find a way to pool what power nations were willing to delegate to prevent aggression and keep the peace. Truman was convinced that without the USSR in the pool there would be no United Nations, so he made strenuous efforts to compromise UN charter issues with the Soviets.[5]

Truman followed up his initial decision to support the UN by meeting with the American UN delegation, which included Republican and Democratic leaders. He kept in touch with them daily by telephone. In going over their instructions with Secretary of State Stettinius, moreover, Truman insisted that if the veto were to be used in the UN Security Council, some way should be found to let the General Assembly consider the question. This provision was incorporated in the UN Charter. Later, in Truman's administration, the United States used this provision to permit the UN General Assembly to supervise the war in Korea after the Soviet Union blocked action in the Security Council.

The San Francisco Conference met on April 25, 1945, before the end of the war. Fifty nations attended, including Belarus and the Ukraine. It was a major conference with 282 delegates from 50 countries plus 1,500 staff and a 1,000-person Secretariat to translate the documents in the five official languages. About 2,600 reporters from the press and world media attended. Within two days the conference agreed to negotiate on the basis of the Dumbarton Oaks draft, and one week was set for submitting amendments of the draft except on trusteeship matters, which involved former colonies. The principal committees on the General Assembly, the Security Council, and the World Court were open to the public. There were 12 other committees on drafting and ironing out differences on the draft charter that were not open to the public.

One of the most controversial issues at the conference concerned the veto of any of the five great powers in the Security Council. Australia led the charge to modify the Yalta formula and prevent the veto from being exercised against attempts at peaceful settlement. Under Article 27, finally approved by the conference, a party to a dispute could not block discussion and proposals by the Security Council for peaceful settlement, but beyond that one of the permanent members could veto proposals for action. The Soviets were adamant, and Stalin rejected a special appeal, so the smaller nations reluctantly gave up the attempt, and Article 27 was approved.[6] There was a similar attempt by the Soviets to limit discussion of the General Assembly, but this was finally settled by the Soviets agreeing to Article 10, which permits the Assembly to discuss any matter within the scope of the Charter, except those being considered by the Security Council, and to make recommendations on such matters.

Within two months the conference had approved the Charter. It is notable that all provisions were approved by at least a two-thirds vote in committee.

By July 28, 1945, the U.S. Senate had approved the Charter by a vote of 89 to 2; the United States was the first nation to ratify it. By October 24 the five big powers and a majority of nations at the conference had ratified, so October 24 is considered the birthday of the United Nations. John D. Rockefeller donated land in the middle of New York City along the East River for the headquarters. This helped the nations of the world to agree that the United States would be the headquarters. Most nations were convinced that one reason for the failure of the League of Nations had been U.S. nonparticipation, so there was little opposition to locating the headquarters in New York City. Moreover, the United States granted the United Nations a $65 million interest-free loan to start building the headquarters building. The point is, at this time President Truman and the Americans were strong supporters of the UN.

Although the UN Charter avoided reference to, and language of, the League of Nations Covenant, there were basic similarities: (1) the major purpose was to maintain peace and security and to take collective measures to implement that aim, (2) its basic organization consisted of a concert of great powers in the council, an assembly of all members, and a permanent Secretariat, (3) the United Nations coordinated international economic and social activities and specialized agencies as did the League.

The basic differences were: (1) UN membership is "universal" and not dominated by Europe, (2) voting in the Security Council and other UN organs is not by unanimity but by majority or qualified majority, (3) the UN is more political and flexible than the League, (4) the UN has more emphasis on economic and social affairs and on self-determination for nations, (5) human rights are emphasized, and (6) the UN provides somewhat more power for the secretary general.

MAJOR PROVISIONS

It is useful to summarize the following major provisions of the UN Charter in order to understand its operation (see Fig. 1; see also Appendix B for the text of the UN Charter).

Purposes and Principles

The preamble and Articles I and II set forth the following major purposes and commitments:

Figure 1. The United Nations System (Courtesy: The United Nations Association of the United States)

1. To maintain peace and prevent war by collective measures and a respect for international law and to refrain from the use of force against another state.

2. To develop friendly relations and a respect for self-determination of peoples.

3. To achieve international cooperation in economic, social, and cultural matters including a respect for human rights.
4. Not to intervene in matters essentially of domestic jurisdiction (this includes civil wars).

The General Assembly

Major provisions for the General Assembly are listed below. The proposals in the economic and social fields for the most part are considered initially by the Economic and Social Council, which reports to the General Assembly.

1. The General Assembly shall consist of all of the members of the United Nations; under Article 10 it may take recommendations on any matters within the scope of the Charter.
2. It may discuss and make recommendations on any questions relating to the maintenance of international peace and security under Article 12 provided that the General Assembly shall not make recommendations when that dispute is being considered by the Security Council, unless the Security Council so requests.
3. Article 11 gives it responsibility for regulation of armaments and making recommendations on them.
4. Article 13 indicates it should make recommendations on promoting international cooperation in economic, social, and related fields.
5. Article 15 states that it shall receive and consider annual reports from the Security Council and other organs of the United Nations.
6. Article 17 delegates the Assembly the power to approve the budget and to apportion expenses.
7. Decisions of the General Assembly on important questions including the budget are made by a two-thirds majority, with decisions on other questions by a majority of members present and voting (Figure 2).

The Security Council

The UN Charter confers on the Security Council the primary responsibility for the maintenance of international peace and obligates members to submit disputes to it if they cannot settle them peacefully. The Security Council originally consisted of 11 members, but the Charter has been amended to increase the membership to 15 members. The permanent members are the Republic of China (now the People's Republic of China), France, the Union of Soviet Socialist Republics (presently Russia), the United Kingdom, and the United States. The

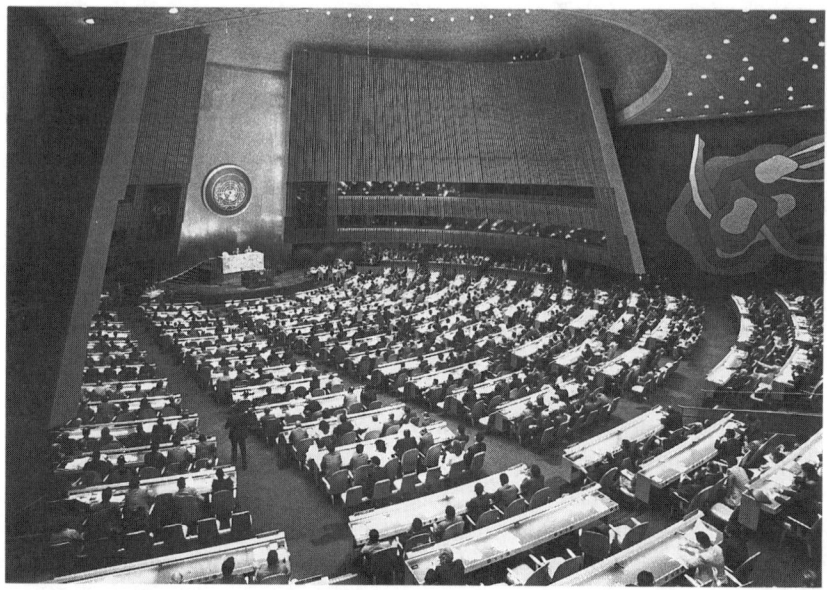

Figure 2. The General Assembly—September 20, 1988 (Courtesy: UN Photo 172.801/Yutaka Nagata)

10 nonpermanent members, according to a General Assembly resolution, are to consist of five from Africa and Asia, two from Latin America, one from Eastern Europe, and two from Western Europe and other areas (Figure 3).

The major provisions of the Charter for the Security Council are:

1. The Security Council is organized as to be able to function continuously.
2. Chapter VI gives detailed provisions for its pacific settlement of disputes, including negotiation and judicial settlement.
3. Articles 30 to 42 (see Chapter VII) provide for deciding on measures including economic and military pressure to maintain and restore international peace and security. Members of the United Nations agreed to make available armed forces and facilities for this purpose, but the agreements are negotiated with the Security Council and are subject to ratification by the states involved. This latter provision reflected the insistence of the U.S. Congress that it not give up its constitutional rights to approve the president's use of armed force.
4. It also is responsible for establishing a system for regulating armaments.
5. Article 47 provides for a military staff committee under the Security Council for strategic direction of any armed forces placed at the disposal

Figure 3. The Security Council Voting on a Resolution to Deplore Israel's Invasion of Lebanon—December 14, 1988 (Courtesy: UN Photo 173852/M. Grant)

of the Security Council. The catch was that establishment of this committee was subject to a veto. With the deterioration of the relations between the Soviet Union and the Western powers in the Cold War, this committee never functioned as it was intended.

6. Article 51 is a key article, stating that nothing in the Charter shall impair a member's inherent right of individual or collective self-defense if an attack occurs against a member of the United Nations, but this does not affect the authority of the Security Council.

7. Regional arrangements may be used for maintaining international peace or even enforcement action. Until the Bosnian crisis, military alliances such as NATO had not been considered "regional arrangements."

The principle purpose of the United Nations is to maintain peace and security and to take collective measures to that end. The next two chapters evaluate how successful it has been in achieving this goal. Until recently, 90 percent of the budgets of the UN System was spent for economic and social development, so we also examine its activities in those fields. In assessing its peacemaking function, keep in mind one of our initial hypotheses—that the United Nations is basically a forum and an instrument to be used rather than a supranational authority to enforce the peace.

MEMBERSHIP ISSUES

The drafters of the UN Charter were convinced that the United Nations would have to include the major powers of the world if it were to be a success. The leaders of the wartime alliance against the Axis wanted to preserve it to help keep the peace, and many of those involved in the tragic events of the 1930s believed that the rise of Hitler could have been prevented by cooperation of major powers within the League of Nations. It was also commonly believed that the failure of the United States to join the League seriously hindered its efforts to oppose the aggression of the Axis powers.

Secretary of State Cordell Hull, in making plans for drafting the UN Charter, sold President Roosevelt on the principle of a "universal" organization rather than an association of the victorious powers, which would divide the world into spheres of influence. The universality principle was not strictly observed immediately after World War II because the enemy states were not admitted. The United Nations idea and name came out of the 1940 United Nations Declaration of the wartime alliance against the Axis. This in turn was based on Roosevelt and Churchill's Atlantic Charter of the year before. Article 4 of the UN Charter stated that it was open to all "peace-loving" states, and this article was used to exclude the defeated enemy powers until their occupation ended and new states were set up. Within 10 years the enemy states had received their own constitutions, and moves were under way to admit them.

Article 4 also states that members will be admitted by a decision of the General Assembly upon recommendation of the Security Council. This meant that this action was subject to a veto in the Security Council. This lent itself to Cold War politics with the Soviets advocating membership for the Eastern European states under its domination, whereas the Western powers supported the membership of Italy, Germany, and Japan as well as other friendly states. The logjam was finally broken in 1955 with a package deal in which 16 states were admitted simultaneously, including four Eastern European states and 12 non-Communist states. (Poland and Yugoslavia were admitted in 1946 as original members.) Both East and West Germany were admitted many years later. By 1996 there were 185 members.

The major issue of Chinese representation in the United Nations was not a "membership" but a credentials issue. The Republic of China as a major ally against the Axis was one of the original permanent members of the United

Nations with a right of veto. The Soviet Union maintained correct relations with the Republic of China until 1949, when the Communist government took control of mainland China, while the Nationalist government fled to the island of Taiwan (Formosa). The new Communist government was officially recognized by only 15 members; the Nationalist government on Taiwan at that time continued to be recognized by 43 members. Moreover, the year after its establishment, the People's Republic of China became involved in the war in Korea opposing the UN forces under the command of the United States. For the next 20 years the United States successfully led the effort to isolate China in punishment for its participation in the Korean War and to keep it out of the United Nations.

The major elements of this complicated legalistic-political issue are as follows. Both the People's Republic of China and the government on Taiwan insisted that they alone represented China, and neither would accept the idea of two Chinas. The United States succeeded in getting approval of a resolution designating the China issue as an "important question"; this procedural resolution requires a majority vote. This meant that the vote on the substantive issue—the "important question" of accepting the credentials of the People's Republic of China—would require an affirmative vote of two-thirds in the General Assembly. Some nations respected the Charter enough to vote the China issue as an "important question," even though they would vote for accepting the credentials of the People's Republic of China while it was not able to obtain a two-thirds vote.

The U.S. efforts to keep the People's Republic of China out of the United Nations, and later to admit it only if it allowed the Republic of China to stay in the General Assembly, failed in 1971 after Henry Kissinger flew to Peking to arrange a visit by President Nixon to the People's Republic of China. With this informal recognition of the People's Republic, it was obvious from informal tallies that the votes could no longer be mobilized to block its admission. In 1971, therefore, the representatives of the government on Taiwan walked out of the General Assembly when they saw their cause was lost. The General Assembly then voted to expel the Republic of China representative and admit the delegate of the People's Republic of China. Similar action eventually followed in the Specialized Agencies as their governing boards followed the political lead of the UN General Assembly. (To confuse the issue further, the Charter still reads as if the "Republic of China" is a permanent member, but it is interpreted to mean the People's Republic of China, because it is so cumbersome to amend the Charter.)

With the admission of Vietnam in 1977 and the two Koreas in 1992, all major states had become members. The Democratic Republic of Vietnam (North Vietnam), after its victory in the Vietnam War in 1975, had tried to get two

Vietnams admitted to the United Nations, but this was vetoed by the United States. After Vietnam's official unification in 1977, it applied for membership as one state, and the United States did not veto its membership. The two Germanies were admitted in 1975 after Chancellor Willy Brandt succeeded in West Germany's initiative to formally recognize the boundaries remaining after World War II.

Until 1991 North Korea had refused to recognize splitting Korea into two governments. In 1948 after a free election in South Korea (the Republic of Korea), the General Assembly had recognized it as the only legitimate government in Korea, but the Soviets vetoed its membership in the United Nations. South Korea, nevertheless, was able to join UN subsidiary bodies such as the UN Conference on Trade and Development (UNCTAD) and the Specialized Agencies. However, responding to the threat of the Soviets to allow South Korea to enter the UN, North Korea agreed that both could become members, and they were admitted in July 1991. Switzerland for many years did not join the UN because of a strict policy of neutrality, although it joined UN Specialized Agencies. In 1992 it, too, applied for membership.

The major change in UN membership in which Russia took over the seat of the former Soviet Union was accomplished with amazing ease. In the fall of 1991, after the Eastern European satellites attained independence, the internal empire of the Soviet Union split into 15 independent republics. Russia remained as the largest republic with about half of the population and 70 percent of the land area. On December 24, 1991, after the General Assembly had finished its fall business, President Boris Yeltsin of Russia in a letter to the United Nations stated that Russia as the "continuing state" of the former Union of Soviet Socialist Republics would now occupy its seat in the United Nations; this included its seat as a permanent member of the Security Council. He was following the precedent of British India which took over India's seat after it split into Pakistan and India in 1947. The letter was not challenged. President Yeltsin and his foreign minister pledged to promote the United Nations in every way.

The Ukraine and Belarus, which had been members since the UN's birth, began to assert independence from Russia's positions. Latvia, Estonia, and Lithuania, which had been taken over by the Soviet Union at the beginning of World War II, after they were admitted as members, at every opportunity demanded the withdrawal of Soviet troops from their territory.[7]

To sum up, for practical purposes the United Nations is now a universal organization organized to meet and consider world crises. In a sense, this makes it stronger than the League of Nations, but as we see in the next chapter, there is a price for this. The United Nations, in order to maintain universal membership, refused to take important enforcement action against a major power such as the Soviet Union when it violated the Charter by its invasion of Afghanistan.

In the eyes of some critics, this seriously compromised the usefulness of the United Nations. However, we will see that there was a happy ending to this story when the Soviets withdrew from Afghanistan as a result of negotiations under United Nations auspices.

Notes to Chapter 3

1. R. Sherwood, *Roosevelt and Hopkins* (New York: Harper, 1948), p. 359.

2. As a college student I participated in one such conference at Ohio Wesleyan University in the spring of 1942. This was sponsored by the Federal Council of Churches of Christ and included Dr. Leo Pasvolsky from the Department of State, John Foster Dulles, later Secretary of State, and Karl J. Hambro, president of the Assembly of the League of Nations. Their proposals stressed the interdependence of nations and the need for a world organization after the war (see *Time*, March 13, 1942, pp. 44–48).

3. R. Russell, *A History of the United Nations Charter* (Washington, DC: Brookings, 1958), pp. 469–470.

4. H. Truman, *Years of Decision* (New York: Doubleday, 1956), p. 280.

5. W. Harriman and E. Abel, *Special Envoy to Churchill* (New York: Random House, 1979), p. 448.

6. Russell, *History*, pp. 719–742.

7. J. Tessitore and S. Woolfson (eds.), *A Global Agenda* (New York: University Press of America, 1992), pp. 16–19.

Chapter IV

COLLECTIVE SECURITY
BEFORE DETENTE

The principal goal of the UN Charter is to maintain international peace and settle disputes peacefully in conformity with international law. To evaluate the effectiveness of the United Nations, we first examine cases in the early years when the United States worked through the United Nations to help maintain peace within the framework of international law. Later, power politics dominated the world scene, and the United Nations tended to be used as an instrument in the Cold War. After the end of the Cold War, the United Nations in the 1990s expanded its peacekeeping activities. We examine in detail those peacekeeping operations in order to dispel the myth that the United Nations was not effective. We then examine the international agreements for nuclear arms control, many of which reflect initiatives of UN bodies. Next we evaluate the importance of international law and the work of many UN organs dealing with economic and social activities. Finally, we conclude with an evaluation of UN successes and failures and its potential for the 21st century.

THE IRANIAN CONFRONTATION

The Iranian dispute came before the Security Council in January 1946 in its first meeting after the United Nations was founded. Early in World War II the Soviets and British invaded Iran to establish a supply route to the USSR, because Hitler's forces blocked the normal European supply routes. Reza Shah was deposed and his son installed as the new Shah. The United States, as the main supplier of war materiel, had considerable leverage to put pressure on the Soviets and Britain to sign a treaty committing them to withdraw after the war. This was in line with the traditional U.S. policy of supporting the sovereignty of Iran. The Soviets suspected American intentions, however, because Iran had offered oil concessions in the north to U.S. firms. (Incidentally, oil was never found there.)

After the war, in September 1945 President Truman received reports that Soviet army units were preventing Iranian police and its military from moving into the area of Azerbaijan in a section of Iran along the Soviet border, where the Iranian Communist Party (Tudeh) was promoting a rebellion of Azerbaijan to achieve independence. The Soviets at first refused to discuss withdrawing their forces. Iran, therefore, brought the matter up before the Security Council at its first meeting, charging the USSR with interfering in Iran's internal affairs. The Security Council could not pass a resolution supporting the charge because of the Soviet veto, but it was able to pass one calling on the parties to negotiate the issue.

Iran, the United States, and others on the Security Council raised a major fuss, with the news media giving the crisis wide publicity. In addition, President Truman sent a stiff note in March 1946 expressing the earnest hope that the Soviets would withdraw troops as had been promised in the 1942 treaty. Meanwhile, the Iranian prime minister indicated that the Soviets also could obtain an oil concession in northern Iran. Finally, several weeks after the deadline, the Soviets announced that they would withdraw. They left advisers there, and the Iranian government was not fully able to exercise its authority until the end of 1946 when it moved its troops into the area.[1]

The fuss raised in the United Nations, which embarrassed the Soviet Union, was an obvious factor in its decision to withdraw. Moreover, at this time it was still hoping to preserve the United Nations as an instrument to prevent future German aggression, and, even more important, to maintain a relationship with the United States that would permit the USSR to share in the control of Germany. Thus Iran was successful in using the United Nations, accompanied by U.S. diplomatic pressure, to preserve Iran's sovereignty in the first major crisis faced by the Security Council.

THE GREEK CRISIS

At the end of 1946 and during 1947, Greece, the United States, and others also raised a hue and cry about Communist countries' support of a rebellion in Greece. British troops had liberated Greece after World War II and stayed on to maintain order—that is, to prevent a Communist movement from taking control of the country. The Soviets and other Communist countries complained to the Security Council, but Britain replied that its troops were there on the invitation of the Greek government. The Greek government denied any interference, which put British action within a framework of international law since they were there with the consent of the Greek government.

After the British troops withdrew, Greece asked the Security Council, on

December 3, 1946, to consider the situation caused by aid provided to Greek guerrillas from its northern neighbors, Albania, Yugoslavia, and Bulgaria. These countries denied the charges. On December 19 the Council established a commission with one representative of each member of the Council to investigate. The commission submitted a report approved by 9 of the 11 members confirming the charges. The Security Council was blocked by a Soviet veto from accepting the report, so it passed the issue to the General Assembly. In 1947 and 1948 the Assembly called on Albania, Bulgaria, and Yugoslavia to stop aiding the rebels. The General Assembly, moreover, established a UN Special Committee on the Balkans (UNSCOB) to investigate. In the course of the investigations by the Security Council and General Assembly, volumes of evidence were obtained proving without a doubt that the Communist countries were supporting the rebellion against the Greek government. The General Assembly passed resolutions every year until 1954 condemning this intervention.

Meanwhile, the United States provided massive aid to Greece in the forerunner of the Marshall Plan of aid to Europe, and Yugoslavia broke out of the East European bloc, expelled Soviets advisers, and asserted its independence. These developments, plus the UN actions to observe the Greek border and report on violations of international law, brought an end to the intervention by Greece's Communist neighbors, and in 1954 the General Assembly dropped the matter. Greece has been a full member of NATO since 1980 and of the European Economic Community since 1981, and there has been no question of its independence from the Soviet bloc.

THE KOREAN WAR

The UN was a center of action for the Korean War. This conflict was long, costly, and unpopular, but it could have been much worse. The United States played the leading role through the United Nations in accordance with international law to mobilize support for South Korea against aggression by North Korea. Despite the terrible cost, the aggressor was defeated and the principle of collective security was upheld. President Truman played a leading role in using the United Nations to contain the conflict.

At the beginning of this century, Japan won the colonial competition for Korea and formally annexed it in 1910. Subsequently, a strong independence movement arose, and in the 1930s Syngman Rhee, a Korean who had studied at Harvard, took over the movement's leadership from abroad.

In line with the principles of the Atlantic Charter, the United States and the Soviet Union agreed that Korea would be given its independence after the war.

The Soviets proposed a four-power trusteeship with no foreign troops, but the United States did not accept this proposal, in part because the Chinese government informed it that the Soviet Union had been training two Korean divisions in Siberia during the war, as well as political personnel who could be brought into Korea to set up a Communist government. The United States and the Soviet Union could not agree on four-power control, so at Potsdam they agreed to divide Korea at the 38th parallel with the Soviets temporarily occupying the North and the United States the South. Kim Il Sung and his followers came in with the Soviet troops and took over control of the Korean Communist Party in North Korea, just after the party leader was conveniently assassinated.

It seemed clear to U.S. observers that the Soviets were consolidating their control of the North with their military and political advisers. President Truman decided, therefore, in November 1947 to turn the issue over to the UN General Assembly. The General Assembly with the nonparticipation of the Communist bloc created a nine-member commission to establish an all-Korean government. The commission was opposed by the Soviets, who refused to permit it to enter North Korea. The commission, therefore, turned its attention to South Korea and arranged for elections to a national assembly in 1948. Syngman Rhee was elected president, and the UN General Assembly recognized the Republic of Korea as the only "lawful government." The General Assembly then established a seven-member commission to bring about unification, which stayed on to observe developments. This was important, because it confirmed that one aim of the United Nations was to unify Korea. It was also an important action in recognizing South Korea as a state, so that the later attack by North Korea was an international war under the jurisdiction of the United Nations and not a civil war of only local concern.

In 1949 following the withdrawal of Soviet troops from the North, the U.S. National Security Council (NSC) in line with a recommendation of General MacArthur proposed the withdrawal of U.S. forces from South Korea. The withdrawal was accomplished in 1949, and only 500 officers of the U.S. military advisory group remained behind.

General MacArthur, on March 1, 1949, in a speech that left out Korea, stated that the U.S. defense perimeter included the Philippines, Okinawa, and Japan, and the Aleutian Islands. About a year later Secretary of State Acheson drew a similar line but added:

> . . . so far as the military security of other areas of the Pacific is concerned, it must be clear that no person can guarantee these islands against military attack. . . . Should such an attack occur . . . the initial reliance must be on the people attacked to resist it and then upon the commitments of the entire civilized world

under the Charter of the UN, which has so far not proved a weak reed to lean on by any people who are determined to protect their in dependence against outside aggression.[2]

The statements by MacArthur and Acheson leaving South Korea out of the U.S. defense perimeter may have played a part in encouraging Stalin and Kim Il Sung to attack the south on June 25, 1950. Khrushchev's memoirs, which describe the meetings between Kim Il Sung, Stalin, and Mao, who together planned the war, indicate that they were confident that the United States would not come to South Korea's assistance. Khrushchev's memoirs indicate that Kim's aim was to start a war of liberation to liberate all of South Korea and bring it under North Korea's control.[3]

The United Nations commission was uneasy about reports of North Korea's aggressive intentions, and in the months before the war it expanded observation teams along the 38th parallel, the dividing line at the time between North and South Korea.[4]

On June 25, 1950, UN Secretary General Trygve Lie was informed by the United States and the UN Commission on Korea that North Korean forces had attacked the Republic of Korea all along the 38th parallel. In view of the UN role in helping form the South Korean government, the June 1950 invasion was an attack on the United Nations as well as South Korea. On that same day the UN Security Council, at the request of the United States, by a vote of 9 to 0 with one abstention (Yugoslavia) and one absent (the USSR), stated that an "armed attack" had occurred and called for immediate cessation of the hostilities, the withdrawal of North Korean forces, and assistance of UN members in carrying out the resolution. Two days later the UN Security Council by a vote of 7 to 1 adopted a U.S. resolution calling on all members to furnish such assistance as necessary to repel the armed attack. On that same day the United States announced that it had ordered land and sea forces to support the Republic of Korea (Map 1). Although the announcement of U.S. assistance took place a few hours before the second resolution was passed, the first resolution by calling North Korea's action an "armed attack" made clear that collective self-defense was justified under Article 51 of the Charter.

Subsequently, 51 UN members supported the Security Council's action; five, including the USSR, said it was illegal because it had been adopted in the absence of two permanent members of the Security Council, the USSR and the People's Republic of China. The Soviet Union was absent during the first meetings of the Security Council because it objected to the Republic of China, instead of the People's Republic of China, representing China on the Security Council.

The Soviet Union argued that a strict interpretation of Article 27 indicated

Map 1. The Korean War

action beyond procedural matters required the presence of the Soviet Union. On the other hand, the Security Council had passed a number of resolutions previously when a permanent member had "abstained" from voting and had passed two resolutions in 1946 when the Soviets were absent. Since the 1950 war the practice has been accepted that absence or abstention does not constitute a veto.[5] The Soviets returned to the Council on August 1, but the Security Council in accordance with Article 11 of the Charter in a procedural vote passed action to the General Assembly, which authorized continuing military support for South Korea.

On July 8 the Security Council in line with the secretary general's suggestion passed a resolution requesting the United States to command the UN forces, and authorizing them to use the UN flag under a Unified Command, which was not under the authority of the secretary general.[6] The United States designated General MacArthur as the commander. Combat units for the Unified Command were provided by Australia, Canada, Belgium, Colombia, Ethiopia, France, Greece, Luxembourg, the Netherlands, New Zealand, the Philippines, Thailand, Turkey, the Union of South Africa, the United Kingdom, and the United States. Denmark, Italy, India, Norway, and Sweden supplied medical units. However, it took time to mobilize these forces, and the North Korean forces had swept through Seoul and down through the end of the Korean peninsula to Pusan before U.S. and UN assistance became effective. While UN forces held on to a small defense perimeter in Pusan, General MacArthur carried out a surprise amphibious landing at Inchon near Seoul. This caught the North Koreans off balance, and they fell back from the Pusan perimeter in a disorderly retreat (Map 1).

President Truman had reacted quickly to the challenge of the North Korean attack. In his memoirs he points out the heavy influence in his thinking of Hitler's aggression in World War II:

> There was no suggestion from anyone that either the United Nations or the United States could back away from it. This was a test of all the last five years of collective security. . . . Communism was acting in Korea just as Hitler, Mussolini, and the Japanese had acted 10, 15, or 20 years earlier. If the Communists were permitted to force their entry into the Republic of Korea without opposition of the free world, no small nation would have the courage to resist threats and aggression by stronger Communist neighbors. If this was allowed to go unchallenged, it would mean a third world war, just as similar instances had brought on the Second World War. It was also clear to me that the foundations and principles of the United Nations were at stake unless this unprovoked attack on Korea could be stopped.[7]

Secretary of State Acheson came to the same conclusion, but he reached it by a different philosophy, that of power politics. Nevertheless, he was loyal to Truman and he recognized the usefulness of the United Nations. He regarded it as an

> open, undisguised challenge to our internationally accepted position as protector of South Korea, an area of great importance to the security of American-occupied Japan. To back away from this challenge in view of our capacity for meeting it, would be highly destructive of the power and prestige of the United States. By prestige, I mean the shadow cast by power, which is of great deterrent importance.[8]

These statements show how supporters of international law and proponents of power politics can unite to support collective security.[9]

China did not participate in the Korean attack initially, but at the time it seemed to be preparing to attack Taiwan and this helped convince Truman and Acheson to take a strong stand against Communist aggression in Korea.

The China issue soon became a major issue in the Korean War. On September 27, 1950, Truman approved instructions to MacArthur, which included as an objective "the destruction of the North Korean armed forces." MacArthur was authorized to conduct military operations north of the 38th parallel as long as there was no threat of Chinese or Soviet intervention. A few days later the United States obtained UN General Assembly authorization in a resolution that recommended that "all appropriate steps be taken to insure conditions of stability throughout Korea." The resolution established the UN Commission for the Unification and Rehabilitation of Korea (UNCURK) of seven states to establish a unified, democratic, and independent government of all Korea. The UN delegates in discussing this issue realized that this was authorizing operations north of the 38th parallel.[10] On October 2, as the first South Korean units crossed north of the 38th parallel, the State Department received a number of messages all reporting the same thing—the Chinese Communists were threatening to enter the Korean conflict if UN forces crossed the 38th parallel. However, Truman chose to ignore this, thinking it was a bluff designed to affect the UN vote on the resolution.[11]

In the middle of October, Truman flew to Wake Island to meet General MacArthur. One of Truman's concerns was the threat of intervention by Chinese Communist forces. MacArthur assured him there was very little chance of Chinese entry, and if the Chinese troops did so, they would be easily defeated. However, as MacArthur was making this statement, the first Chinese troops were crossing the Yalu River into Korea, and by the end of October they had mounted their first attack. The Chinese called their troops "volunteers" to avoid declaring war on the United States and other UN forces, but the volunteers were obviously those of the Communist Chinese government.

After November 6 a representative of the People's Republic of China participated in the Security Council discussion of the Korean War. On November 28 the representative of the People's Republic of China asserted that the U.S. announcement that its navy would protect Taiwan constituted "aggression" because Taiwan was a part of China. The United States replied that the action was designed to keep the peace and that the U.S. navy was also instructed to prevent attacks on the mainland by Marshal Chiang Kai-shek's forces.

At the beginning of November, the General Assembly institutionalized its authority to supervise collective security when the Security Council is tied up with a veto. The General Assembly adopted the Uniting for Peace Resolution calling for the Assembly to meet in an emergency session when a veto prevents action to meet a threat to the peace. The resolution established a Peace Observation Commission of 14 members including the five permanent members of the Security Council to report on the situation. Also, a Collective Measures Committee of 14 members was established to report on methods that might be used to maintain peace. In the Korean War this committee consisted of those who provided troops to Korea.

MacArthur's troops pressed on toward the Yalu with the expressed hope of ending the war by Christmas. On November 28, 1950, the Chinese volunteers mounted mass attacks. As the UN troops fell back into disorderly retreat, MacArthur indicated that he might have to evacuate his forces from the Korean peninsula unless he was authorized to attack and blockade China, to obtain reinforcements from Formosa, and to have the option of using atomic weapons against North Korea.[12] Despite this statement of near panic, General Ridgeway, MacArthur's field commander, was able to establish a line below Seoul and then fight back to the 38th parallel north of Seoul.

The General Assembly, in considering the "intervention" of the People's Republic of China in Korea, established a Cease-Fire Group of the president of the Assembly, Canada, and India to arrange a cease-fire. On January 31 the Security Council, stymied by a Soviet veto, again removed the Korean War from its agenda, leaving the way for General Assembly actions. China rejected the Cease-Fire Group's proposals, and on May 18, 1951, the Assembly recommended an embargo against China of all shipments of arms and items useful for war.

Meanwhile, U.S. officials were carrying out a series of delicate negotiations for a truce that eventually succeeded, but only after the firing of General MacArthur. Publicly, and in a letter to the House of Representatives' minority leader, MacArthur called for the use of Chinese Nationalist troops in the war. This was directly in opposition to the president's view and that of the United Nations, which did not want to expand the nature of the war to a war against China by such a step. Truman asked for and obtained MacArthur's resignation in April 1951.

The secretary general maneuvered cease-fire negotiations to the military commanders to avoid political demands such as the admission of China into the United Nations. The armistice negotiations formally began between the military commanders of the opposing sides on July 10, 1951. The main stumbling block preventing agreement was what to do with about 25,000 Chinese and North Korean prisoners of war. Difficult negotiations were carried out by the military commanders of both sides and in the United Nations. Finally, agreement was reached providing for a UN Repatriation Commission including Czechoslovakia, India (chairman), Poland, Sweden, and Switzerland to interview the prisoners. Some observers suggest that Eisenhower's veiled threat to use nuclear weapons played a part in reaching agreement on this final issue holding up the armistice.[13]

The Armistice Agreement was signed on July 27, 1953. It established a cease-fire zone between the two sides, and a Military Armistice Commission with representatives of the two sides was set up to supervise the agreement. Subsequently, the Geneva Conference of 1954 failed to reach agreement on a peace treaty, but it agreed that failure to reach this agreement did not prejudice the armistice. Since the truce there have been tension and incidents along the demilitarized zone, and there has been no permanent settlement. The United States maintains a sizable number of troops along the northern border of South Korea, and periodic verbal conflicts take place in the Mixed Armistice Commission. The United States continues to report periodically to the Security Council on the implementation of the 1958 Armistice Agreement.

The cease-fire has held with minor exceptions, and there has been no war. South Korea has prospered. With a larger population it appears capable of defending against any renewed threat from the North, particularly since it is buttressed by thousands of U.S. troops still stationed in South Korea. There has never been a peace treaty, and Korea has not been unified. There have been periodic attacks and even terrorist incidents instigated by North Korea against the South. However, most observers regard the UN action to defend Korea as a high point of supporting collective security under the UN Charter. Some suggest that this was an accident due to the Soviet Union's absence from the Security Council, but others note that the General Assembly during this crisis established the machinery and precedents for it to act when the Security Council is stymied by a veto. It is true that the United States dominated the military action, but this reflects a fact of life in the United Nations that it needs the support of major powers, particularly the United States.

THE ARAB-ISRAELI WARS

The Middle East is a highly strategic area that has been a cockpit of power politics since the beginning of written history. Even before the Suez Canal was built, it was a corridor to Africa and Asia. Since the Suez Canal, Britain and France have regarded the area as a lifeline to their colonies and former colonies in Asia and Africa. Since World War II airlines have used the Middle East airspace for their routes. In recent decades the Middle East has become a major source of oil and the world's energy. It is ironic that the United Nations, which is based on international law, inherited the Palestine issue and was thrust into the middle of the power politics and conflicts of this strategic region.

The depth of feeling in the conflicts of the Middle East reflects thousands of years of religious history. The tribes of the area have been fighting for thousands of years over historical and religious claims. The book of Genesis tells of

God's covenant with Abraham to give him and his descendants the land of Canaan, which later became known as Palestine. The problem is that Arabs, Jews, and Christians claim Abraham as their father and also claim his inheritance. The Jewish Zionist movement, stimulated by persecution of Jews in France, began to reassert the Jews' claim to Palestine at the end of the last century.

During World War I the British Cabinet approved a statement called the Balfour Declaration, which read as follows: "His Majesty's Government views with favor the establishment in Palestine of a national home for the Jewish people, and will use its best endeavors to facilitate the achievement of this object, it being clearly understood that nothing may be done which may prejudice the civil and religious rights of existing non-Jewish communities in Palestine, or the rights and political status enjoyed by Jews in any other country." This declaration was later accepted by the League of Nations as part of the British Mandate for Palestine.

Different British officials had different reasons for encouraging Jewish immigration into Palestine by granting the Balfour Declaration to the British/Jewish community. Some officials favored it for religious reasons, believing that such a refuge was ordained in the Bible. Others wanted to use the declaration to get more enthusiastic support for World War I from the Jewish communities in Britain, and also in the United States and the Soviet Union. Other British officials probably wanted to create a rationale for continued British rule over the area of Palestine, which was close to the vital Suez Canal link to Britain's colonial empire in Asia and Africa. The declaration did promote unrest in the mandate, and Arab terrorists attacked the Jews to discourage their immigration into Palestine, forcing Britain to act as a referee.

In 1922 Britain defined the area of the Palestine Mandate as separate from TransJordan, and since that time the area of Palestine has generally been regarded as west of the Jordan River. At the time of the Balfour Declaration, Jews made up about 10 percent of the population of the Palestinian Mandate. During the 1920s and 1930s, limited immigration was permitted and Jews managed to buy up a considerable part of Arab farmlands in Palestine. By World War II Jews constituted about 30 percent of Palestine's population.

The First Arab-Israeli War

The Arab-Israeli conflict in Palestine came to a boil after the end of World War II. At that time the world was horrified by the reports of the Nazi extermination of 6 million Jews in the Holocaust. This gave tremendous momentum to attempts of the Zionists to establish a refuge in Palestine for the remaining hundreds of thousands of Jews in Europe. The Arabs of Palestine, however, were determined that their land should not be used to repay the Jews for the horrors suffered under Hitler. As fighting broke out, Britain was left holding the bag with the Palestine Mandate, and it tried to keep the lid on by limiting the immigration of Jews into Palestine. The British policy was opposed violently by Menachem Begin's Irgun, which attacked the British military for its policies of restricting Jewish immigration. A surge of opposition to British policy occurred after the British sent the ship *Exodus*, with 4,493 Jews, back to Germany after it tried illegally to discharge its passengers in Palestine. In frustration the British Cabinet, on April 2, 1947, approved a letter to the secretary general of the United Nations stating that Britain would withdraw within a year and asking that the question of Palestine be placed on the agenda of a regular session of the General Assembly, at which time Britain would submit a report of its administration of the mandate. Britain also asked that the General Assembly session appoint and instruct a special committee to make a study with recommendations on the issue. This was an orderly way to dispose of this issue because the United Nations had inherited the League of Nation's responsibilities for mandates.

On May 15, 1947, the special session of the General Assembly established a UN Special Committee of 11 members—Australia, Canada, Czechoslovakia, Guatemala, India, Iran, the Netherlands, Peru, Sweden, Uruguay, and Yugoslavia—to study the issues. Note that none of the great powers were included. The Jewish Agency maintained liaison with this committee, but the Arab Higher Committee refused to cooperate. The Arab states objected to the fact that no reference was made in the covering resolution to the interests of the inhabitants of Palestine. The committee visited Palestine, Lebanon, Syria, and TransJordan, and also displaced persons camps in Germany and Austria. Representatives of the Arab states presented their views in hearings in Lebanon.[14] On August 31, 1947, the committee reported to the General Assembly with two sets of proposals, both recommending partition of Palestine. The majority recommendation by Canada, Czechoslovakia, Guatemala, the Netherlands, Peru, Sweden, and Uruguay was that two separate states be established with Jerusalem as the capital under international trusteeship. India, Iran, and Yugoslavia proposed a federal state of an Arab state and a Jewish state with Jerusalem as the federal capital. Australia abstained, stating that the proposal went beyond the terms of reference of the committee. On September 23, 1947, a special ad hoc committee of the General Assembly, composed of all member states, heard the three parties. The General Assembly then adopted the majority plan by a vote of 39 to 13 with 10 abstentions. Countries voting for the majority plan were Australia, Belgium, Bolivia, Brazil, Belarus, Canada, Costa Rica, Czechoslovakia, Denmark, the Dominican Republic, Ecuador, France, Guatemala, Haiti, Iceland,

Liberia, Luxembourg, the Netherlands, New Zealand, Nicaragua, Norway, Panama, Paraguay, Peru, the Philippines, Poland, Sweden, Ukraine, Union of South Africa, the USSR, the United States, Uruguay, Venezuela, Lebanon, Pakistan, Saudi Arabia, Syria, Turkey, and Yemen. The countries abstaining were Argentina, Chile, China, Colombia, El Salvador, Ethiopia, Honduras, Mexico, the United Kingdom, and Yugoslavia.

The Assembly resolution provided for the Trusteeship Council to prepare a statute for the city of Jerusalem and for the UN Palestine Commission to carry out the recommendations of the General Assembly. Following this resolution, the Arab states began preparing for war. By April the Security Council established a Truce Commission to try to prevent war between the Arab and Jewish communities. Violence increased in Palestine as the end of the mandate drew near.

During this period the U.S. position was confused, with President Truman for a while losing control of U.S. policy. The United States approved the partition, but it refused to support it with a UN force, although the Soviets probably would have agreed. Then, as violence increased and war threatened, the United States UN delegation proposed a trusteeship for Palestine, apparently trying to stop the partition from going into effect. The Arabs were delighted at this proposal, but it did not garner support. On the day the British withdrew, the Jews declared Israel a state, and the United States from the White House immediately gave it *de facto* recognition. The next day the Arab states attacked. The Jews managed to hold on to Jerusalem, although their forces were greatly outnumbered by the armies of their Arab neighbors. Jews had manufactured a number of small arms and managed to buy other arms on the black markets of the world.

The Security Council established a Truce Commission for Palestine consisting of Belgium, France, and the United States. It initially worked closely with UN mediator of Palestine Count Folke Bernadotte, the head of the Swedish Red Cross, to establish a truce.

There were so many rivalries among the Arab states that they were not able to get their act together to defeat Israel. On June 11 with the support of a Security Council resolution that threatened sanctions, Count Bernadotte was able to arrange a cease-fire for only 30 days. During this period the Jewish forces were able to regroup and get more supplies into Jerusalem. Fighting broke out again, but by July 15 the Security Council obtained another truce. By this time the Jews had gained an area more than double the size of the original UN partition plan.[15]

The Security Council established the UN Truce Supervision Organization (UNTSO), a team of 63 U.S., Belgian, French, and Swedish military observers to help the mediator. In September 1948 Count Bernadotte was killed by Jewish terrorists. The Council appointed another mediator, Ralph Bunche, a black American, and reinforced UNTSO under him. By a series of bilateral negotiations he got Israel and Egypt to sign a general armistice agreement in February 1949. Agreements followed with Israel and Lebanon on March 23, Jordan and Israel on April 3, and Syria and Israel on July 20.

Meanwhile UNTSO was increased to a strength of 700 to observe the armistices and report to the Council. It was assisted by Mixed Armistice Commissions chosen by both sides and chaired by the chief of staff of UNTSO. In August 1949 the Security Council ended the role of the mediator and made UNTSO an autonomous organ of the Security Council with the UNTSO chief of staff in command. It still operates in the area with a force of about 300 from Argentina, Australia, Austria, Belgium, Canada, Chile, Denmark, Finland, France, Ireland, Italy, the Netherlands, New Zealand, Norway, Sweden, Russia, and the United States. The participation of many countries in UNTSO and other organs of the United Nations in the Middle East gives the organs a genuine international character, which obtains respect that would not be given to groups made up of parties who take sides in the conflicts. It suffers casualties, which are incurred as a result of high-risk patrols and mediating in the area (Table 1).

It is important to note that the new state of Israel was recognized by action of the Security Council and by more than a two-thirds vote of the General Assembly. Israel was formally admitted to the United Nations on May 11, 1949. (At that time, the Soviet Union supported Israel and did not veto its admission.) The Arab nations were furious and frustrated, but they have not been able to turn back the clock and get the world community to withdraw recognition of the state of Israel.

The 1956 War

The principal events leading to the 1956 Suez War were the decision of President Nasser of Egypt to nationalize the Suez Canal Company, which managed the operation of the canal, and the violent response of the British and French to this act. As a prelude to this crisis, the United States and the International Bank had engaged in a long, complicated negotiation to help Nasser finance building the Aswan Dam, a huge project on the Nile that Nasser hoped would bring power and irrigation to Egypt, permitting it to enter the twentieth century. At the last minute, however, the United States, in July 1956, withdrew its offer in frustration over the antagonistic policies of Egypt, which opposed U.S. efforts to build an alliance against the Soviet Union in the Middle East. Nasser had openly courted the Soviet Union and arranged to buy arms from Czechoslovakia, at the same time supporting nationalist rebels in Algeria against France.

Table 1
UN Coalitions and Peacekeeping Operations (1945–1996)

	Peak number of UN personnel			Deaths	
	Military	Civilian	(U.S.)	UN	U.S.
UN peacekeeping					
India-Pakistan (UNMOGIP), 1949–	39	2		6	3
Israel (UNTSO), 1948–	224	17		28	7
Suez I (UNEF I), 1956–67	6,000	0		90	0
West Irian (UNSF), 1962–63	1,500	0		0	0
Yemen (UNYOM), 1963–64	164	0		52	0
Cyprus (UNFICYP), 1964–	7,000	38	0	163	0
Suez II (UNEF II), 1973–79	7,000	0		52	0
Golan Heights (UNDOF), 1974–	1,218	0		31	0
Lebanon (UNIFIL), 1978–	5,280	520	0	193	0
Afghanistan (UNGOMAP), 1988–	50	0		0	0
Iraq-Iran (UNIIMOG), 1988–90	320	188	0	1	0
Angola (UNAVEM), 1991–	75	143	0	3	0
El Salvador (ONUSAL), 1991–	380	250	0	2	0
Uganda-Rwanda (UNOMUR), 1993–	81	24	0	11	0
Mozambique (ONUMOZ), 1992–	7,500	0		8	0
Cambodia (UNTAC), 1992–	22,000	4,500	33	55	0
Western Sahara (MINURSO), 1991–	348	100	30	3	0
Kuwait-Iraq (UNIKOM), 1991–	367	188	15	0	0
Namibia (UNTAG), 1988–90	4,900	1,600	0	0	0
Liberia (UNOMIL), 1993–	300	0	0	0	
Georgia (UNOMIG), 1993–	88	0	1	1	
Macedonia (UNPROFOR), 1993–	1,190		584	0	0
UN enforcement					
Congo (ONUC), 1960–64	25,000	1,300	0	234	0
Yugoslavia (UNPROFOR), 1992–	60,000		647	59	1
Somalia (UNOSOM), 1993–	35,000	2,800	25,800	83	26
UN collective defense					
Korean War, 1950–54	1,100,000		480,000	116,000	55,000
Kuwait-Iraq War, 1990–91	670,000		425,000	480	50

Note: The above figures do not include civilian personnel in the extensive aid operations by UN Specialized Agencies. Blanks indicate figures are not known. The Macedonian force is for the former Yugoslav republic.

Sources: *UN Chronicle*, September 1992, p. 17; *UN Chronicle*, September 1993, pp. 40–41; R. L. Sivard, *World Military and Social Expenditures 1993* (Washington, DC: World Priorities, 1993), p. 21; *World Book* 1993; United Nations, *The Blue Helmets* (UN Publications, 1990); *Peacekeeping and International Relations*, Jan/Feb 1994, pp. 2–3. Detailed figures for each country as of September 30, 1993, are given in *Peacekeeping and International Relations*, Nov/Dec 1993, pp. 2–3, and also see p. 19.

Nasser had added to the tensions by preventing Israeli ships from going through the Suez Canal and by supporting fedayeen raids from Gaza into Israel.[16] As the raids and reprisals had mounted, the UNTSO chief of staff had warned the Security Council that such incidents could spread like brushfire. The UN secretary general had undertaken extensive negotiations in the spring of 1956 and had managed to obtain an uneasy cease-fire along the armistice lines, but the withdrawal of the offer to finance the Aswan Dam and the nationalization of the Suez Canal completely undermined these efforts.[17]

After Nasser nationalized the Suez Canal Company on July 26, 1956, the French and British secretly began to plan with Israel to attack the canal and reestablish British troops in the canal zone. Meanwhile, American Secretary of State John Foster Dulles attempted to mediate the controversy by establishing a "users committee" of major nations using the Suez Canal that would oversee Egyptian management of the canal and ensure that this vital transportation link would not be closed. Dulles appeared on the verge of getting final approval, when, on October 29, Israel, in a secret league with France and Britain, attacked Egyptian forces in the canal zone. In accordance with their plan, British and French troops moved in to "protect" the Suez Canal. This was in line with a 1954 treaty that permitted them to protect it in the event of war.

President Eisenhower and Dulles saw through the scheme and were furious with the British and French for having misled the United States on this issue. Eisenhower took the high road of international law in supporting the U.S. position. He explained his position in his memoirs by stating that Nasser was within his rights in nationalizing the canal company, since it lay completely within Egyptian territory. He added that Egypt had an inherent right to do so provided that just compensation was paid to the owners of the property so expropriated. Moreover, he added, resort to force was unjustified. During the crisis, he made these views known in strong terms to British Prime Minister Eden.

The day before the British, French, and Israeli attack, the Soviets moved to suppress a rebellion in Hungary. The United States condemned this Soviet move. Eisenhower, in the middle of a presidential campaign, explained that "we cannot—in the world, any more than in our own nation—subscribe to one law for the weak, and another for the strong." The United States immediately asked for a meeting of the Security Council on the Suez question. General Burns, the chief of staff of UNTSO, in the early hours of October 30, requested Israel to withdraw its troops from the Sinai and stop firing.[18]

The British and French vetoed a Security Council resolution to oppose their aggression. The Council then passed the issue to the General Assembly under the "Uniting for Peace Procedure." On November 2 the General Assembly at 4:20 A.M. approved a U.S. cease-fire resolution by a vote of 64 to 5, opposed only by Britain, France, Australia, New Zealand, and Israel. Also, by a vote of 50 to 8, the General Assembly demanded that the Soviets withdraw their troops from Hungary. Under strong pressure from the United Nations, supported by economic pressure from the United States, the fighting in the Sinai and the canal area came to an end within a few days.

Meanwhile, on November 4 the General Assembly asked the secretary general to form an emergency force supervised by the chief of UNTSO. By November 6 Secretary General Hammarskjöld had negotiated the arrangements for a cease-fire and international force to supervise the withdrawal of Israeli, French, and British forces. He accepted offers from 10 states—Brazil, Canada, Colombia, Denmark, Finland, India, Indonesia, Norway, Sweden, and Yugoslavia—to provide contingents. The United States offered the airlift. By November 7 the fighting had stopped. By early 1957 the UN Emergency Force (UNEF I) had been brought to its full complement of 6,000 officers and men. In connection with pressuring Israel to withdraw, the force undertook to patrol the border between Egypt and Israel in order to prevent terrorist raids against Israel.

Britain, France, and Israel completed evacuation of all occupied areas by March 8, 1957. During the next 10 years, UNEF I maintained peace along these borders. It was lightly armed, whereas UNTSO observers are not armed. It is important to note in connection with the 1967 war that Hammarskjöld, in setting up UNEF I in 1956, pledged that it was stationed on Egyptian territory only with Egyptian consent.[19] With the putting into effect of the agreements for UNEF I, the reputation of the secretary general reached an all-time high. He had arranged a face-saving device for three major powers for withdrawing their forces from the Suez Canal and established a basis of cooperation of Egypt with UNEF patrols that worked smoothly for a decade.

The negotiations for clearing the canal of ships sunk by the Egyptians were difficult because of Egypt's initial objections to accept British salvage ships. The canal was cleared by March 29, 1957. The arrangements for occupying Gaza were even more difficult because of Israel's insistence that the United Nations administer Gaza and that Egypt not take control, whereas Egypt insisted on administering the area. Israel finally accepted a minimum Egyptian presence in Gaza.

The secretary general maintained that the expenses of UNEF were expenses of "the organization," according to Article 17, paragraph 2 of the Charter. However, the Soviets and their Eastern European allies did not agree, claiming that the force under the General Assembly was established in violation of the Charter provisions, which required that such force be a responsibility of the Security Council. The General Assembly and the secretary general obtained an advisory opinion from the International Court supporting their position that the cost of this force should be borne by the UN members according to the general provisions for financing UN expenses. (The Court ruled, however, that UNEF had no power of "enforcement"; such powers are reserved for a force of the Security Council.) The Soviets still refused to pay, and as the total expenditures of UNEF mounted, the United Nations faced a major financial crisis. The UN nations were reluctant to try to force the Soviet Union to back down. The financial crisis was alleviated ultimately only by voluntary contributions and the issuance of UN bonds to pay the expenses of the emergency force. UNEF I kept the peace for over 10 years, but it was terminated as a result of the 1967 war, as indicated below. At its peak it consisted of 6,000 officers and men. It suffered 90 fatalities. Its total cost over 10 years was $213 million, which was microscopic in comparison with the military budgets of major powers during those years. However, its Achilles' heel was revealed in the 1967 crisis when Egypt requested it to leave and it complied.

The 1967 War

The 1967 war was a major disaster that laid the basis for the 1973 war and created lasting impediments to achieving peace in the area. In the spring of 1967 there were increased fedayeen raids against Israel encouraged by Nasser's *Voice of Cairo*, a radio broadcast that blanketed the Middle East. Israel retaliated with raids against Syria and Jordan. This added to the pressures against the moderate pro-Western governments of Jordan and Lebanon, which refused to ally with Nasser and accept his leadership. Israel's relations with Syria were particularly bad. Syrians had fired into Galilee from the Golan Heights, and Israel retaliated in dogfights in which six Syrian planes were shot down. The radical Arab press made sarcastic remarks about the inaction of President Nasser, who had a defense pact with Syria. In this explosive atmosphere the Soviets spread rumors that Israel was about to attack Syria. This added to the tension even though the United States investigated and found the report untrue. Israel proposed that the Soviet ambassador tour the northern part of the country to confirm that the Israelis were not mobilizing forces, but he refused. The cynicism of the Soviet Union, after spreading rumors about Israel preparing an attack, was demonstrated when it said on May 24 that the situation was not serious enough to warrant convening the Security Council. The Soviet Union and Egypt apparently were overconfident of the latter's military power.[20]

Within the Egyptian government, General Amer put increasing political pressure on Nasser to act against Israel, and on May 16 Nasser declared a state of emergency for the Egyptian armed forces. The Egyptian government then requested General Rikyhe, the UNEF commander, to withdraw his forces. Secretary General U Thant called an advisory committee meeting of the countries that provided the force. Opinion was divided between India, Pakistan, and Yugoslavia, which wanted immediate withdrawal, and Canada, Denmark, Norway, Sweden, and Brazil, which wanted to appeal to Egypt to change its mind and then to put the question to the General Assembly. However, the committee did not propose to convene the General Assembly to consider the crisis. The legal validity of Egypt's demand to withdraw UN forces was recognized since those forces were stationed there with the consent of that government.[21] It will be recalled that UNEF forces were under the General Assembly, which did not have the authority to put troops in Egypt without its agreement. Under the UN Charter, Security Council forces would have had that authority, since the Council acts on behalf of the entire membership on such issues (Article 25, Chapter VII).

U Thant tried without success to get Egypt to withdraw its demand and to get UNEF forces stationed in Israel. On May 18 he expressed deep anxiety to the UN advisory committee for UNEF I about the dangerous deterioration of the situation, but he continued with the evacuation of the 3,378 troops of UNEF.[22] He replaced them with a few UNTSO observers to maintain a UN presence.

Anwar Sadat's memoirs report that Nasser knew that his actions were being provocative. On May 22 Nasser declared the blockade of the Strait of Tiran, and in a cabinet meeting he admitted that this action made war "100 percent" certain. Nasser asked if General Amer was prepared, and Amer answered that everything was in tip-top shape.[23] During this tense period Egyptian spokesmen made threats about destroying Israel.

Britain proposed to the United States that a naval task force be established to keep the strait open. On May 30 Israeli Prime Minister Eshkol told the United States through the Israeli ambassador that it was essential that a naval escort move through the strait "within a week or two." Meanwhile President Johnson, who was embroiled in the escalation of the war in Vietnam, asserts in his memoirs that he was trying to get congressional and UN support for such a commitment of forces to the strait. With his immersion in Vietnam, Johnson refused to give a clear commitment to keep the strait open without strong allied and congressional support.

The secretary general in his report to the Security Council of May 26 said that he had expressed his "deep concern" about Egypt's restricting innocent passage through the Strait of Tiran. In the Security Council debates Ambassador Goldberg of the United States also pleaded with Egypt to forgo the act of belligerence of closing the Strait of Tiran, but in vain. This belligerence gave Israel the excuse that Egypt had committed the first warlike act, even though in the 10 years the strait had been open only five Israeli ships had used it.[24] The Council debates asked for restraint, but it made no move to establish the international naval escort the Israelis had demanded.

On June 5 Israel attacked, wiping out the Egyptian and Syrian air forces, and Israeli forces drove into the Sinai. Within a week the Israelis had taken the Sinai, the Golan Heights, Gaza, and the West Bank. By June 10 the way was open to Damascus, but the Israelis called a halt. The Security Council in a series of meetings and resolutions demanded a cease-fire. By June 10 fighting had stopped, and the UNTSO was observing a cease-fire under instructions of the Security Council. Israel now controlled the Sinai, the Gaza Strip, the West Bank including Jerusalem, and the Golan Heights (see Map 2).

The Security Council met in July and October to consider complaints by both Israel and Egypt about violations of the cease-fire. In November the Council considered Egyptian complaints of Israel's failure to withdraw its forces from the occupied territory.

On November 22 the Security Council unanimously passed Resolution 242, a landmark. Lord Caradon of Great Britain drafted it after months of discussion in the Council and General Assembly, and after extensive discussion with the Arabs, Israelis, and other delegates. It was later accepted as a basis for the Camp David negotiations that established peace between Egypt and Israel. At the same time, the Security Council appointed a special representative to assist in efforts at a peaceful settlement.

The major points of the resolution, whose full text is in Appendix C, are as follows:

> 1. The Security Council affirms that fulfillment of Charter principles requires the establishment of a just and lasting peace, which should include the application of both the following principles:
>
> (i) Withdrawal of Israeli armed forces from territories occupied in the recent conflict;
>
> (ii) Termination of all claims or states of belligerency and respect for and acknowledgment of the sovereignty, territorial integrity, and political independence of every State in the area and their right to live in peace within secure and recognized boundaries free from threats or acts of force;
>
> 2. Affirms further the necessity
>
> (a) For guaranteeing freedom of navigation through international waterways in the area;
>
> (b) For achieving a just settlement of the refugee problem;
>
> (c) For guaranteeing the territorial inviolability and political independence of every State in the area, through measures including the establishment of demilitarized zones.

Map 2. Israel after the 1967 War

Resolution 242 is intentionally vague about whether Israel should return *all* territories that it occupied in the 1967 war, with the Arabs insisting it should and Israel refusing to agree. The Palestinians object to the resolution because it does not mention the rights of the Palestinian people. Nevertheless, the resolution has stood the test of time and was still being used as the basis of the U.S. initiative in 1992 to try to bring about a settlement of the basic causes of the Palestinian uprising against the Israeli occupation of the West Bank and Gaza.

The 1973 War

Vice President Anwar Sadat became president of Egypt after Nasser's death in 1970. Sadat was obsessed and humiliated by the 1967 war and determined to get back Egyptian territory. In 1971 he expelled 20,000 Soviet military advisers because the Soviets were involved in plotting a coup against him. However, Sadat continued to get military equipment from the Soviet Union to replace that lost in 1967. After the loss of Soviet military advisers, few if any took the threat of Egyptian military action seriously. Even Sadat's own commanders did not believe him when he asked them to prepare to attack Israel.[25] But Sadat insisted, and on October 6, 1973, Egyptian forces surprised the Israelis by attacking along the Suez Canal, while Syrian forces mounted an attack at the Golan Heights. For a while the Syrian tanks threatened to break through into Galilee, but the Israeli air force and defenders turned back the attack. Then the action shifted to the south where General Aric Sharon led a counterattack across the canal and threatened to cut off the Egyptian Third Army, which had established a bridge-head in the Sinai. This fighting recorded the biggest tank battle in history, and the Israelis lost hundreds tanks to the new Soviet antitank missiles. The Israelis also suffered heavy losses to their aircraft from new mobile antiaircraft weapons provided by the Soviets.

On October 22 the Security Council adopted Resolution 338 calling on parties to cease fire and to start implementing Resolution 242. As fighting continued President Sadat appealed for a joint Soviet-American force to be sent to the area. This precipitated a nuclear crisis. The Soviet Union in response to Sadat's plea had sent a letter from Brezhnev to President Nixon calling for joint Soviet-U.S. contingents to police the truce, adding that if the United States found it impossible to act in this matter, the Soviets would consider acting unilaterally. Henry Kissinger, Nixon's national security adviser, interpreted this in the worst way because he did not want Soviet troops in the area, and his fears were increased by intelligence that the Soviets were alerting airborne divisions. With a phone call to the president, who was in the middle of the Watergate crisis, and to the secretary of defense, Kissinger raised the alert status of U.S. nuclear forces from a normal DEFCON 4 or 5 to a DEFCON 3. Soldiers were called back from leave and B-52 bombers were put on emergency alert. These signals were received in the Kremlin, but fortunately the crisis did not escalate further.

The next day the UN Security Council approved establishing UN Emergency Force II (UNEF II), without soldiers from the superpowers. The force, which eventually numbered about 7,000 soldiers, was sent promptly to monitor the truce. Because the Security Council set up this force, it could have been authorized to take enforcement action, in contrast to UNEF I set up under the General

Assembly, which did not have this power. The acceptance of this UN force without question contrasted with the nuclear crisis that occurred when the Soviets proposed a Soviet-U.S. force, and the incident demonstrates the neutral nature of the United Nations as a source of peacekeeping units.

Secretary of State Kissinger began shuttling back and forth between Cairo, Jerusalem, and Damascus to try to achieve a cease-fire. These efforts succeeded, and the cease-fire was formally endorsed by the Peace Conference on the Middle East under the cochairmanship of the Soviet Union and the United States on December 21, 1973. This conference was under the auspices of the United Nations. Egypt, Israel, and Jordan attended, but Syria refused.

During the crisis the Arab states had put pressure on the United States by cutting back on their oil exports, while insisting that there be a withdrawal of Israeli forces. This helped motivate Kissinger in his shuttle efforts. Also, a military working group under the chairmanship of the UNEF commander in December 1973 and January 1974 reached agreement on provisions for the disengagement of forces from the Sinai and establishing a buffer zone between Egyptian and Israeli troops. This disengagement was supported within Israel by General Dayan, now the foreign minister, and by the efforts of Secretary of State Kissinger.

UN military observers in October began observing the cease-fire in the Golan Heights. On May 31, 1974, an agreement mediated by Kissinger was signed on the disengagement of forces between Israel and Syria along that border. The Security Council subsequently then set up the UN Disengagement Observer Forces (UNDOF) of UN members to patrol a cease-fire line and neutral zone. This consisted of about 1,250 lightly armed military personnel at a cost about $1.7 million a month. Both the UNDOF and the UNEF II forces were renewed periodically by the Security Council. They were responsible to it and the secretary general.

On September 4, 1975, Kissinger succeeded in mediating a second disengagement agreement between Egypt and Israel providing for further withdrawal of Israeli forces to east of the Gidi-Mitla passes in the Sinai and from the oil fields along the Red Sea. This agreement established a large buffer zone between Israeli and Egyptian forces patrolled by UNEF II troops, and it prohibited an Egyptian military buildup. It is significant that Kissinger as a foremost practitioner of power politics found that the United Nations peacekeeping forces were essential to his diplomacy in the Middle East.

These agreements set the stage for Camp David. Following a visit by Sadat to Jerusalem in November 1977, President Jimmy Carter began negotiations that led to two agreements. The September 1978 agreements, which were based on principles of UN Resolution 242 (Appendix C), set a framework for a peace treaty in which Israel would return the Sinai. The second one set a framework for peace in the Middle East between Israel and the Palestinians by providing for self-government on the West Bank. These agreements were incorporated in treaties signed on March 26, 1979.[26] Israeli forces withdrew from the Sinai on April 25, 1982, with General Sharon's troops dragging out the last Israeli settlers. Originally, the agreements called for UNEF II to patrol the Sinai, but, as a result of opposition by Arab states, the Soviet Union, and the Palestinian Liberation Organization (PLO), UNEF II was terminated on July 24, 1979.

President Carter then set up a new multinational observer force modeled after the UN units to monitor the provisions of the peace treaty. The multinational force patroled the Strait of Tiran, which is internationalized by the treaty. During the first year, the force had 2,600 personnel from 10 countries, and it was commanded by a Norwegian. Its budget was $103.5 million with one-third each contributed by Egypt, Israel, and the United States.

The Camp David agreements stabilized the situation in the Middle East by making peace between Israel and Egypt, by far the largest and most powerful Arab neighbor. With its southern border protected, Israel was much less threatened by Syria, Jordan, and Lebanon. For this reason the agreements were attacked by other Arab states, which broke off normal diplomatic relations with Egypt.

War in Lebanon

There was no peace in the area, however. The tensions were reflected in terrorist attacks against Israel mostly from Lebanon followed by retaliatory strikes. On March 15, 1978, following a Palestinian commando raid in Israel that killed 37 Israeli civilians, Israel invaded southern Lebanon. Israel and Lebanon both requested a meeting of the Security Council. Four days later the Council passed a resolution calling on Israel to cease immediately its military action against Lebanon and setting up a UN Interim Force in Lebanon (UNIFIL). The Israeli forces completed their withdrawal on June 13, 1978. The Security Council continued to extend UNIFIL every six months, and it has remained in southern Lebanon despite receiving heavy casualties and at times being circumvented by Israel.

The 6,000 soldiers of UNIFIL managed to help keep the lid on until June 1982, when Israeli forces mounted a major attack to destroy PLO bases in southern Lebanon. The Israeli leaders were alarmed at the continued buildup of PLO arms and strength in southern Lebanon, which it controlled. Israeli forces used the excuse of an attack on the Israeli ambassador in London by Palestinians to invade southern Lebanon again and destroy the PLO bases. Some UNIFIL positions were bypassed or overrun; one Norwegian soldier was killed. The

Israeli forces moved into Beirut where heavy fighting took place. Also, military clashes occurred with Syria during which Israel shot down 88 aircraft and destroyed Syrian surface-to-air missiles in Lebanon. The Security Council called for a cease-fire and endorsed the continued presence of UNIFIL. The Council's action was reinforced by efforts of U.S. Ambassador Philip Habib, who over a period of months negotiated an agreement on a withdrawal of about 10,000 PLO forces from Lebanon.

The United States, along with Britain, France, and Italy, sent a multilateral defense force into Lebanon to monitor the agreement negotiated by Ambassador Habib. These were not UN forces, but UN observers did monitor the situation in Beirut. The 10 UN observers were named the Observer Group Beirut. Later the Security Council increased the number to 50. At the beginning of 1983, however, 241 U.S. marines, who were part of the multilateral defense force, were killed in their Beirut headquarters by a terrorist bomb. Subsequently the United States withdrew its forces, eventually followed by those of Britain, France, and Italy. These troops were not under the United Nations, and their failure contrasts with the ability of the UN peacekeeping forces in the Middle East to maintain their positions.

After about two years of violent clashes between contending factions in Lebanon, a government backed by Syria was established that ended the open warfare but not periodic terrorist actions. Israel withdrew its forces finally at the end of 1985, but it periodically patrolled a "security zone" in a 25-mile strip within Lebanon's southern border. Violence and retaliation continued in the area, but UNIFIL forces provided an authority to which leaders who wished to end fighting in the region could appeal.

A new crisis broke out at the end of 1987 with the uprising of Palestinians against the Israeli occupation of the West Bank and Gaza. Israeli troops over the following years killed hundreds of demonstrators demanding a Palestine state and an end to the occupation. More than 1.2 million Palestinians live in the West Bank and Gaza. In November 1988 the PLO's Palestine National Council compromised by accepting UN Resolution 242, which indicated a willingness to recognize and negotiate with Israel. Arafat then applied for a U.S. visa to speak before the General Assembly, but it was refused by the United States on the grounds that he was associated with terrorist organizations. The General Assembly then voted to move its session temporarily to Geneva to hear Arafat speak. In ensuing negotiations Arafat drafted a statement acceptable to the United States denouncing terrorism and accepting UN resolutions. The United States then agreed to carry on conversations with him.

Secretary of State Baker in 1991 with repeated visits to the Middle East negotiated the breakthrough of face-to-face talks among Israel, the Arab states, and the PLO. The first session took place in Madrid followed by bilateral nego-tiations between Israel and its neighbors. Although at the insistence of Israel the United Nations was excluded, the conference was based on UN Resolutions 242 and 338. The General Assembly in its 1991 session affirmed rights of the Pales-tinians, but also repealed the "Zionism is racism" resolution, which had been offensive to Israel. Finally, under President Clinton and after repeated visits by Secretary of State Christopher, a peace agreement was negotiated between Israel and the Palestinians that involved turning over most of the West Bank to the Palestinians, with a final agreement to be negotiated after elections. At the end of 1995—ahead of schedule—Israel turned over West Bank cities to the new Palestinian authority. Again with Christopher's mediation negotiations started between Israel and Syria on the Golan Heights issues.

The United Nations inherited the Palestine problems from the League of Nations, and the United Nations has been at the center of Arab-Israeli wars and controversies since that time. It did not prevent these wars or solve the prob-lems, but it did prevent the wars from escalating into conflicts involving forces of the major powers. The UN peacekeeping forces helped end the wars and monitor cease-fires. The UN efforts set the stage for collateral efforts at Camp David and other venues for the peace agreements between Israel and its neigh-bors. This success for the United Nations is due in large part to support from the United States. Many other countries have provided peacekeeping forces. Major failures in heading off the 1967 war and bringing an end to the conflict in Lebanon in the 1980s were associated with the failure of the United States to act within a UN framework.

The United Nations' peacekeeping units still patrol southern Lebanon and the Golan Heights and the UNTSO observers patrol throughout the area. Peace spread to Lebanon in the 1990s. Thus, the United Nations and its peacekeeping forces are helping keep a lid on the Mideast, despite the actions of terrorists and opponents of the peace process.

THE CONGO OPERATION

In the Congo crisis that began in 1960 the secretary general of the United Nations acted as commander-in-chief of a UN military force at times engaged in conventional military operations. Secretary General Hammarskjöld anticipated trouble as the Congo achieved independence and sent Ralph Bunche there by Independence Day to be available to advise the new government. The crisis started on July 5, 1960, 35 days after the Congo (now named Zaire) achieved independence from Belgium. Congolese soldiers mutinied against their officers, who were exclusively Belgian, and for the first time killed Europeans. Belgian troops came back into the Congo to restore order, despite opposition by the new head of state, Patrice Lumumba.

On July 14, the UN Security Council, in a resolution instigated by the secretary general, called upon Belgium to withdraw its troops from the Congo, and authorized the UN secretary general to provide military and technical assistance to the Congolese government until its security forces could "meet fully their tasks." It was mostly a civil war but outside powers including the Soviets and Belgium were intervening. The secretary general formed the UN Operation in the Congo (ONUC), which rapidly built up to more than 14,000 troops, most of them from African nations. No troops of the permanent members of the Security Council were included in the force. The Security Council resolutions authorized ONUC to use force to get Belgian troops to withdraw, to maintain law and order, and to prevent a civil war.[27] The Security Council action reflected the common anticolonial attitude of the Security Council members.

Several years of confused actions occurred during which members of the Security Council were often at odds. The major political problem was that Katanga, the mineral-rich province, wished to secede with the help of Belgian forces. When Katanga resisted the entrance of UN troops, it took Hammarskjöld's personal intervention to persuade the province to accept the troops and obtain the evacuation of Belgian forces. The other major problem was that the Soviet Union and the United States supported different factions in the Congo.

Hammarskjöld's attempt to steer a middle course and prevent Soviet military support to the radical faction in the Congo enraged Khrushchev. He attacked Hammarskjöld personally in a speech before the General Assembly and proposed replacing him with a troika, a three-person executive. Hammarskjöld's moderate and measured response defending the integrity of the position of the secretary general was greeted with a standing ovation. The following day Khrushchev personally "buried the hatchet" and warmly received him at a Soviet reception. The Soviets did not stop their attacks on Hammarskjöld, however, or their support for the troika. Khrushchev's behavior can be explained by his frustration over the power the secretary general was exercising, which was not subject to the Soviet veto.[28]

The secretary general was able to take initiatives under the original resolutions, which were backed by the General Assembly's continued support for the central government of the Congo since the Security Council could not reach agreement. In September 1961, Secretary General Hammarskjöld was killed in a plane crash on his way to confer with President Tshombe, head of the Katanga province. Hammarskjöld was probably the most popular secretary general the United Nations has ever had.

The new acting secretary general, U Thant, received a strong mandate from the Security Council. Katanga, at first, did not cooperate and even fired on ONUC positions. By 1963, however, a new federal government of the Congo including Katanga was established. General Mobutu took over as president and was able to end the civil war. The United Nations provided major technical and economic assistance to the new government, and it has maintained its integrity since that time.

The successful initiatives of Secretary General Hammarskjöld during the crisis cost him his life. The world lost a great public servant. And there were other costs. Although he prevented Soviet and other intervention in the Congo, at times by closing all the airports with UN forces, he alienated the Soviet Union. Moreover, the heavy monetary costs of the operation added to UN financial strains. The Soviet Union and France did not regard the costs of the Congo operations as regular expenses of the United Nations and refused to pay. After the Congo crisis the secretary general did not take major initiatives to carry out peacekeeping operations without the approval of the Security Council, but the debts accumulated by the original Congo operations continued to threaten the financial position of the United Nations.

THE CUBAN MISSILE CRISIS

Officials making decisions in the Cuban missile crisis were concerned that the crisis would get out of control and escalate into nuclear war. The confrontation between the superpowers originated in the spring of 1960. At that time President Kennedy approved a plan started by President Eisenhower for the CIA to support the landing of Cuban exiles in Cuba with the aim of overthrowing Fidel Castro, who had established a communist-style government. When the landing occurred, the poorly trained force of about 1400 exiles, only indirectly supported by the U.S. military, failed miserably, with more than 1100 Cubans taken prisoner. Subsequently, U.S. covert support for attacks against Cuban targets and attempts to assassinate Castro continued.[29] However, such intervention violated international law, which is based on respect for the sovereignty of nations. The attacks together with belligerent statements and actions of the U.S. Congress created a concern in Cuba and the Soviet Union about future attacks against Cuba.[30]

According to Khrushchev's memoirs he got the idea of placing the missiles in Cuba when he was visiting Romania. He was concerned, he said, about the U.S. threat to Cuba and he added: "In addition to protecting Cuba, our missiles would have equalized what the West likes to call 'the balance of power.'"[31] It was high time, he wrote, that Americans knew what it felt like to have their own land and people threatened. Since the American long-range missiles outnumbered the Soviet long-range missiles 10 to 1, the USSR's placing 80 intermediate-range missiles plus medium-range missiles in Cuba would have helped redress the imbalance. Moreover, Khrushchev during his visit publicly criticized the U.S. missiles in Turkey, and he noted with concern Kennedy's statement that the United States would be willing to be the first to use nuclear missiles if attacked by another country. The primary reason for the Soviet move is still disputed, but the threat of U.S. missiles in Turkey was an important possible cause.

On October 16, 1962, Kennedy saw the first CIA pictures of the Cuban missile sites. During the next six days the high-level executive committee advising him debated what response to make. On Monday, October 22, Kennedy announced the United States would impose a "quarantine" on the shipment of offensive weapons to Cuba. The concept of a quarantine, or very limited blockade, was proposed by the committee to avoid imposing a "blockade," which is an act of war. Abram Chayes, the State Department's legal adviser during the crisis, points out in his book, *The Cuban Missile Crisis*, that over half of the executive committee were lawyers, which helps to explain the committee's concern about international law. For this reason, and in order to get support for the U.S. position, the United States took the matter to the United Nations and to the Organization of the American States (OAS), which can have regional responsibility for security matters under the United Nations Charter. The Executive Committee was relieved that the OAS gave the United States unanimous support on the quarantine. The U.S. state department produced a legal justification of U.S. action that was so popular with the media it had to be reissued.

This is not to say that legal arguments persuaded the Soviets to withdraw the missiles in return for a pledge not to invade Cuba. It seems clear from their statements that they believed Robert Kennedy, speaking for the president, had given them an ultimatum that they remove the missiles within 48 hours or the United States would act to remove them. Nevertheless, the unanimous support by the OAS for the quarantine and the widespread belief in NATO and by other nations that the United States' action was justified legally and politically probably helped persuade the Soviets to remove the missiles.

On October 28 Khrushchev announced that the Soviets would withdraw the missiles because the United States had pledged not to invade Cuba. Some years later it was revealed that the president's brother, Bobby Kennedy, during the crisis had committed the United States to remove its missiles from Turkey within a few months if the Soviets kept this commitment secret. Then, in March 1987 Kennedy's Secretary of State Dean Rusk revealed at the Hawk's Cay conference in Florida that during the crisis President Kennedy asked Rusk to request the former deputy secretary general of the UN, Andrew Cordier, to approach Secretary General U Thant and suggest that U Thant propose that the United States withdraw missiles from Turkey and the Soviets withdraw them from Cuba. If this were kept secret, it would give the United States an excuse to remove the missiles without seemingly breaking a commitment to NATO on the Turkish missiles in the face of a Soviet threat. Khrushchev yielded before this ploy was put into effect. This would have been a last-ditch option to use the United Nations as an impartial umpire to propose a solution that both sides could accept without losing face. Although fortunately the crisis was resolved without this effort to solve the issue, the incident demonstrates how important a role the United Nations could have played in one of the most serious crises the United States ever faced.

THE INDIA-PAKISTAN CONFLICTS

In 1948 the United Nations was involved in its first major ethnic conflict after World War II, when India and Pakistan were formed from the British colony of India. The differences were rooted in religion—the Hindus worship many gods whereas the Moslems believe in one god. When the Moslems came to India about 1000 A.D., they destroyed Hindu temples and sculptures as idolatrous. Their food laws were also different. To Hindus, the cow was sacred and they would not eat beef, but Moslems eat beef and consider pork unclean. There was virtually no intermarriage between Moslems and Hindus.

As Britain ended its colonial rule in India, a terrible civil conflict broke out, the most serious religious conflict of our era. More than 800,000 civilians were killed as Moslem refugees moved into Pakistan and Hindu refugees moved into areas of India. Lord Mountbatten stayed on as viceroy to referee the division of India. After the British Empire drew lines between the new states, there were two Pakistans—East Pakistan and West Pakistan—separated by 1000 miles of India.

The United Nations was not involved in the original civil war until after the lines between the two countries were determined. The state of Jammu Kashmir, a beautiful resort area in northern India, was controlled by a Hindu prince, but its population was mostly Moslem. The Hindu prince decided to join India, which antagonized the new Pakistan, a Moslem state.

The Indians were furious when Pakistani tribesmen, obviously supported by the new Pakistan government, attacked the cities of Kashmir. India wanted to retaliate with its army, which could have caused a major war. The matter was brought before the Security Council by India on January 1, 1948. Pakistan entered a counter-complaint, charging that Indian forces had unlawfully occupied part of Kashmir and that the genocide of Moslems was being carried out in a prearranged plan.

On January 20, 1948, the UN Security Council established a three-member UN Commission for India/Pakistan (UNCIP), which included a U.S. member, to investigate and mediate. The Commission arrived in July 1948 and on August 13 proposed a cease-fire, with the disputed area being administered under UNCIP. There was a withdrawal of troops and both governments finally accepted the cease-fire line in July 1949. Following this, the parties could not agree on the details of a plebiscite for a permanent settlement of the problem. Probably, India was afraid that it would lose control if the issue came to a vote of the largely Moslem population. In March 1950 the Security Council terminated UNCIP and established a UN representative to mediate. In March 1951 Frank Graham, an American, was appointed the UN representative for these issues.

In 1949 the United Nations had also established the UN Military Observer Group in India and Pakistan (UNMOGIP) to supervise the cease-fire. That unit, under the authority of the secretary general, continued to operate, reporting violations and trying to prevent violence along the cease-fire line.

In 1965 a major war broke out again in Kashmir. In August 1965 Pakistan crossed the UN cease-fire line in an invasion of Kashmir. Indian forces retaliated successfully in an invasion of West Pakistan. The secretary general received reliable reports from UNMOGIP and appealed to the Indian and Pakistan representatives, and personally to the prime minister of India and the president of Pakistan, for a cease-fire. Both India and Pakistan accepted his pleas on September 22. At the same time, the secretary general created the UN India/Pakistan Observation Mission (UNIPOM) to supervise the cease-fire and to assist UNMOGIP.

At the end of 1965, and the beginning of 1966, the secretary general and his representatives supervised talks on the withdrawal of forces from Kashmir. These talks were largely successful and were assisted by the good offices of the Soviet Union. On January 10, 1966, India and Pakistan agreed on a joint declaration that all armed personnel of their countries would be withdrawn. The UNIPOM was then disbanded. Ironically, the cease-fire line was virtually the same as had been established by the United Nations in 1949.

The above conflicts were a continuation of the original civil war, which were contained with the help of UN mediation, particularly by the secretary general. The 1971 war involved a different ethnic conflict and a new international dimension, one that threatened to bring about a confrontation between the superpowers (Map 3). East Pakistan was a very poor area, and the Bengalis of East Pakistan believed that they were neglected by West Pakistan, where the capital

Map 3. India and Pakistan, 1971

was. In 1970 a violent cyclone from the Bay of Bengal killed more than 200,000 people. The West Pakistan government was slow to aid the devastated areas. This exacerbated the differences between the two parts of Pakistan, which had different languages and cultures, although they both were Moslem.

Meanwhile President Yahya Kahn was preparing to establish a democratic government. In March 1971 the elections were held. In East Pakistan, the Awami League representing the Bengalis won 167 out of 169 seats, a strong vote for independence. The 167 seats would have given it a majority in the new Pakistan parliament, which could have forced a division of the two countries. Yahya Kahn did not want to preside over the splitting up of Pakistan, so he postponed the convening of the new parliament. The Awami League responded with a campaign of civil disorder and a general strike.

West Pakistan moved in its troops to suppress the rebellion, but 70,000 West Pakistani soldiers could not pacify 30 million East Pakistanis. In this civil conflict several hundred thousand Bengalis were killed, and raping and pillaging were extensive. About 10 million Bengalis fled in terror from this conflict to the Bengali area of eastern India, where the Bengalis were Hindu not Moslem. The UN secretary general with the consent of the two governments set up two large-scale humanitarian programs—one for East Pakistan and the other for India—to assist the Bengali refugees.

During 1971 Indian Prime Minister Indira Gandhi informed the United Nations and its members that India could not continue to support 10 million Bengali refugees in the poorest part of India. Tensions rose when a study of an Indian research organization pointed out it would be cheaper to wage war than for India to continue to support the refugees.[32] One of the most serious sources of tension was that the leader of the Awami League had been arrested and imprisoned in West Pakistan. On July 20, 1971, the secretary general directed the attention of the president of the Security Council to the deteriorating situation and described it as a threat to the peace. He continued to offer his good offices, but there was no move by Pakistan to pacify the situation and accept the return of the refugees.

On November 26, 1971, Indian troops were reported to be participating in probes against East Pakistan. On December 3 Yahya Kahn claimed that Indian forces were dismembering his country, and he launched a surprise attack in the West on Indian airfields, hoping to wipe out their air arm. The secretary general, in an almost unprecedented move, used Article 99 to bring the matter before the Security Council. On December 6 there was an eight-power resolution calling for a cease-fire and withdrawal of troops, but it was vetoed by the Soviet Union in the Security Council. The Security Council then referred the matter to the General Assembly, which on December 7 adopted a resolution by an overwhelming vote of 104 to 11 calling for an immediate cease-fire and withdrawal of troops. Only India, Bhutan, and the Soviet bloc voted against the resolution.

By December 16 Indian troops forced West Pakistan troops in East Pakistan to surrender to the Indian forces. By this time the matter was again before the Security Council, which voted 13 to 0, with the Soviets abstaining, for a cease-fire. Indian troops obeyed the Security Council resolution and withdrew from East Pakistan. UNMOGIP supervised the cease-fire in West Pakistan.

As a result of the ending of resistance by West Pakistan, the new state of Bangladesh was established in East Pakistan. President Yahya Kahn of West Pakistan generously released the Awami League leader, who came back to be president of Bangladesh. On December 21 the Security Council adopted a resolution demanding strict observance of the cease-fire and the withdrawal of armed forces to the agreed-on cease-fire line in Kashmir. In July 1972 the prime minister of India and the president of Pakistan confirmed these agreements at Simla, again confirming the cease-fire line of 1949 with only minor deviations.

The United Nations, by representing the world community, helped bring about an early end to the 1971 war. It followed this with a massive relief program to help resettle 10 million refugees created by the war. This efficient and rapid resettlement of refugees contrasts with the decades of strife that resulted from the displacement of 1 million Palestinian refugees.

In the above cases, the United Nations restrained the aggressor and helped contain the crises. In assessing the success of the United Nations in achieving its main aim of maintaining international peace, it is useful also to examine cases during that period where the United Nations played a minor role and initially was not effective. We will then look at the new era of the 1990s with successes assisted by cooperation of the Soviet Union and China on the Security Council.

SOVIET CONTROL OF EASTERN EUROPE

After World War II the nations of the world recognized as a fact of international life the Soviet domination of a group of East European states. When the war ended, Soviet troops were occupying these countries, some of which had allied with Hitler. In summit meetings before the end of the war and before the United Nations was founded, a line was drawn through Europe dividing the areas occupied by the Soviets and those by the armies of the Western allies. The Soviets did not keep their commitment in the Yalta agreement to form governments representative of their democratic elements through free elections. As the Western armies rapidly demobilized, the Western allies realized that they could not enforce the Yalta agreement or force the Soviet armies out of Eastern Europe without resuming the war.

When Hungary in 1956 and Czechoslovakia in 1968 tried to break out of the East European bloc, Soviet armies invaded to restore order. In the case of Hungary, the new revolutionary government of Imre Nagy requested assistance of the Security Council in negotiating the withdrawal of Soviet troops. The Soviet Union vetoed a draft resolution in the Security Council, and action was transferred to the General Assembly. During the Assembly meeting, another new Hungarian government just installed by the Soviets informed the secretary general that all communications from the previous government were invalid. The General Assembly, on November 4, adopted a resolution calling on the USSR to withdraw, affirming the right of the Hungarian people to form their own government and requesting the secretary general to investigate. The Soviets ignored this and subsequent resolutions. Finally, in 1962, after numerous UN resolutions, the matter was dropped. Meanwhile, about $20 million was provided through the UN for about 200,000 refugees fleeing from Hungary.

In Czechoslovakia in 1968 Dubcek, a new leader of the Communist Party, started to implement a series of liberal economic and political reforms including holding elections, reestablishing a parliament, and giving workers a stronger voice in management. The Soviets, alarmed by this challenge to the communist systems of Europe, persuaded other Eastern European countries to join them in invading Czechoslovakia. The Czech government protested to the United Nations but ordered the Czech forces not to resist. The invasion was so quick and effective that the matter died in the Security Council after three days of consideration. At the end of that time, the Czech government requested the item be withdrawn from the agenda. A resolution condemning the intervention was vetoed by the Soviets.

These two cases demonstrated the basic weakness of the Charter—it is not designed to enforce a decision against one of the great powers. Theoretically, the General Assembly could have mobilized the world community to oppose the invasions or impose sanctions, but none of the countries were willing to confront the Soviets to that extent or to go to war with the Soviets, who were at the time a nuclear power. Moreover, there was no indication that Hungary or Czechoslovakia wanted to be liberated at the cost of being destroyed in such a war. These issues reflected the fact that the United Nations had inherited a situation in 1945 that could not have been corrected at that time without another world war. Moreover, there was a strong belief it was necessary to keep both superpowers in the organization. The sequel was that the Eastern European countries were liberated peacefully following their 1989 anti-communist revolutions.

THE CYPRUS WARS

Cyprus occupies a highly strategic position at the eastern end of the Mediterranean near the Suez Canal. It was settled by Greeks in antiquity, but conquered by the Turks in the 16th century. Britain took over in 1914 during World War I and established bases to help defend the route to the Suez Canal.

After World War II, Greek Cypriots demonstrated for independence from Britain or for union with Greece. In a plebiscite among Greek Cypriots in 1949, 96 percent of the eligible voters favored union with Greece. The UN General Assembly discussed the issue of self-determination but was not able to muster a two-thirds vote for an agreed resolution.

Demonstrations and violence continued, including fighting between Greek and Turkish communities. Finally, at the urging of NATO, the Greek and Turkish prime ministers and the British negotiated a treaty establishing Cyprus as an independent republic in 1960 with a Greek-Cypriot president and Turkish-Cypriot vice president. The treaty prohibited union with Greece or partition of the island and gave the British sovereignty over two base areas on the island. Small contingents of Greek and Turkish troops were also permitted on the island.

In 1963 after the president, Archbishop Makarios, demanded changes in the constitution that would have lessened the rights of the Turkish minority, fighting broke out between the Greek and Turkish communities. Britain proposed a NATO force for peacekeeping, but Archbishop Makarios insisted that it be under the Security Council. In February 1964 Britain and the government of Cyprus asked for the assistance of the UN Security Council. Heavy fighting continued, and finally after eight meetings the Security Council established, with the consent of the government of Cyprus, a UN peacekeeping force in Cyprus (UNFICYP). Turkey threatened to intervene if peace was not restored. By May 1964 UNFICYP increased to about 7,000 men. After major fighting, including bombing by Turkish air force planes to support Turkish Cypriot forces, UNFICYP managed to stop the violence. There was no other major conflict for ten years.

In July 1974 the Cyprus National Guard, which was controlled secretly by Greek military intelligence forces, launched a coup. President Makarios was almost captured, but British helicopters from a British base on the island evacuated him at the last minute. Turkish troops invaded from the mainland and took control of part of the island for the Turkish minorities.

Within a few days a more moderate government was formed in Cyprus, while the military government of Greece fell and was replaced by a democratic one. The UN Security Council on July 20 called for a cease-fire and for Greece, Turkey, and the United Kingdom to negotiate without delay to restore peace and a constitutional government. There were heavy UNFICYP casualties, but the force maintained control of the island's airport, which prevented reinforcements by air. On August 16 the Council condemned the military action of Turkey. On the same day Turkey and Greece accepted a cease-fire, but Turkey continued to control the northern third of the island. The UN High Commissioner for Refugees began to assist and resettle about 200,000 refugees displaced by the war. Archbishop Makarios returned as president.

UNFICYP and the secretary general tried to mediate the issue and managed to contain the conflict despite sporadic outbreaks of fighting. The Security Council continued to renew the force, but contributions did not meet expenses and the UN deficit increased. In February 1975 the Turkish Cypriots declared their area a "federated Turkish state." It was not recognized by the international community, but it exercised *de facto* control over the Turkish community on the island outside control of the Cypriot government.

In these crises the Security Council, operating in a difficult situation, established the peacekeeping force of 7,000 soldiers, which managed to stop the wars and contain the violence. Its commanders and the secretary general made strenuous efforts over the years to bring about a settlement, but as of the fall of 1992 their efforts were not successful. Greece and Turkey both resisted suggestions for a legal settlement through the International Court of Justice or for arbitration of the issues. (A major legal issue was whether under the 1960 treaty establishing the government of Cyprus the Turkish troops had the right to intervene to protect the Turkish community.) By 1996 the parties were finally coming close to accepting UN proposals for establishing a loose federation of the Greek and Turkish communities.

THE VIETNAM WAR

The United Nations without great power support played no important role in the Vietnam War. After World War II, a communist insurgency led by Ho Chi Minh fought the French, trying to end their colonial rule. In 1954, after being defeated by the communist forces, the French negotiated the Geneva Agreements with Vietnamese representatives that provided for the establishment of the Democratic Republic of Vietnam in the north under Ho Chi Minh and another government in the south under Emperor Bao Dai and his prime minister, Ngo Dinh Diem. The United States, the Soviet Union, China, and Great Britain also participated in the negotiations. The agreements specified no role for the United Nations.

After 1954 South Vietnam was formally recognized as a government by at least 90 nations, which were most of the countries of the world at that time. These included the important nations outside the Communist bloc. The communist nations and a few others formally recognized North Vietnam. The Communist bloc did not recognize South Vietnam, supporting North Vietnam's position that Vietnam should be unified under the Communist government of North Vietnam.

The United States supported the new government of South Vietnam with military and economic aid as the French withdrew. Under the terms of the 1954 agreement U.S. military advisers were limited to several hundred. In the late 1950s, as the Diem government arrested and fought with the insurgents, North Vietnam sent tens of thousands of communist cadres with military supplies to the South. President Kennedy, aiming at stopping the spread of communism in Asia, increased aid and the number of U.S. military advisers to about 17,000.

Vice President Johnson took over after President Kennedy's assassination in 1963. On August 4, 1964, President Johnson requested an urgent meeting of the UN Security Council complaining that U.S. naval vessels had been attacked by North Vietnam in international waters in the Gulf of Tonkin off the coast of North Vietnam. North Vietnam attended the Security Council meeting and responded that U.S. aircraft and warships had bombed and strafed North Vietnamese territory and supported raids by South Vietnam. Action was blocked not only because of the possibility of a Soviet veto, but other nations on the Council realized that the United States and North Vietnam were not willing to accept the judgment of the Security Council on the issues. The United States and North Vietnam continued escalating the conflict, with the United States eventually sending 535,000 of its own troops to South Vietnam.

After major escalation of the war, the United States on January 31, 1966, requested another meeting of the Security Council to consider the "question of Vietnam." The Council, after a debate, decided on February 2, 1966, to include the item on the agenda. The vote was 9 to 2 with 4 abstentions. The president of the Council undertook private consultations and then reported that the members wanted to end the conflict but believed that negotiations should take place in another forum.

Secretary General U Thant, in his annual reports to the General Assembly, explained why the United Nations was not taking initiatives to end the war. He noted the Geneva Agreements of 1954 prescribed no role for the United Nations and that neither North Vietnam or South Vietnam were UN members. He urged a revival of the Geneva Conference of 1954. He said he had, without success, devoted a great deal of effort to getting the parties (North Vietnam, South Vietnam, and the United States) to negotiate, but had failed because the struggle had been dominated by power politics.

North Vietnam was determined to unify the country under its control, and the United States was determined to support the South Vietnam government or a new government set up by free elections. After a long and costly war involving extensive bombing of North Vietnam, a truce was negotiated in 1973 under President Nixon, and the United States withdrew its forces. In the spring of 1975 North Vietnam flagrantly violated the terms of the truce with a full-fledged invasion by its regular forces and within a few weeks had won the war and taken control of the South. But this time the United States was so tired of the war that it accepted the outcome.

The United Nations was virtually powerless in this war. Neither side wanted to yield nor turn the issue over to UN mediation or arbitration. From the early stages of the war, U.S. leaders believed the United States, as the most powerful nation in the world, could defeat the insurgency without complications of UN involvement. France, Britain, and other allies did not want to commit their forces because they had a realistic view of the political and military costs involved.

The United States lost the war because its political system would not have accepted the use of nuclear weapons in that conflict or the conventional escalation needed to "win." Moreover, a conventional escalation to attack North Vietnam might have again triggered participation of Chinese "volunteers" such as in the Korean War. The result was a victory for North Vietnam and a stunning defeat for South Vietnam and the United States.

In the closing days of the Vietnam War, a radical communist movement, the Khmer Rouge, overthrew the military government of Cambodia and imposed a repressive regime. In purging its country of bourgeois elements the Khmer Rouge were responsible for the deaths of more than 1 million Cambodians, as dramatized in the movie *The Killing Fields*. Its regime challenged the forces of the new Communist government of Vietnam in border clashes. At the end of 1978 approximately 120,000 Vietnamese troops invaded Kampuchea. Within a few days, Vietnam had established a puppet regime headed by Heng Samrin, a communist defector from the Khmer Rouge. On February 19, 1979, Vietnam provided a post facto legal facade for the invasion by concluding a treaty providing for all necessary assistance by Vietnam when requested by the government of Kampuchea.

The world then watched in amazement as China and Vietnam, formerly allies in the Vietnam War, quarreled over Kampuchea. The Soviet Union lined up on the side of Vietnam, and China with Kampuchea. China, in the Security Council, denounced the "flagrant" military aggression of Vietnam, claiming its aim was to establish a colonial empire.

The bulk of the Khmer Rouge forces eluded the invading Vietnamese forces and began a campaign of opposition to the invaders. China continued to supply these forces through Thailand, while Vietnam strengthened its alliance with the Soviet Union, which provided large-scale aid.

The Vietnamese-Cambodian war escalated when Chinese forces invaded Vietnam's northern provinces on February 17, 1979. In the 17-day war, approximately 250,000 Chinese troops drove about 12 miles into Vietnam causing extensive damage and tens of thousands of casualties. The Chinese announced their troops were sent to "teach a lesson" to the invaders of Kampuchea and to end Vietnam's incursions into Chinese territory. The Chinese were also retaliating against the Vietnamese government, which had forced more than 170,000 ethnic Chinese to flee the country by nationalizing their shops and through other repressive actions.

After 17 days of bitter fighting and strong resistance by Vietnam, China announced that its mission was completed and withdrew from North Vietnam. During the conflict Moscow made threatening statements, airlifted supplies, and sent a naval task force to the South China Sea.

Vietnam's aggression appeared to be aimed at achieving the historic goal of Vietnam's Communist Party of creating a federation out of the former area of French Indochina. China's attack was classic power politics aimed at forcing Vietnam to withdraw from Kampuchea, and to weaken the Vietnamese alliance with the Soviet Union, which threatened China. In the sense that it was helping defend Kampuchea and opposing aggression it could be argued that China's action was supporting collective self-defense consistent with Article 51 of the Charter. The UN General Assembly recognized the old Khmer Rouge government and refused to seat the representatives of the new Kampuchean regime, regarding it as a puppet of the Vietnamese aggressors. As the former communist allies quarreled, China supported Thailand to deter an attack from Vietnam and drew closer to the United States. China continued to supply the Kampuchean resistance forces through Thailand.

The Southeast Asian neighbors of Cambodia and the United Nations encouraged peace talks in international meetings including the United States, the Soviet Union, Britain, China, and other major powers along with a representative of the UN secretary general. In October 1991 the talks finally bridged the gap between Prince Sihanouk, former prime minister and a spokesman for the resistance, and Hung Sen, the prime minister of Kampuchea.

The final peace agreement provided for the most expensive UN peacekeeping operation up to that time, with about 14,000 participating. Initial estimates of cost exceeded $2 billion. The United Nations was tasked with disarming about 300,000 troops, helping resettle about 350,000 refugees from Thailand, overseeing government ministries, organizing free elections, and helping clear over 1 million mines. An advance UN mission arrived in November 1991 and large numbers of advisers and peacekeeping troops arrived the following spring. The political hatreds arising from the Cambodian holocaust would interfere with the formation of a representative government in the exhausted nation.

Nevertheless, the UN force brought an end to the war and then stayed on to monitor elections. As a result, a moderate democratic government under Prince Sihanouk was established. The UN organs mobilized aid and advice for the new government. By the beginning of 1996 this "mission impossible" could be considered a qualified success. The government was struggling with factional political disputes and economic problems of reconstruction of an economy that had been poorly developed to begin with. However, the dangers of a renewal of the terrible holocaust were over and there were prospects for continued economic progress.

CONCLUSIONS

The Cambodian peacekeeping was a notable UN success that bridged the gap to the new era of cooperation between the Soviets and China with the West. It was originally labeled mission impossible because of the ferocious civil war, but the UN peace settlement was still holding in 1996. Even before the new era of cooperation the UN peacekeeping and coalition building had successes that belie the myth that it was not effective. The UN coalition repelled North Korea's aggression supported by the communist superpowers. President Truman took the lead under the banner of collective security and international law. The United Nations inherited the Palestine problem from the League of Nations, and over the decades managed to settle the wars and set the stage for collateral negotiations that promised to reduce tensions and avoid another world war. The UN Security Council also intervened in major civil wars that breached the peace in a holocaust (Cambodia and India-Pakistan) or threatened to escalate (India-Pakistan, Cyprus, and the Congo).

The above successes contrast with the disastrous failure of power politics in the Vietnam War. Also, power politics in the U.S. attacks against the Castro government helped bring about the Cuban missile crisis during which the world faced the threat of nuclear war. We will now make a case-by-case review of UN coalitions and peacekeeping in the new era of world politics.

Notes to Chapter 4

1. Y. Alexander and A. Nanes, *The United States and Iran: A Documentary History* (Frederick, MD: University Press, 1980), pp. 145–189.

2. D. Acheson, *Present at the Creation* (New York: Norton, 1969), p. 357.

3. N. Khrushchev, *Khrushchev Remembers* (Boston: Little, Brown, 1979), pp. 367–373.

4. T. Lie, *In the Cause of Peace* (New York: Macmillan, 1954), p. 327.

5. S. D. Bailey, *Voting in the Security Council* (Bloomington: Indiana University Press, 1971), pp. 69–73.

6. Lie, *Peace*, pp. 334–336.

7. H. Truman, *Years of Decision* (New York: Doubleday, 1956), pp. 332–334.

8. Acheson, *Present*, p. 405.

9. B. Smith, *Dean Acheson* (New York: Cooper Square, 1962), p. 417.

10. *New York Times*, September 29, 1950, p. 1; October 5, 1950, p. 1; October 8, 1950, p. 1.

11. U.S. Department of State, *Foreign Relations of the United States, East Asia and the Pacific 1950* (Washington, DC: Government Printing Office, 1976), pp. 267–269, 291–298, 374–375.

12. Acheson, *Present*, pp. 477, 514.

13. D. Eisenhower, *Mandate for Change* (New York: Doubleday, 1963), pp. 180–181.

14. D. Wainhouse, *International Peace Observation* (Baltimore: Johns Hopkins University Press, 1966), p. 246.

15. L. Collins and D. Lapierre, *O Jerusalem* (New York: Pocket Books, 1976); G. Pasha, *A Soldier with the Arabs* (London: Hodder and Slaughton, 1957); M. Dayan, *The Story of My Life* (New York: Werner Books, 1966).

16. T. Hoopes, *The Devil and John Foster Dulles* (Boston: Little, Brown, 1973), p. 335.

17. B. Urquart, *Hammarskjold* (New York: Harper, 1981), pp. 132–162.

18. Ibid., p. 173.

19. Ibid., p. 193.

20. A. Lall, *The UN and the Middle East Crisis* (New York: Columbia University Press, 1970), pp. 29–30.

21. R. Seikman, *Basic Documents on United Nations and Related Peacekeeping Forces* (Boston: Martinus Nijhoff, 1985), pp. 4–7.

22. Lall, *The UN*, p. 20.

23. A. Sadat, *In Search of Identity* (New York: Harper & Row, 1977), pp. 215–231.

24. Lall, *The UN*, pp. 34–35.

25. Sadat, *In Search*, pp. 213–233.

26. J. Carter, *Keeping Faith* (New York: Bantam, 1982), pp. 397–403.

27. Urquart, *Hammarskjold*, chap. 15, 16, 18, and 21.

28. Ibid., pp. 462–470.

29. U.S. Congress, Senate Select Committee, *Alleged Assassination Plots Involving Foreign Leaders* (Washington, DC: Government Printing Office, 1975); A. Schlesinger, *A Thousand Days* (New York: Fawcett, 1965), pp. 223–243; D. Phillips, *The Night Watch* (New York: Ballantine, 1977), chap. 4; R. Garthoff, *Reflections on the Cuban Missile Crisis* (Washington, DC: Brookings, 1987).

30. Garthoff, *Reflections*, pp. 54–55.

31. Ibid., pp. 6–7

32. J. Stoessinger, *Why Nations Go to War* (New York: St. Martins, 1974), p. 163.

Chapter V

UN COLLECTIVE SECURITY
IN THE NEW ERA

As President Bush led a UN coalition to repel Iraq's invasion of Kuwait, he called for a "new era" of international politics in which the United Nations "could fulfill the historic vision of its founders."[1] In this new era the five permanent members of the Security Council have cooperated in forming coalitions and peacekeeping units in contrast to the confrontations and vetoes of the Cold War.

The new era started with President Gorbachev's decision to end the Afghanistan War by withdrawing Soviet troops. UN mediators played a central role in that decision. The most controversial actions of the new era have been UN actions to bring peace to Somalia and the former Yugoslavia, which were essentially civil wars. These expanded the scope of UN operations. The UN Charter did not authorize interventions in matters essentially of domestic jurisdiction, which covered civil wars, unless they threatened international peace.

THE WAR IN AFGHANISTAN

The major event leading to the invasion of Afghanistan was a local communist coup in Afghanistan in 1978, which was followed by violent opposition of Islamic nationalists. They infuriated Soviet leaders when they attacked and killed Soviet military advisers to the new communist government of Afghanistan.

The Soviets invaded Afghanistan in December 1979 with the aim of establishing a reliable communist leader. The Soviet troops moved into the capital, killing the prime minister and putting a rival, Babrak Karmal, in his place. The world was shocked by the invasion, and 52 states called for a Security Council meeting. The United States sponsored a Security Council resolution deploring the intervention and calling for the immediate withdrawal of foreign troops from Afghanistan. The vote was 12 to 2 with the Soviets vetoing the resolution and East Germany joining in opposition. The Council sent the issue to the General Assembly. By a vote of 104 to 18 it called for the withdrawal of foreign troops from Afghanistan. The new Afghan representative appointed by the puppet Karmal government joined with the Soviets in opposing the General Assembly resolution.

The United States cut back on exports to the Soviet Union of grain and high-technology goods and organized a boycott of 65 nations to the Olympic Games in Moscow the following summer. Mr. Perez de Cuellar of the UN Secretariat negotiated with the Soviets for a withdrawal until he became UN secretary general on January 1, 1982. He appointed Diego Cordovez to continue that effort.

During the fighting the U.S. Congress openly appropriated hundreds of millions of dollars to support the resistance.[2] The United States insisted its actions were in accord with international law because it was assisting a legitimate government in opposing aggressive action.[3]

The United States worked closely with the UN negotiators, who represented world opinion on this issue. After eight years of negotiations and an exhausting war against the mujahideen resistance, President Gorbachev signed agreements for withdrawing Soviet forces. A plausible motive for this action was a desire to remove an impediment to opening up the Soviet Union to the West for reforming the Soviet government.

The Afghanistan agreements provided for the UN Good Offices Mission in Afghanistan (UNGOMAP) of 50 military officers plus civilians to monitor the withdrawal of Soviet troops and assist in the voluntary return of refugees. The military officers were taken from other UN peacekeeping operations.

Soviet troops withdrew on time as UNGOMAP monitored them, and it successfully assisted in return of refugees. The operation saved face for the Soviet Union by interposing the United Nations between it and the great powers. The secretary general redeployed 10 UN officers to advise his personal representative in Afghanistan and Pakistan, a post established in 1989. They attempted to mediate a peace among various Afghanistan factions, which continued to fight, but the United Nations was not empowered to enforce a peace. Nevertheless, Gorbachev's withdrawal of Soviet troops from Afghanistan opened the door to a new era of detente in international politics.

THE IRAN-IRAQ WAR

The Iran-Iraq war began with an Iraq invasion in 1980 to take complete control of the Shatt al-Arab waterway on their border. President Saddam Hussein's motive appeared also to be to establish Iraq's hegemony in the area. The war, which was waged near the largest oilfields in the world, initially caused petroleum shortages in the world market.

The Security Council repeatedly called for a cease-fire, and the secretary general, working with the Islamic League, tried to mediate the war. Khomeini, the Iranian leader, blocked progress in peace negotiations by insisting the president of Iraq be replaced and that a huge indemnity be paid. The war continued in a bloody stalemate and included the use of poison gas by Iraq, which was condemned by the Security Council. The superpowers and the nations in the area realized that as long as one side did not break the stalemate and decisively defeat the other side, the balance of power in the area would not be disrupted. Other UN members watched with dismay and apprehension, but they could see no lever to force a settlement. They had no stomach for forcefully confronting the fanatical religious and nationalistic emotions involved.

In the fall of 1988, after losing battles and facing unrest, the Iranian government announced it was ready to accept the "poison" of a cease-fire, which had been repeatedly proposed by the UN secretary general. The Security Council established the Iran-Iraq Military Observer Group (UNIMOG) to monitor the cease-fire with about 400 observers from 26 countries, but with none from the great powers.

There were no territorial gains in the war. UNIMOG's day and night patrols covered about 850 miles of the cease-fire lines. It investigated many of the thousands of complaints it received and helped maintain the cease-fire between Iraq and Iran. It was terminated in 1990. At the beginning of 1996 the cease-fire was still holding, although no lasting peace had been agreed on.

IRAQ ATTACKS KUWAIT

Iraq, frustrated by its drive to the east, turned to another border and in 1991 invaded Kuwait. President Bush, who had served as ambassador to the United Nations, called on the Security Council to authorize action to repel Iraq's invasion. Iraq not only took over the large oilfields of Kuwait, but moved its forces to threaten the major oilfields of Saudi Arabia (Map 4).

The attack occurred while Secretary of State Baker and advisers were visiting the Soviet Union. Their strategy was to rally the UN Security Council and a coalition approved by the Security Council to repel the aggression. President Bush and Baker saw Soviet and Chinese support as essential, but this was not easy because the Soviets had been a close ally of Iraq and had supplied it with military equipment. Baker describes how step by step he and his staff spent

Map 4. The Strategic Middle East

most of their visit persuading Soviet leaders to approve a UN Security Council resolution.[4] They later mobilized Arab support for the resolution, which was not as difficult because Saudi Arabia and other countries were threatened by Iraq's aggression.

The Security Council acted quickly and after several hours of debate passed the first of a series of over a dozen resolutions condemning the Iraqi invasion and calling for assistance for Kuwait. The next months were spent in developing congressional and UN support for using military force if necessary to liberate Kuwait, with a deadline for Iraq's withdrawal.

UN Resolution 678 demanded Iraq comply with previous UN resolutions demanding its withdrawal, and it authorized member states cooperating with Kuwait to use "all necessary means" to restore peace to the area. This allowed countries to form a coalition as in the Korean War resolution with the United States in the lead. The new UN military coalition, which included Arab forces, was under U.S. command. After the deadline it easily defeated Saddam Hussein's forces in a brief war that liberated Kuwait.

In accord with the UN Security Council resolutions the UN coalition did not invade and occupy Iraq, but it did impose strict peace terms. These included provisions for disarmament.

The action of the UN Special Commission on Disarmament (UNSCOM) to destroy weapons of mass destruction in Iraq has been one of the most important achievements of international peacekeeping. Its actions were supported by repeated warnings of the Security Council to Iraq that its lack of cooperation would result in continued sanctions. These included controlling billions of dollars of Iraqi funds that were deposited abroad, embargoing exports to Iraq except for humanitarian aid, and using proceeds of Iraqi oil exports to pay for relief and compensation to victims of the war.

The sanctions included an attack on January 13, 1993, by U.S. and British bombers against a few Iraqi military targets. The following day the UN secretary general told the press that the raids were in accord with Security Council resolutions. Despite Iraq's protests, it allowed inspection teams to continue their work. The weapons destroyed by the teams included 2,000 Scud long-range rockets, tens of thousands of chemical weapons, the supergun, and nuclear plants for making weapons-grade materials.[5]

Beginning in April 1991 the United Nations negotiated memoranda of understanding with the Iraqi ambassador to assign 300 UN guards to protect relief convoys to the Kurdish population of four million in the three northern governorates of Iraq. These convoys and the Kurdish population were also protected by daily flights of U.S., British, and French military aircraft north of the 36th parallel.

The Kurds' announced aim of establishing an autonomous region was viewed with alarm not only by Iraqi military forces but by Turkey, which has a Kurdish population of ten million. It and the Kurdish population of Iran for hundreds of years have supported Kurdish independence movements.[6] This issue continues to threaten the stability of the area.

The UN memoranda with Iraq provided for relief convoys in Iraq including areas of minority populations in the south. The memoranda also permitted periodic flights by U.S. planes over the southern provinces to deter attacks against minority populations there that opposed the central government. The United Nations did not prevent, however, the Iraq government's retaliation by diverting the major river from the southern area, which caused a severe water shortage there.

A UN Iraq-Kuwait Boundary Demarcation Commission demarcated the boundary coordinates agreed on by the two sides in the truce agreement after the war. This was the first time the United Nations had drawn a border between two member states.

In February 1993, following provocative actions along the border, the Security Council transformed the Kuwait observation mission into a force that would observe violations of the demilitarized zone between Iraq and Kuwait. The Security Council authorized increasing personnel from 350 to 3,600 for this task.

After the surprisingly rapid victory of the UN coalition against Iraq, the United Nations shared in the credit for the dramatic success. As a result, the number of people in the United States who believed the UN was doing a good job almost doubled to 54 percent compared with 34 percent who believed it was doing a poor job. Only 8 percent believed the United States should withdraw from the United Nations.[7]

President Bush proclaimed that in the new era of international politics with the end of the Cold War the United Nations "could fulfill the historic mission of its founders." The dramatic UN success against Iraq with U.S. support plus the installation of a new activist secretary general was reflected in the increase in UN peacekeeping activities after 1989. The United Nations undertook more peacekeeping than it had in the previous 40 years. Much of it went unreported in the news media. (The best sources of reporting are the UN Association's annual *A Global Agenda* and the UN's *UN Chronicle.*) There was a temporary increase in U.S. public support for the United Nations, but it was not matched by support in the U.S. Congress, which continued to withhold payment of assessments for the UN budget and its peacekeeping activities.

THE WAR IN YUGOSLAVIA

The success of democratic revolutions in Eastern Europe after 1989 encouraged Yugoslavia's republics, which were dominated by non-Serbs, to break away from the Serbian-dominated, communist-oriented central government. Serious fighting broke out in the summer of 1991 as the northern republics of Slovenia and Croatia declared their independence, and the federal army, which was dominated by the Serbian Republic, fought to take over Serbian communities in those provinces. Most of the international community, hoping to deter war, recognized Slovenia, Croatia, Bosnia and Herzegovina, and Macedonia as independent states, so technically the conflicts as they involved these republics became international wars. However, in reality the conflicts were a civil war that arose from the breakup of Yugoslavia.

After European Community representatives failed to achieve a truce in the conflicts, the matter was turned over to the Security Council. Cyrus Vance, former U.S. secretary of state, was named as a UN mediator. He negotiated a cease-fire and the Security Council placed peacekeeping units, 14,000 strong, in the two northern provinces of Slovenia and Croatia, which became recognized as independent states. Sporadic fighting continued with Serbian irregulars keeping control of some areas, but Slovenia and Croatia established their independence.

The focus of fighting then shifted to Bosnia and Herzegovina. It claimed independence and was recognized by many countries, which hoped to discourage an attack by the Serbian-dominated, truncated government of the former Yugoslavia. The new state of Bosnia and Herzegovina consisted of three major ethnic groups—Moslems, 40 percent; Serbs, 33 percent; and Croats, 18 percent. In a referendum boycotted by the Serbs, an overwhelming majority voted for independence, but military units of Serbs attacked, aiming to absorb Bosnia and Herzegovina, or at least its Serbian communities, into a greater Serbia. The Serbian military units were supported by the truncated Yugoslavia, although that government disclaimed responsibility.

Serbs used the term "ethnic cleansing" to describe their ruthless policy of attacking civilians and forcing them to flee from homes in areas claimed by the Serbs. The Moslems and Croats controlling the Bosnian government fought back. In places Croats, supported by the Republic of Croatia, and Moslems attacked each other as they staked claims to Bosnian areas.

The Security Council established the UN Protection Force (UNPROFOR) in the area to deliver humanitarian aid to civilians who were a major target of fighting, particularly in the Bosnian capital of Sarajevo. As fighting continued, the United Nations extended the UNPROFOR mandate to deter attack against "safe areas" established by the UN negotiators. The mandate included promoting withdrawal of forces, occupying key areas, and using all necessary measures to carry out the UN mandate.

As Serbia continued to defy UN resolutions and the cease-fire, the United Nations imposed a strict embargo on Serbia that included all but humanitarian aid. Serbia's economy was severely affected in 1994 with runaway inflation and a severe shortage of food. On April 7, 1993, the Security Council recommended Macedonia, another Yugoslavian republic, for UN membership, and on June 18 the Security Council authorized deployment of troops there, including 300 from the United States, to reinforce the UN presence and deter a Serbian attack.

Representatives of the United Nations and the European Community were frustrated as they attempted to mediate peace among the warring factions. The mediators were criticized for not intervening by force to stop the fighting, but no governments were willing to commit the huge armies and resources that would have been needed to overpower the warring factions. The UN forces numbered about 27,000. They arranged for thousands of relief flights and hundreds of convoys of food and medical supplies to the besieged civilians but they were not able to stop the killing and atrocities. These escalated as the fighting continued and various factions sought revenge. At times UN peacekeepers were ignored or even taken as hostages. Nevertheless, the UN convoys prevented mass starvation until NATO nations in February 1994 finally authorized NATO to support the United Nations in lifting the siege of Sarajevo.

The Security Council on May 25, 1993, established an international tribunal to prosecute violations of international humanitarian law. A UN Commission of Experts was established in 1992 to investigate and report on atrocities.

At the beginning of February 1994 the logjam holding up a cease-fire and peace settlement was broken when a mortar shell killed about 70 people in Sarajevo's market. UN secretary general Boutros Boutros-Ghali requested NATO to take the necessary action to respond to a UN request for air strikes. Public outrage at the action galvanized the NATO countries in concert with the United Nations to approve an ultimatum demanding the withdrawal of artillery and mortars from Sarajevo and an end to its siege. With Soviet diplomatic pressure Serbian units agreed to the ultimatum and to a cease-fire in certain other areas.

With U.S. sponsorship Croats and Muslims in February 1994 agreed to form a federation as part of Bosnia-Herzegovina and also agreed in principle to a confederation with the state of Croatia. The agreement was signed in Washington, DC, and provided a balance against Serbia for negotiating a peace. However, fighting continued in strategic areas until the fall of 1995, when the United States, in September 1995, persuaded the Yugoslav (Serb), Croat, and Bosnian governments to send top officials to Dayton, Ohio, to negotiate a peace agreement. The agreement at the beginning of November confirmed the existence of Bosnia-Herzegovina consisting of a Croat-Bosnian federation with a Serbian republic, resettlement and compensation for displaced persons, protection of human rights, and a NATO force of 60,000 authorized by a UN Security Council resolution to separate the forces and enforce the peace.

Many in the U.S. Congress and news media could find much to criticize in the four years of conflict in the former Yugoslavia. Hundreds of thousands were killed for ethnic reasons, at times UN resolutions were ignored and its peacekeepers attacked, and there was lack of support for UN efforts by the United States and others. On the other hand, the UN efforts including economic sanctions supported by the world community prevented the conflict from spreading into neighboring countries, which had strong ties to various factions, the UN convoys prevented mass starvation, and the UN provided an international framework for the final peace negotiations and agreement. The alternative could have been a Vietnam-type war involving Eastern European nations and Muslim countries.

SOMALIA

Secretary General Boutros-Ghali in his first months in office in 1992 challenged the Security Council to provide aid and assistance to Somalia. Somalia was wracked by wars between tribal factions and a severe drought, with estimates that hundreds of thousands had starved from lack of law and order. Relief convoys of the United Nations and private relief organizations were attacked by irregular forces, and there was no governmental authority to establish order.

In March 1992 UN representatives brokered a cease-fire between two of the major factions and then established the UN Operation in Somalia (UNOSOM) to monitor it. However, irregulars continued to attack deliveries of relief and looted warehouses.

On December 3, in response to an appeal from the secretary general, the Security Council sanctioned the use of force to deliver humanitarian aid in Somalia. In the next week U.S. forces led those of 20 countries in securing the airfield and port in Mogadishu and in protecting relief shipments. The operation consisted of 37,000 troops at its peak with 21,000 U.S. troops as part of the Unified Task Force (UNITAF). Its mandate was from the Security Council. UNITAF quickly established security in most of Somalia and ended the attacks on relief workers. Most of the U.S. units were then withdrawn, and the Security Council established UNOSOM II to take over from UNITAF.

After Somalia irregulars ambushed and killed 24 Pakistani peacekeepers of what remained of UNITAF, the Security Council on March 26, 1993, adopted a resolution authorizing the secretary general "to take all necessary measures" to establish the authority of UNOSOM throughout Somalia and to arrest, try, and punish those responsible for the attack. Additional U.S. forces were introduced into Somalia.

However, the UN forces were not able to establish their authority in Mogadishu, the capital. After 18 American soldiers were killed in their attack on General Aidid's headquarters in October 1993, the United States announced it would withdraw troops in March 1994. Eight other nations including France, Germany, and Italy followed suit, leaving 19,000 troops mostly from developing nations. The UN mediator then worked out an agreement among the tribal factions to establish a new government. By March 1994 the Americans left the country with security "vastly improved" and a "patina of normal life to return" in the countryside. However, in subsequent months the Somalian military and political factions did not agree on forming a new government, and by the fall of 1994 the situation had deteriorated. U.S. Marines reentered Somalia in January 1995 to assist in the withdrawal of remaining UNOSOM units. A few UN and other relief agencies remained at airports and ports for limited relief.[8]

Until 1996, UNITAF and UNOSOM restored order and protected relief supplies in most of Somalia, except in the part of the capital controlled by General Aidid's forces. UNOSOM and UNITAF stopped mass starvation and saved hundreds of thousands of lives by protecting relief convoys. However, the withdrawal of U.S. and other forces in 1994 and 1995 cut back the efforts of remaining UN and other relief agencies. General Aidid was killed in July 1996, and fighting among clans again undermined stability. It will take years to evaluate the final results of the peacekeeping and relief efforts.

OTHER AFRICAN CONFLICTS

At the beginning of 1994 the United Nations was carrying out peacekeeping in Angola, the Western Sahara, Rwanda, and Mozambique.

Angola

The UN Angola Verification Mission (UNAVEM) was set up by the Security Council in December 1988 to oversee withdrawal of Cuban troops from Angola. This had come about as a result of persistent negotiations led by Chester Crocker of the U.S. State Department, who negotiated the withdrawal in connection with South Africa's finally agreeing to the independence of Namibia. The elections were held in Angola on September 30, 1992, with UN monitoring. UNITA President Jonas Savimbi, who had led an insurrection against the Angolan government for many years, was decisively defeated. He refused to accept the results and continued to lead the insurrection.

The Security Council kept UNAVEM in the country. In adopting Resolution 834 it expressed readiness to expand the force in the event of significant progress in the peace process. By the summer of 1995 there was enough progress to reinforce the peacekeeping force, called UNAVEM III, and it continued to monitor an uneasy truce.

Western Sahara

The UN Mission for the Referendum in Western Sahara (MINURSO) was established by the Security Council on April 29, 1991, to monitor a cease-fire and to oversee a referendum to settle whether the Western Sahara would choose independence or integration with Morocco. The Security Council also established an Identification Commission appointed by the secretary general to register voters for a referendum issue. At the end of 1995 MINURSO was maintaining a cease-fire, but the Identification Commission was having difficulty in registering eligible voters.

Rwandan Civil War

In February 1993 the Rwandan government and the Rwandan Patriotic Front (RPF) rebels of the ethnic Tutsi tribe reached a cease-fire agreement. They requested UN observers to monitor the agreement, which provided for not infiltrating rebel forces across the border from Uganda. The United Nations established the UN Observer Mission Uganda-Rwanda (UNOMUR) in June 1993, consisting of 81 military observers. They worked with a larger mission from the Organization of African Unity (OAU).

On October 5, 1993, the UN Security Council established the UN Assistance Mission Rwanda (UNAMIR) of 2,500 troops to establish a weapons-free zone in Kigali, to monitor elections, and to help demobilize rebel and government forces. In 1994 UN agencies helped resettle 900,000 refugees from the Rwandan civil war.

On April 7, 1994, an airplane with the Burundi and Rwandan presidents was shot down in Kigali as it returned from a summit meeting. The Hutus, who were the majority ethnic tribe in Rwanda, blamed the Tutsis for the deaths. Hutu military units assassinated Tutsi officials including top officials and supported genocidal attacks against Tutsis in Rwanda. By April 8 UN representatives had helped negotiate a new interim government and cease-fire, but local massacres did not end. Despite Rwandan pleas for an increased UN presence, the UN secretary general, faced with opposition from the United States and others, indicated that they were planning to withdraw.

In May, after hundreds of thousands had been killed and more than a million Rwandan refugees had fled to neighboring countries, the Security Council approved the secretary general's request to reinforce the UNAMIR mission, but to a limited financial extent at the insistence of the United States. On June 8, 1994, however, the United States offered to contribute 1,600 troops to the operation. In July 1994 there were renewed massacres in Rwanda. There were 1 to 1.5 million refugees, many dying of starvation and from disease caused by impure water. Many were Hutus, including those forced by Hutu leaders to flee to Zaire to camps so they could be drafted to fight in the civil war.

On July 22 President Clinton directed military assistance for Rwanda. The United States in two days flew in construction equipment and expanded the airstrip at Goma and airfield at Entebbe to accept and refuel planes for a major airlift of relief supplies and peacekeepers from other countries. A major task of the Americans was to coordinate the relief effort and the incoming flights, which included those of the Russian civil air transport. The U.S. Air Force replaced the antiquated UN air controller system, which consisted of one air controller in Geneva, Switzerland, and a radio. The U.S. military used construction equipment to bury the bodies, which were a health hazard. By July 28 the U.S. military was producing clean water for the refugees.[9] There was no functioning government entity in Kigali, which held mostly soldiers and dead people.

On December 12, 1995, the UN Security Council extended for three months the UN peacekeeping mission although the Tutsi-dominated government of Rwanda said it did not want it there. It also reduced the peacekeeping force from 2,100 to 1,400, although Security Council members, particularly Canada, with forces on the ground, expressed the fear that reducing the UN force might lead to new cycles of massacres by Tutsis wanting revenge on Hutus. The Rwandan government expelled private relief organizations, and human rights groups feared that the government's aim was to expel possible witnesses to future revenge killings. On December 12 the first eight indictments for genocide were handed down by the international tribunal created by the Security Council.

The U.S. participation in ending the Rwandan holocaust indicated the United States can make a valuable contribution to stabilizing a situation at a relatively small cost even in a very messy civil conflict. Because of the United States' unique air transport and logistics capability its support is critical in assisting the United Nations to settle conflicts.

The U.S. forces worked well with the United Nations. American forces gave a sense of security to field workers and to the Rwandan people. The U.S. operation was conducted efficiently and with remarkable speed. The U.S. and British forces have a high standard of conduct in such situations and discourage misconduct such as looting. The only casualty was an American sergeant who injured himself playing volleyball.

Although the U.S. Congress cut dues in half for the UN regular budget and peacekeeping budget and has tried to prevent U.S. participation in peacekeeping, President Clinton managed in 1996 to continue U.S. participation in Rwanda.

Mozambique

Africa's longest civil war started in 1975 when a Marxist government seized control as Mozambique achieved independence from Portugal. The resistance was supported by South Africa. In October 1992 the two sides concluded a General Peace Agreement with the UN to monitor a cease-fire and withdrawal of foreign troops and to supervise elections. About three million people had died and more than five million refugees had been displaced in more than a decade and a half of civil war. The UN Operation in Mozambique (ONUMOZ) was established on December 1, 1992, to implement the agreement. Nineteen countries contributed to the UN military elements. Under the Peace Agreement government and resistance forces were to be demobilized with UN monitoring. A UN representative chaired the commission for forming a new defense force.

In 1993 Mozambique for the first time in 17 years enjoyed a combination of peace and rainfall, and elections were scheduled. On November 21, 1995, the secretary general in reporting the results of the elections to the Security Council declared they had been free and fair. ONUMOZ had also overseen the demobilization of 78,000 combatants and helped establish a new defense force. The UN agencies and private relief organizations had resettled 4.3 million refugees and initiated reconstruction projects.[10]

CAMBODIA

In the aftermath of the Vietnam War, the Khmer Rouge overthrew the military government of Cambodia and established a repressive regime. This regime challenged Vietnam in border clashes, and Vietnam responded by invading and establishing a puppet government. The new government was aided by the Soviets, while the Khmer Rouge forces, who began a campaign of opposition to the invaders, were helped by China.

The UN General Assembly in a controversial decision refused to recognize the aggression by continuing to accept credentials of the old Khmer Rouge government, which was by then represented in the United Nations by a moderate delegation under Prince Sihanouk. Initially he had opposed the Khmer Rouge, but his faction had reached an understanding with them because he was even more opposed to the Vietnamese invaders and their puppet government.

The Southeast Asian neighbors of Cambodia involved the United Nations in peace talks that included, in addition to the warring factions, the United States, the Soviet Union, Britain, China, and a representative of the UN secretary general. In 1991 a peace agreement was reached that provided for the most expensive UN peacekeeping mission in previous history (UNTAC). In 1992 about 22,000 military and 4,500 civilian personnel were assigned to the operation. UNTAC monitored elections and worked with the UN High Commissioner for Refugees to coordinate a major relief and reconstruction effort.

As of the beginning of 1994 the United Nations had helped convince the Vietnamese troops to withdraw, supervised free elections, and helped set up a new government under the moderate leadership of Prince Sihanouk. However, Khmer Rouge guerrillas were still a minor threat to the new government, which was struggling with factional problems and fighting corruption. The UN peacekeepers had withdrawn, and UN organs and government donors had been mobilized to provide aid for development and reconstruction.

NICARAGUA AND EL SALVADOR

When President Reagan took office in 1980 Nicaragua was dominated by a procommunist government. Reagan authorized the CIA to support insurgents (contras) against the government, and threatened the Guatemalan government with U.S. military exercises in neighboring Honduras. This was classic power politics, and Nicaragua in 1982 succeeded in getting the Security Council, the General Assembly, and the World Court to condemn the U.S. action.

The United States originally claimed it was trying to block shipments of arms through Nicaragua to insurgents trying to overthrow the El Salvador government, but the actions of the contras showed their aim was to overthrow the Nicaraguan government. The Security Council and General Assembly by overwhelming votes condemned U.S. intervention and urged support of the Contadora Group (Costa Rica, Mexico, Panama, Guatemala, and Honduras) to negotiate a solution. The Contadora Group reached agreement with the Sandinista government for a UN Mission for the Verification of Elections to monitor February 1990 elections. Violetta Chamorro won those elections and took office. The Sandinista government stepped down and became the parliamentary opposition, while still controlling the armed forces.

Meanwhile, the El Salvador insurgents had agreed that the UN secretary general would mediate their conflicts. By 1991 the UN secretary general had mediated an end to the long-standing civil war. The peace agreement provided for elections monitored by the United Nations. The United Nations established an observer mission of 380 military and police plus 250 civilian staff. Its mission was to verify implementation of agreements that covered a cease-fire, reform and reduction of armed forces, creation of a new police force, reform of the judicial and electoral systems, and monitoring of elections.

In the 1994 elections the candidate of the right easily won the presidency but the left won about half the seats in parliament. On April 28, 1994, the Security Council recognized that El Salvador "had evolved from a country driven by conflict into a democratic and peaceful nation," and on May 1 it terminated ONUSAL, the UN operation in El Salvador.

HAITI

Before 1990 Haiti's history was marked by military dictatorships that ruined the country. For a short time in 1990 there was an elected government under President Aristide. Later that year military rulers took over and forced Aristide and other officials to leave the country. The military leaders arrested and killed hundreds of opponents.

After the military takeover, tens of thousands of Haitians tried to flee to the United States, but most were sent back to Haiti by the U.S. Coast Guard. Many people died in rafts and small boats off the coast of Florida. The UN General

Assembly and the Security Council condemned the rulers of Haiti, but did not consider invading Haiti. Instead the Security Council imposed an embargo except for necessary food and medicine.

At the end of 1994 in negotiations managed by the United Nations the military rulers agreed to let President Aristide return to office, but they soon denounced the agreement (Governors Island Agreement). Conditions worsened and thousands fled from the country—as many as 5,000 in one week. Tens of thousands were kept in camps in Guantanamo, a U.S. military base in Cuba. The United States appealed to the Security Council for help.

The Security Council in Resolution 940 condemned Haiti's not keeping its agreement and for violating human rights. The Security Council authorized member states to form a UN multinational force, which could "use all necessary means to facilitate the departure from Haiti of the military leadership." The United States formed the force and threatened to invade. As the forces prepared to occupy Haiti, former President Jimmy Carter, along with Senator Sam Nunn and General Colin Powell, persuaded the military leaders to step down and let President Aristide return by October 15, 1994.[4]

About 21,000 troops of the 17-nation UN coalition occupied Haiti, mostly from the United States. President Aristide returned to Haiti. There was no important resistance but one American soldier was killed in a shoot-out in a police station. UN Resolution 940 provided for 6,000 peacekeeping troops to help Haiti keep order until the government could assume full responsibility. In March 1995 the United States withdrew all of its coalition force, leaving 2,400 as part of about 6,000 UN peacekeepers.

At the beginning of November 1994 the Haitian parliament approved Aristide's cabinet and plan of action, including elections and promoting a market economy. Elections were held as scheduled at the end of 1995. The candidate supported by President Aristide won, and Aristide stepped down as provided in the constitution. At the beginning of 1996 Haiti's capital was bustling again and there was no significant violent opposition.

GEORGIA

The Security Council on August 24, 1993, established a small peacekeeping unit in Georgia to verify compliance with the July cease-fire agreement between Georgia and separatist forces in Abkhazia. The force would attempt to resolve incidents between the parties. The UN presence had psychological value, but the settlement of the conflict came only with Russian assistance. Georgia, despite its desire for independence, agreed to pay the price of permitting Russia to train the Georgian army and establish bases on the border with Turkey.[11]

CONCLUSIONS

Not listed in the above peacekeeping efforts were civilian operations by observ-ers and UN officials who were attempting to mediate other conflicts and dis-putes. These included the civilian UN mission to Haiti, a Special Representative for Liberia to investigate a massacre, a Special Envoy for the Sudan to help assist refugees displaced by civil conflict, and 100 UN civilian observers in South Africa to help local police contain violence.

Although the United Nations in the first forty years did not achieve the ambitious aims of its founders to remove the scourge of war, it made consider-able progress toward that goal. Even when agreement was not reached in the Security Council it worked as designed to contain and end wars in the Middle East, Korea, the Congo, and India and Pakistan. These wars had a danger of serious escalation. Failures to settle all international wars were not the fault of the United Nations, which is only an instrument of its members in the area of collective security. The Soviets violated the UN Charter numerous times, in-cluding materiel support for North Korean aggression and Nasser's wars against Israel, and invasion of East European satellites. Great Britain and France joined Israel in aggression against Egypt in the Suez War. The United States violated the Charter by supporting covert attacks against Cuba and Nicaragua. The other powers, however, realized they could not effectively challenge the great powers in these crises without shattering the United Nations. The United Nations was not at fault. Rather, the major powers with a veto failed to support the UN Charter and international law in these crises. Conflicts are deterred in the inter-national arena, just as in domestic societies, by building up a respect for law, and the great powers failed to build up that respect by using power politics when it suited them.[5] The question is whether the process of building respect for international law will be effective in the new era of international politics.

Gorbachev's cooperation with the United Nations in ending the Afghanistan War began the new era of cooperation in the UN Security Council. It was consolidated in the dramatic success of the UN coalition in defeating Saddam's attack on Kuwait. This was followed by UN teams destroying his weapons of mass destruction. With no more important international wars to address, the United Nations in the following years embarked on more peacekeeping mis-sions than in the previous 40 years in what were essentially civil wars. The legal justification was that the Security Council could intervene in major civil con-flicts if they had major international implications, including genocide.

The efforts to end civil wars included a huge peacekeeping force in Cambo-dia that at the beginning of 1994 had supervised free elections and established a government that challenged remnants of the notorious Khmer Rouge, which had carried out the Cambodian holocaust after the Vietnam War. The UN peace-keepers also helped to bring peace to Haiti, Nicaragua, El Salvador, Uganda-Rwanda, Angola, and Mozambique, where civil conflicts had involved outside powers. The UN interventions in Somalia and the former Yugoslavia also stopped the fighting, but at the beginning of 1996 peace was still not assured there.

The UN successes were not recognized in the barrage of political criticism in the United States and the tendency of the news media to focus on problems that remained in the devastated societies. Moreover, the United States continued to hold back from paying its share of UN budgets. The secretary general had to negotiate with many countries for each of the peacekeeping forces. The chains of command were confused in part because of the voluntary nature of the peace-keeping units. Only in 1993 was the secretary general able to obtain a command center to keep track of the many UN operations.

Meanwhile, the U.S. Congress not only refused to pay the full annual assessment for peacekeeping operations but it tried to block U.S. troop support for the Bosnian Peace Agreement the U.S. had mediated. Why was there such strong opposition? After the end of the Cold War the United States was no longer threatened by a nuclear attack and the American voters could see no reason for the United States to take the lead in addressing world crises. This new isolationism was reinforced by politicians' calls for cutting back on government spending for social services and for reducing spending abroad for peacekeeping and related aid activities. Some of the trauma from the Vietnam War still existed among the public, and Congress played on fears of escalation of fighting in Bosnia. It found a big response among voters to rhetoric about not sending American boys abroad to risk their lives. Moreover, the Congress was ignorant of the intricacies of building coalitions and international cooperation under a UN framework, in contrast to the executive branch under Presidents Bush and Clinton, which carried out efforts to build a system of collective security. These pressures for Congress to play politics on the Bosnia issue increased as 1996 and its presidential election approached.

Despite the above opposition, President Clinton assigned 20,000 troops to the Bosnian peacekeeping force and supported other peacekeeping operations. Hopefully, support for the United Nations would not become an election issue. Bipartisanship in the U.S. Congress would be needed in the new era to strengthen the system of UN collective security.

Notes to Chapter 5

1. *New York Times*, March 7, 1991, p. A-8.
2. *Washington Post*, January 12, 1985.

3. *UN Chronicle*, June 1988, pp. 4–17.

4. J. A. Baker, III, *Politics of Diplomacy* (New York: W.P. Putnam Sons, 1995), chap. 1, 13–21.

5. *UN Chronicle*, September 1994, pp. 36–37; September 1992.

6. *UN Chronicle*, March 1993, p. 20; *New York Times*, January 21, 1993, p. 1.

7. *Gallup Poll Monthly*, Gallup, 1990, pp. 15–16.

8. *UN Chronicle*, September 1993, pp. 4–7; June 1993, pp. 13–17; *Economist*, April 2, 1994, p. 42. (*Source*: United Nations Association of the USA, *A Global Agenda*, p. 49, GA.)

9. Briefing by Colonel Bob Killebrew, U.S. Army Training and Doctrine Command at Mershon Center of Ohio State University, November 29, 1995. Colonel Killebrew participated in the Rwandan operation.

10. *UN Chronicle*, April 1993, pp. 25–56.

11. *Economist*, February 12, 1994, pp. 55–56.

Chapter VI

AGREEMENTS ON LIMITING NUCLEAR AND OTHER ARMS

After World War II international politics centered on the Cold War and the ultimate threat of a nuclear holocaust. World leaders looked into the abyss several times during the Cuban missile crisis and other crises. In the era of the nuclear threat there was a running debate on how to avoid nuclear war. Strategists of the nuclear powers believed in deterrence, which meant frightening potential enemies. During the ensuing arms race the Soviets and the United States made about 50,000 nuclear warheads, each one capable of destroying a city. Other leaders, reflecting the force of public opinion, including pressures by UN bodies, believed the way to peace was to negotiate limits on nuclear weapons, and some said they hoped eventually to abolish all nuclear weapons. Perceptive observers bridged the two strategies by stating that the process of negotiating nuclear arms agreements was more important than the agreements themselves. They said that leaders who are negotiating arrangements to abolish weapons and to avoid a nuclear holocaust are not likely to initiate such a war. After the democratic revolutions of 1989, the process permitted drastic reductions in nuclear arsenals and helped end the Cold War. After the Cold War ended, negotiators then shifted their attention to chemical weapons of mass destruction, which are much easier and cheaper to make and much more difficult to control.

The Soviets initiated the arms reduction process at the beginning of this century. There was no progress until after World War I, and those efforts ended with the outbreak of World War II. Beginning with the 1960s a network of more than a dozen important nuclear arms control agreements were negotiated and put into effect. Many of these agreements were linked with UN agreements. In the 1980s the Reagan administration accepted the agreements but did not extend the network until toward the end of its term. In the summer of 1986 President Reagan was so concerned that U.S. security was undermined by proposed limits of the second strategic arms limitation treaty (SALT II), he announced the United States would no longer honor those ceilings on strategic nuclear missiles. In October 1986, however, at a meeting in Iceland, President Reagan and General Secretary Gorbachev revived the nuclear arms negotiating process, and a historic agreement abolishing all intermediate-range missiles was ratified in Moscow in June 1988. After the 1989 democratic revolutions, negotiations accelerated to the point it was difficult to keep track of nuclear arms reductions.

EARLY EFFORTS AT LIMITING ARMS

The Russian tsar took the initiative at the beginning of the century to call the two Hague conferences of 1899 and 1907. These conferences are not taken seriously today because of the cataclysm of World War I that followed, but events precipitating that war showed the potential of the conference process for preventing war. (See also Chapter 2.) The Russian tsar probably was inspired to call the Hague conferences by his great-grandfather who had concluded the Holy Alliance. That alliance, which had been proposed in 1815, called for the great powers to base their relations upon the "sublime truths" of the Christian religion. The Holy Alliance is often confused with the Quadruple Alliance of that time, which was used to suppress radical movements that could threaten the principal monarchs of Europe.

The 1899 invitation was accepted by all 26 major governments to whom it was addressed, including the United States. Three major conventions were adopted relating to the pacific settlement of international conflicts, the laws of war, and maritime warfare. Three additional declarations were adopted that prohibited launching projectiles and explosives from balloons, using poison gas, and using dumdum bullets. The Convention on the Pacific Settlement of Disputes obligated powers to solve disputes by legal methods including a commission of inquiry and arbitration. It established a Permanent Court of Arbitration with a panel of arbitrators for this purpose. During the next 15 years three major disputes were settled by the court.

The tsar called a follow-up conference in 1907, which was attended by 54 nations including those from Latin America. Important conventions were adopted again on the pacific settlement of international disputes and restriction of force for recovering contract debts as well as on laws of warfare. This conference agreed that the contracting powers should have recourse as far as possible to good offices or mediation of disputes by other powers. Unfortunately, the great powers did not observe these agreements, and they blundered into World War I as a result. Many historians and diplomats of that time believed that if the great powers could only have met together and discussed the relatively minor problem of the assassination of the Austrian archduke by Serbian terrorists, which triggered the war, World War I could have been avoided. Periodic peace conferences obviously were not enough.

As indicated in Chapter 2, the surviving leaders designed the League of Nations to remedy this gap by providing for a permanent organization of nations to prevent war. The Versailles Treaty, which established the League, also provided for strict limits on German rearmament including demilitarizing the Rhineland. The League Covenant called for measures of disarmament, and in the 1920s and particularly in the 1930s, there were major meetings to try to reach agreement on limiting arms. The Versailles Treaty and the negotiations sponsored by the League of Nations were shattered by the Axis powers in their drive for world domination.

The United States, whose failure to join the League seriously weakened it, demonstrated to the world that it did not need the League for measures of disarmament by calling the Washington Naval Conference of 1921 and 1922. Secretary of State Hughes, chairman of the conference, startled the delegates and the world by an audacious proposal to scrap major naval vessels of the three great powers so that their strength and tonnage would be left at a ratio of 5-5-3 (United States, United Kingdom, and Japan). This proposal involved the destruction of 30 American ships and a total of 66 ships with a total tonnage of almost 2 million tons. One British reporter stated that this was more than all the admirals of the world had sunk in a cycle of centuries.[1] After further negotiations, France and Italy joined with smaller limits on their ships. The agreement stayed in effect almost 15 years. It may be noted that the number and tonnage of naval ships was relatively easy to verify by counting, so that there was little suspicion that the limits would be exceeded. (Today, limits on strategic delivery systems like submarines and bombers are checked by counting by satellites.) In 1930 a subsequent treaty was signed in London that limited other classes of warships and provided for a third naval conference in 1935. The above naval treaties expired in 1936 following the Japanese refusal to continue the arrangements.

There was one other major arms limitation agreement of that era, the Geneva Protocol prohibiting the use of poison gas and bacteriological weapons in war. This was concluded in 1925, and it was generally observed during World War II, although Italy used poison gas during the 1936 war against Ethiopia. The United States, however, did not ratify the agreement until 1975. One of the major issues in 1975 was whether riot control agents and herbicides were included, and the U.S. government when ratifying indicated that it did not consider these weapons covered by the protocol.[2]

The experience of the 1930s made a deep impression on that generation. Some were convinced that nations should rely on military strength including nuclear deterrence. Others were convinced that a strong international organization and persistent efforts to limit arms were the ways to peace. The initial efforts on arms control focused on controlling nuclear weapons.

AGREEMENTS TO LIMIT NUCLEAR ARMS

The nuclear destruction of Hiroshima and Nagasaki at the close of World War II gave a new emphasis to arms control efforts. World War II was the first major war of our era in which civilians suffered many more deaths than the military, and it was evident with the nuclear weapons of destruction that world civilization was threatened if there should be another war. Most writers emphasize the terrible dimensions of the nuclear threat, and it is true that Hiroshima and Nagasaki demonstrated the awesome power of nuclear weapons. However, during the 1920s and 1930s there was a comparable fear of the threat of poison gas as demonstrated in World War I, but the threat of that terrible weapon did not deter war.

At the end of World War II there was hope that the two powerful victors could cooperate to establish a system of peace, but, as indicated in previous chapters, the Cold War dominated international politics. It hindered but did not prevent slow progress toward nuclear arms control.

Article 26 of the UN Charter gives the Security Council the responsibility for formulating plans for disarmament, whereas Article 11 provides that the General Assembly may also consider this issue. The General Assembly in its first resolution, on January 24, 1946, established the International Atomic Energy Commission with instructions to submit proposals for the elimination of atomic weapons and other weapons of mass destruction. At its first meeting in June the United States submitted the Baruch Plan calling for an international authority to own all uranium mines and plants capable of producing atomic weapons. Inspection teams under the United Nations would not be subject to the great power veto of the Security Council. Many Americans took the plan seriously, not realizing that the proposal was a nonstarter from the beginning. Not only were suspicious hard-liners in charge of negotiations, but in retrospect it is clear that the Soviets at that state in history would not have allowed inspectors free reign within their borders. The Soviets criticized the plan as a capitalist plot to interfere with Soviet industrial production. In fact, the U.S. president and his advisers anticipated that the Soviets would not accept the control plan. The verification and control issues have continued to be the most difficult to negotiate.

The Soviets countered with their own proposal and propagandistic peace campaign. They called for prohibiting the manufacture of nuclear weapons and destroying present stocks of weapons with no provisions for verification. Meanwhile, they pressed on with developing their own weapons and exploded their first atomic bomb in 1949, earlier than had been anticipated by the West. Their propaganda campaign continued with the World Peace Congress out in front supported by communists and many well-meaning people anxious to eliminate the threat of nuclear war. Millions of signatures were mobilized under the Soviet campaign.

The victorious Western allies were anxious to include German armies in a defensive NATO alliance but at the same time to ensure that Germany never again would be able to threaten aggression in Central Europe. They solved this dilemma by persuading the German authorities to accept the ABC Agreement, which is still in effect and which prohibits certain powers of the Brussels Pact (the Netherlands, Belgium, Luxembourg, and Germany) from making or obtaining atomic, bacteriological, or chemical weapons. The Western European Union of 1948 succeeded the Brussels Pact. In 1955, with French fears alleviated, the Germans joined NATO and provided the major forces of that alliance. The Soviets countered with the Warsaw Pact.

Meanwhile, the Soviets, alarmed at German rearmament, proposed reducing conventional forces and destroying nuclear stockpiles. Their proposal provided for control posts at the big ports, railway junctions, motor roads, and airfields to see that no dangerous concentration of land, air, or naval forces was effected. Their proposals were not accepted by the NATO powers, which believed both German arms and nuclear arms were necessary for their defense.

The Soviets also advocated a nuclear test ban at this time. It had first been proposed by Indian Prime Minister Nehru in 1954. The problem of verification prevented negotiations making headway since the United States was convinced with the technology of that era that it would require hundreds of inspectors to check on such an agreement.

In 1957 the Polish foreign minister, Adam Rapacke, called for a denuclearized zone in Central Europe. His proposal was to prohibit manufacturing or stockpiling of nuclear weapons or materials in East and West Germany, Poland, or Czechoslovakia. The West attacked the plan because it believed that it needed nuclear weapons based in Germany for the defense of Western Europe.

In 1958 the United States and the Soviet Union observed a voluntary nuclear test ban. In 1961, as a result of tensions over Berlin and other issues, the United States announced that it would no longer be bound by the informal agreement, and the Soviets then broke it by testing nuclear weapons. In 1963, however, as a result of the Soviet initiative, the Kennedy administration negotiated the partial nuclear test ban treaty.

In its first meetings the General Assembly established a commission for negotiating disarmament of nuclear and conventional weapons. This and subsequent UN conferences with varying membership, usually meeting in Geneva, have pressured the major and minor powers to conclude agreements on disarmament. The most ambitious plans have failed to win approval of the major powers, but the General Assembly and its commissions have initiated action and mobilized support for the International Atomic Energy Agency, the Nonproliferation Treaty, the Latin American nuclear weapon-free zone, the Seabeds Treaty, the Outer Space Treaty, and test ban treaties. These are described below.

The United Nations has also initiated and approved authoritative reports on the economic and social consequences of the arms race (1971 and 1977); a report on the ways of implementing an agreement on reducing military budgets (1974 and 1977); reports on the effects of atomic radiation (1958, 1966, and 1969); and a comprehensive study on nuclear weapons (1980).

In 1961 the General Assembly declared that the use of nuclear weapons would violate the UN Charter. In 1964, when China exploded its first nuclear device, China announced that it would never be the first to use nuclear weapons. In 1982, at the second special General Assembly session on disarmament (the first was in 1976), the foreign minister of the Soviet Union announced that his country would not be the first to use nuclear weapons, and he called for similar commitments from other nuclear states. The United States refused to make such a pledge, believing it was necessary to reserve the use of nuclear weapons for defending against possible Soviet aggression in Western Europe.

The UN commissions, the UN conferences on disarmament, and the General Assembly have also called for a freeze in the production of nuclear weapons, and the General Assembly in 1982 called especially for the two major nuclear weapons states to proclaim an immediate freeze on the production and testing of nuclear weapons. The United States refused, pointing out that American and Western defensive strategy viewed nuclear weapons as a means of deterring war. In 1983 and 1984 the General Assembly adopted additional resolutions calling for a freeze.

The millions of words in meetings and reports of UN bodies proposing nuclear disarmament and freezes have had direct and indirect impacts on the negotiation of nuclear arms agreements. Set forth below are the highlights of the important agreements that were finally concluded after the ambitious Baruch Plan under President Truman failed to receive support. The agreements are also listed and described in Table 2.

The first nuclear agreement established the important International Atomic Energy Agency (IAEA). President Eisenhower proposed it in a 1953 speech before the UN General Assembly as a means of promoting the peaceful use of

Table 2
The Network of Nuclear Arms Agreements

Agreement and date in force	Comments
International Atomic Energy Agency. July 1957. Eisenhower	Promotes peaceful use of nuclear energy. Checks by NPT (see below). Reports to Security Council.
The Antarctic Treaty. June 1961. Eisenhower	Prohibits nuclear weapons in Antarctic. All buildings open for inspections.
The Hot Line Agreement. June 1963. Kennedy	Establishes communications between White House and Kremlin.
Limited Test Ban Treaty. October 1963. Kennedy	Prohibits tests causing fallout in neighboring countries.
The Outer Space Treaty. October 1967. Johnson	Prohibits placing weapons of mass destruction in outer space.
The Latin American Nuclear Weapons-Free Zone. April 1968. Johnson	Prohibits the stationing of weapons in Latin America.
Nonproliferation Treaty (NPT). 1970. Extended without limit. 1995.	Commits countries not to build or help countries build nuclear weapons.
Agreement to Reduce Risk of Nuclear War. September 1971. Nixon	Safeguards against accidental launch prohibits nuclear threats.
The Seabeds Treaty. May 1972. Nixon	Prohibits nuclear weapons on seabeds, but not on submarines or ships.
SALT I. October 1972. Nixon	Provides ceilings on intercontinental (ICBMs) and submarine-launched ballistic missiles (SLBMs).
Antiballistic Missile Treaty. October 1972. Nixon	Prohibits antiballistic missile (ABM) tests and more than one ABM site.
Agreement on Prevention of Nuclear War. June 1973. Nixon	Parties agree to consult, to not use force, and to keep UN informed.
Threshold Test Ban Treaty. 1974. Senate approval 1990.	Prohibits tests of nuclear weapons of over 150 kilotons.
The Vladivostok Agreement. November 1974. Ford	Joint U.S.–Soviet statement setting framework for SALT II.
SALT II. Signed 1979. Carter	Not ratified but its ceilings were observed on strategic weapons.
The Intermediate Nuclear Force Agreement. June 1988. Reagan	Abolishes all intermediate and "shorter range" nuclear missiles.
Peaceful Nuclear Explosions Treaty. Senate approval 1990.	Provides verification of nuclear explosions for peaceful purposes.
START I. July 1991. Bush	Cuts strategic weapons 25–35%.
Unilateral Cut. September 1991. Bush	Reduces tactical nuclear weapons in Europe, except for those on aircraft.
START II. Initialed Jan. 1993. Bush	Cuts strategic weapons 50–66%.

nuclear energy by nonnuclear powers and discouraging the proliferation of nuclear weapons. By 1956 the draft of the agreement was unanimously approved by a conference at UN headquarters, and within three months it had been signed by 80 nations. In 1996 the IAEA has 112 members and a staff of 1,900. The IAEA's staff of inspectors monitors the use of nuclear materials for peaceful uses to see that they are not diverted for weapons, establishes safety standards, and provides technical advice. After the Chernobyl nuclear disaster in Russia in 1986, the IAEA inspected the site and offered advice on how to avoid future disasters of this nature. The IAEA was given the additional task of providing inspectors for the nonproliferation treaty, which was concluded 13 years after the IAEA treaty came into force. It also helped in inspecting and destroying Iraq's nuclear installations after the Gulf War.

For years the General Assembly discussed banning nuclear weapons from certain areas of the world. The first agreement of this nature was initiated under Eisenhower in 1958. The Antarctic Treaty, which prohibits nuclear weapons in that area, came out of the cooperation of 12 nations in the UN International Geophysical Year. The treaty calls for cooperation in Antarctic research with Specialized Agencies of the United Nations. Eisenhower, in an address to the General Assembly in 1960, also initiated the negotiation of the Outer Space Treaty, which prohibits weapons of mass destruction being deployed in outer space including celestial bodies. Both treaties allow open inspection to verify their provisions.[3]

The next major treaty was the Limited Test Ban Treaty, which grew out of a UN initiative of 1954. At that time the United States tested a fusion bomb in the Pacific on the Bikini Atoll. The explosion spread radioactive fallout for hundreds of miles, some of which fell on the Japanese ship *Lucky Dragon*. The sailors did not know what had hit them until after they returned to Japan and sold some of the contaminated fish in the local market. By that time some of them were ill, and one of the men actually died. As a result of the outcry and other objections to fallout from nuclear tests, about a dozen resolutions were passed in the General Assembly calling for an end to atmospheric tests. The subject of test bans received more attention in UN bodies than any other subject of nuclear disarmament.

Negotiations between the Soviet Union and the United States made little progress until 1963, when Chairman Khrushchev proposed a compromise of prohibiting nuclear tests of a kind where the fallout would be detected in a neighboring state. This solved the verification problem and was acceptable to President Kennedy. An agreement was negotiated in about a week in Moscow between the Soviets, the United States, and Britain to prohibit such tests. These nations subsequently conducted their nuclear tests underground. President Nixon negotiated a follow-up treaty prohibiting all tests over 150 kilotons, which is about 10 times the strength of the Hiroshima bomb. The General Assembly and the Conference on Disarmament have not reached agreement on all the issues for a comprehensive test ban treaty, but the five major nuclear powers pledged to reach an agreement by September 1996.

The Hot Line Agreement came out of the Cuban missile crisis. Kennedy and Khrushchev's personal communications were key factors in solving that crisis. They saw the need to speed up communications in the future because each side had been only one-half hour away from destruction by intercontinental ballistic missiles (ICBMs). Direct communication lines serviced by interpreters were established between the White House and the Kremlin under this agreement to permit direct talks between both locations during a serious world crisis. The agreement was signed in 1963 by the U.S. and Soviet representatives to the UN Eighteen-Nation Conference on Disarmament in Geneva.

President Nixon also concluded the important Nonproliferation Treaty (NPT); negotiations had been started by President Johnson. This agreement arose from pressure by the General Assembly, which more than ten years earlier by a vote of 69 to 0 had called for such a treaty. The major issue preventing early agreement was that the Soviets did not want the United States to deploy nuclear weapons in other countries of Western Europe. The United States, on the other hand, insisted that NATO must have these weapons. After about 10 years of negotiations, the Soviets accepted the fact that U.S. nuclear weapons would be deployed in Europe. The United States explained that these were placed under U.S. control by requiring a U.S. officer to insert a key for launching such a nuclear missile. The treaty pledges countries not to produce or help another country to produce nuclear weapons, and commits them to extensive verification from IAEA inspectors mentioned above. Article 6 requires the nuclear powers to pursue negotiations to cease the nuclear arms race and complete disarmament under strict and effective international control. The major INF and ABM agreements discussed below between the Soviet Union and the United States acknowledge their commitment under the NPT. The countries signing the NPT pledge not to develop nuclear weapons hoped to avoid any reason for a nuclear power to involve them in a nuclear war, to prevent a possible enemy from developing nuclear weapons, and to put pressure on the nuclear powers to end the arms race. A UN Security Council resolution of 1959 pledges assistance by its permanent members to a nation threatened by a nuclear power if the threatened nation is nonnuclear and a party to the NPT. On May 12, 1995, after intense lobbying by the United States, the conference for reviewing the NPT agreed by unanimous consent to extend it indefinitely.

The Seabeds Treaty of 1972, which prevents emplacement of nuclear weapons on the seabed, was also begun by a resolution in the General Assembly of

1967. In December 1970 the General Assembly called for such a treaty by a vote of 102 to 2. The treaty was negotiated by the UN Eighteen-Nation Disarmament Committee that later became known as the Conference of the Committee on Disarmament. It went into effect in 1972.

President Johnson, toward the end of his term, pressed the Soviets to begin strategic arms limitation talks. The Soviets held back, however, not wanting to waste their bargaining strength on a lame-duck president. Ambassador Dobrynin on the day Nixon took office proposed to set a date for such talks. President Nixon and his national security adviser, Henry Kissinger, held back, wanting to link the negotiations with other issues. However, political pressure from the news media and the Congress as well as international pressures forced them to open discussions.[4]

Nixon and Kissinger became concerned as they studied the problem that the Soviets, who were catching up rapidly in numbers of strategic missiles, would keep their production lines open and surge ahead. Kissinger and Nixon, therefore, negotiated the SALT I agreement, which froze the numbers of ICBMs and SLBMs (submarine-launched ballistic missiles).[5]

The Soviets ended up with a higher ceiling of ICBMs, but this was balanced by the U.S. lead in heavy bombers, which were not covered by the agreement. The preamble of the agreement noted the obligation of the two superpowers to take such effective measures to cease the nuclear arms race under Article VI of the nuclear Nonproliferation Treaty, which as noted above was sponsored by the United Nations.

SALT I was an "interim" agreement, not a treaty, and both sides began negotiating a new agreement that would include bombers and also put a limit on MIRVs (multiple independently targeted reentry vehicles) and on the Soviet heavy missiles. President Ford and General Secretary Brezhnev set the framework with the Vladivostok Agreement. President Carter then negotiated the SALT II agreement with such limits. Although it was not formally ratified, its ceilings were observed by both sides until late in the Reagan administration.

The Antiballistic Missile (ABM) Treaty was closely associated with SALT I. This treaty and a later protocol limited deployment of ABM systems to one each, and it strictly limited ABM radar and tests. The net effect was that in case of a nuclear war only one small area of each of the superpowers would be protected or partially protected from nuclear attack. The purpose of this "mutual assured destruction" (MAD) policy was to prevent, by the threat of mutual suicide, nuclear war between the superpowers. This treaty also recognized the obligation to take effective measures to cease the nuclear arms race under Article VI of the nuclear Nonproliferation Treaty. The treaty was ratified by an overwhelming vote in the U.S. Senate.

Nixon and General Secretary Brezhnev in 1973 also signed the Agreement on Prevention of Nuclear War. In this agreement they pledged to refrain from the threat or use of force and urgently to consult together in the event of a risk of nuclear war. Each party in such a case is free to inform the UN Security Council and the secretary general of the progress of such consultation. They also agreed that nothing in the agreement should impair the provisions of the Charter of the United Nations. This agreement is often overlooked by commentators, but since the time it was negotiated, the United States and the Soviet Union have not threatened to attack each other, as in the days of Khrushchev, or in the days of Dulles and the "massive retaliation" doctrine. As in the case of the other agreements, this agreement reflects the common interest of the two superpowers.

Table 2 summarizes the above agreements. They restrained the arms race for 14 years, but by 1986 the network of agreements had begun to tear apart. The basic problem appeared to be that President Reagan believed that the Soviets had superior strength in nuclear weapons, particularly in the heavy missiles, and that theoretically in a first strike they could wipe out the U.S. Minuteman ICBM force, leaving the United States at the mercy of a further strike that could annihilate its cities. Reagan's initial negotiating proposals to limit strategic arms were nonstarters. They would have canceled the SALT II agreement, which had been agreed on by the Carter administration, and would have reduced Soviet heavy missiles, where they had an advantage, without comparable reductions by the United States. The Soviets, on the other hand, called for a freeze in further installation of nuclear weapons and also a ban on testing of nuclear weapons.

In 1986 the Soviets voluntarily halted their tests, calling for a freeze on testing. In April 1986 the Reagan administration continued its series of nuclear tests, rejecting the chance for a freeze on the tests. The U.S. rationale for continuing the tests was to ensure that the nuclear warheads it possessed would work and thus preserve a "deterrent" against a Soviet attack and to develop new weapons. Press reports indicate that the United States was also interested in testing nuclear devices that could create laser beams for the Star Wars program, discussed below. In the summer of 1986 Reagan announced that the United States would no longer be bound by the SALT II ceilings. This threatened a serious tear in the network of nuclear arms control agreements and little prospect for future agreements.

On March 22, 1983, President Reagan had proposed creating a total defense against ballistic missiles, thus implying a radical change in nuclear doctrine. The speech called for futuristic weapons in space and was called the Strategic Defense Initiative (SDI). Before that U.S. doctrine had been based on the previously discussed MAD policy to deter war. As noted above, the ABM Treaty is associated with this MAD doctrine of deterrence. The USSR had chosen Moscow for its one ABM site, whereas the United States chose Grand Forks, North Dakota, to protect its Minuteman missile field there. The United States subsequently decided that it was so expensive and impracticable to develop such weapons that it did not even activate the one defensive site. Meanwhile, the Soviets placed nuclear-capable defensive missiles in a ring around Moscow to defend it. The ABM Treaty also severely limited radars capable of tracking incoming missiles. Research and limited ABM systems, however, are permitted if located at present test sites. Reagan's Star Wars, or SDI, proposals would have violated the ABM Treaty by expanding ABM systems into outer space. (State Department officials tried to persuade Congress without success that the treaty approved by the Senate did permit such space systems.)

Opponents of the Star Wars program argued that the side creating an effective defense could threaten the other side with the possibility of a first strike and thus encourage the other side to create more offensive missiles to offset the possible defensive potential of an ABM system. The other argument against Star Wars accepted by many scientists was that an ABM system is impracticable. The technical problems of shooting down with a high degree of certainty thousands of missiles fired from space as well as from submarines and cruise missiles are impossible to solve. Even if a system were put in place, scientists argued, it would be easy to disrupt it by decoys and an attack on key elements of the system. If only a few missiles got through, they continued, this would still be adequate to devastate the defenders.

The Soviets violently attacked the Star Wars program as designed to give the United States nuclear superiority that could threaten the Soviets with a first strike. They opposed an arms race in space because it would be costly for them to try to keep up with the new defense techniques. They initially linked any negotiated limits on nuclear weapons with ending the Star Wars program, because they did not wish to have their offensive capability offset by a U.S. lead in defensive technology.

In a related series of negotiations the United States and Soviets had discussed the possibility of limiting or eliminating intermediate-range missiles in Europe. In the late 1970s, as a result of a decision under Carter, the United States decided to deploy cruise and Pershing missiles in Europe to offset the intermediate-range Soviet SS 20s that were being installed there. As the United States started to deploy these Pershing and cruise missiles under the Reagan administration, the Soviets made various offers to try to stop this threat to their command centers. The Soviets reasoned that the Pershing missiles could reach their command centers and major cities in seven minutes and, therefore, represented a more serious threat than the long-range intercontinental missiles from the United States, which take about a half-hour in flight.

As policymakers faced rising political pressures and the no-win situation of a nuclear arms race, there was a dramatic development in nuclear arms negotiations. President Reagan and General Secretary Gorbachev met for two days in October 1986 in Iceland and agreed on a general framework of concessions on the following major issues:

Intercontinental Missiles

1. The two leaders agreed to a 50 percent reduction in strategic missiles and warheads over a period of five years. (Later their spokesmen disagreed whether they had agreed to go on from that point and eliminate all "nuclear strategic weapons" or all "ballistic missiles," which would not include bombers and cruise missiles.)
2. The Soviets agreed to major cuts in their biggest missiles, which the United States considered the most threatening.

Intermediate-Range and Short-Range Missiles

1. The Soviets agreed to remove all their SS 20s, and the United States agreed to remove all Pershing and cruise missiles from Europe.
2. The Soviets would keep only 100 SS 20s in Asia; the United States would keep only 100 intermediate-range weapons in the United States.

Nuclear Tests

1. The two sides agreed on improved verification.
2. The United States did not agree to stop tests, but it agreed to negotiate a reduction in tests with the aim of ultimately eliminating all tests.

The major issue not settled was the Soviet demand to limit strictly SDI testing, and they conditioned the above proposals on settling the SDI issue. First reports indicated that the Soviets took a more restrictive position on SDI than that of the ABM Treaty, although this was not clear because both sides had a different interpretation of the treaty. Both sides agreed, however, to continue negotiations in Vienna to try to clarify and settle the above issues.

The breakthrough came in the following year when the Soviets yielded on the Star Wars issue in the context of the intermediate-range missiles. At a Washington summit they signed an agreement (the Intermediate Nuclear Force Agreement [INF]) for completely eliminating *all* medium-range and "shorter range" nuclear missiles with a range of 300 to 3,400 miles. There were detailed provisions to monitor destruction of the missiles and to make detailed on-site inspections in more than 100 places in the USSR and 30 places in Europe and the United States in order to verify that the missiles were actually destroyed. The Star Wars issue was left unresolved with both sides agreeing to conduct research, development, and testing of ABM systems as permitted by the ABM Treaty.

The implications of the INF treaty were breathtaking, although some commentators tended to downplay its importance. For the first time entire classes of nuclear missiles totaling about 2,000 were to be destroyed. For the first time the Soviets and the United States would permit extensive inspections of military facilities. The agreements took place in the framework of friendly and business-like meetings including extensive media coverage in the Soviet Union. Both leaders appeared determined to press forward with an agreement to cut strategic missiles by 50 percent, and agreement was reached on many issues involved. The experience from inspections and verification under the INF Agreement would help in negotiating the strategic arms reduction treaty (START).

The above network of negotiations and agreements are important not only because of their carefully drafted provisions but also as a continuing process under international law to limit the nuclear arms race. The INF negotiations were a dramatic reversal of the Cold War atmosphere that had prevailed at the beginning of the Reagan administration, and this put an end to the Cold War tensions. START II, signed in Moscow in January 1993 by Presidents Bush and Yeltsin, requires reductions of nuclear arsenals by two-thirds and elimination of MIRVs. The United States and republics of the former Soviet Union have continued to implement the agreement.

The INF treaty was further evidence of the Soviet Union's movement toward more respect for international law and world opinion calling for an end to the nuclear arms race. In the week following the INF Agreement Soviet Foreign Minister Shevardnadze in a speech at the United Nations called for involving the United Nations in verification of nuclear agreements. He also offered again, if the United States would reciprocate, to end all nuclear testing in line with the extensive record of UN resolutions demanding this. The United States did not accept the offer because it wanted to continue testing.

Political pressures, particularly U.S. congressional pressures and international pressures to reduce nuclear arms and SDI budgets, had helped to persuade President Reagan to negotiate for reductions in nuclear arms. Not all groups calling for nuclear arms reductions would call themselves strong supporters of the United Nations and international law, but they were allies with similar objectives. The most important factor in the INF Agreement was the change in outlook of the Soviet Union, with Gorbachev making major concessions in the nuclear arms negotiations. These included not counting the British and French intermediate-range missiles, allowing for the first time foreign inspectors access to Soviet military bases, and dropping the demand to tie the agreements to the Star Wars issue. The advantages of opening up their society and limiting the arms race, as well as a hard-headed evaluation of the threat of the U.S. buildup of arms obviously played an important part in Gorbachev's decision.

After 1989, with the breakup of the Soviets' East European and internal empires under Mikhail Gorbachev, negotiations on nuclear arms control accelerated. They were aided by the termination of the Warsaw Pact military alliance in 1991 and agreements on major reductions of Soviet and American troops and conventional weapons in Europe.

In July 1991, after about nine years of negotiations, Presidents Bush and Gorbachev signed START I, cutting U.S. strategic nuclear warheads by 25 percent and the comparable Soviet weapons about 35 percent. Verification procedures included on-the-spot inspections.

Then, as Gorbachev made a last-ditch struggle to keep his position and to hold the Soviet Union together in the fall of 1991, President Bush announced the United States would unilaterally withdraw and destroy its nuclear weapons in Europe and cut back on strategic weapons. This included withdrawing and destroying all nuclear artillery shells and warheads for short-range missiles, removing all tactical nuclear weapons including nuclear cruise missiles from surface ships and nuclear submarines, removing tactical nuclear missiles from naval aircraft, and dropping plans to deploy the strategic mobile MX missiles and smaller Midgetman missiles. He completed the above reductions by July 2, 1992. However, the United States retained tactical nuclear weapons for aircraft. Bush invited the Soviets to make similar concessions.

On February 17, 1992, Yeltsin, the new president of Russia, and U.S. Secretary of State Baker announced agreement on U.S. technical assistance in dismantling Russia's nuclear arsenal, including providing special boxcars and containers to transport nuclear warheads. The highly enriched uranium and plutonium would be entombed in underground bunkers to be monitored by the IAEA or converted to use for power or research. Meanwhile, former Soviet republics that had achieved independence agreed to a joint nuclear command with Russia and to accept the arms limitation treaties of the former Soviet Union. They also accepted U.S. technical assistance in removing their nuclear weapons.

In January 1993, President Yeltsin and President Bush signed a treaty for further drastic cuts in nuclear weapons. Each side would reduce its long-range weapons from the START ceiling of 6,900–8,600 to 3,000–3,500. The job of destroying those weapons is so time consuming it was estimated it would take until the year 2000 or 2003 to complete the task. Secretary of State Baker pressed the Senate for approval of this arrangement as well as the 1991 START I, which would provide machinery to help implement the later cuts. Technical assistance for arms reductions was worked out in NATO with the former Soviet republics. The Soviets' desire to open their society to foreign investment and aid and to limit the costly arms race, as well as an end of paranoia about the German threat, influenced Gorbachev's and Yeltsin's decisions to make concessions in the arms negotiations.

CONTROL OF NONNUCLEAR WEAPONS

In 1993, after almost 25 years of negotiations, the Chemical Weapons Convention (CWC) was signed. It prohibited the development, production, and stockpiling as well as the use of chemical weapons. It would enter into force 180 days after the 65th signatory had ratified it. As of 1996 less than half of the states had ratified it, with many waiting until the United States, Britain, Russia, and China ratified.

In 1975 the United States finally approved the Geneva Protocol, which prohibited the use of poison gas and bacteriological weapons in war, and President Nixon made a public commitment not to provide such weapons. A major problem was how to verify compliance with the agreement, because bacteriological weapons could be made in a small room converted to a laboratory. In 1996 a UN Special Committee met to discuss transparency measures to exchange information and visits to increase confidence in compliance with the agreement.

For conventional weapons the UN Register of Conventional Arms of 1994 enjoyed support, with more than 80 countries submitting detailed data on their exports and imports of arms. However, the arms trade continued with relatively few restrictions.

The increased attention of the Security Council to internal wars with international implications was reflected in concerns about the terrible toll taken by land mines. In line with a General Assembly resolution, negotiations began in 1995 on measures to prohibit manufacture of such mines.

CONCLUSIONS

The process of arms limitation was as important as the actual reduction of weapons. Countries consolidated detente in these arms control agreements, which proved their good faith and their respect for treaties and international law. The world finally seemed safe from a nuclear holocaust, although a few minor powers appeared to have such weapons in their arsenal. It was clear, however, that those countries would be condemned and opposed by the world community if they used them, and would probably face strong Security Council action. There have been no important limits set on manufacturing and trade in conventional weapons, which are the weapons of ethnic conflicts, but there is hope that a UN agreement might be negotiated to limit or end the manufacture of land mines, which take a terrible toll in such conflicts.

Notes to Chapter 6

1. Arms Control and Disarmament Agency, *Arms Control and Disarmament Agreements* (Washington, DC: U.S. Government Printing Office, 1980), p. 4.

2. T. Bailey, *A Diplomatic History of the American People* (New York: F.S. Crofts, 1945), p. 691.

3. U.S. Arms Control and Disarmament Agency, *Arms Control*, p. 80.

4. H. Kissinger, *Whitehouse Years* (Boston: Little, Brown, 1979), pp. 130–138.

5. Kissinger, *Whitehouse*, p. 197.

Chapter VII

THE UNITED NATIONS AND INTERNATIONAL LAW

There are two major types of international law. The first is called public international law. It is practiced mostly by diplomats and lawmakers who draft and negotiate treaties and other international agreements such as the INF treaty, the Canadian free trade agreement, the Panama Canal Treaty, and many other international agreements. Their international agreements for the most part cover problems of relations between states, and they are a major source of international law.

The other type is concerned with "conflict of laws" and is called private international law. It is practiced by lawyers who are largely concerned with international business arrangements and problems arising from different provisions of laws in different countries, particularly for foreigners and foreign business concerns. Its practitioners are mostly lawyers who deal with the laws of various nations and use the court systems when necessary. These lawyers help individuals and firms, because one of the principles of international law is that the individual should first try the local courts and local officials for assistance before diplomats of his or her government take the case. This is called exhausting the local remedies.

American and other courts practice the principle of comity, or recognizing and enforcing legal actions of foreign courts and governments, unless there is reason to believe they were not fair. This means that jurisdictional conflicts are seldom submitted to dispute-settlement procedures.

This chapter deals mostly with public law, and particularly how international law relates to the major issues of war and peace. It also examines several important examples of the use of international law, including how nations have cooperated to reduce international terrorism, to promote human rights, and to establish a body of law for issues relating to the sea.

World leaders and academics have severely criticized as idealists the leaders and diplomats who have tried to use international law as a guide for diplomacy and build a system of collective security based on it. President Wilson, a liberal internationalist, was severely criticized by some writers for supporting a framework of international law of the League of Nations. Presidents Truman and Eisenhower to a large extent escaped such criticism when their policies supported the United Nations and international law, because they also used a blend of power politics with international law to reinforce their positions, and the United Nations supported them in their efforts. President Carter was severely criticized for being weak in the Iranian hostage crisis because he resorted to diplomacy and the United Nations rather than force. President Reagan attacked Carter for this and became one of the most popular presidents largely because of his macho stance against the communists. In 1986 he rejected the World Court and United Nation's condemnation of the United States for supporting the contras' attacks against Nicaragua, which Reagan accused of being communist. He later confounded critics of his hard line by making one of the most far-reaching treaties on nuclear arms control, which was linked to the extensive network of nuclear arms control agreements originating in the UN System.

President Reagan demonstrated a lack of respect for international law and the United Nations by the attacks against Nicaragua and Grenada. His lawyers' assertions were not convincing, that the intervention was for self-defense and in support of insurgents fighting for the UN Charter's principles of self-determination.[1] Reagan's officials distrusted trying peaceful means through the United Nations because they believed it was dominated by third-world nations opposed to U.S. policies. However, after Secretary of State Shultz negotiated a carefully drafted INF treaty on nuclear arms, respect for international law naturally followed. He requested Congress to stop slashing the UN budget, and it complied.

There was hope when President Bush took office that U.S. support for the United Nations would be strengthened. He formerly had served as U.S. ambassador to the UN and knew how to work within its framework. That hope was undermined when the United States unilaterally invaded Panama at the end of 1989 to capture its military leader and bring him to trial on narcotics charges. That violation of Panama's sovereignty and international law was condemned by the General Assembly.

However, at the end of 1990 when Kuwait was overrun by Iraq, and Middle East oil was threatened, President Bush and Secretary of State Baker mobilized UN Security Council support with the slogan of supporting the "rule of law." This helped mobilize international support including that of Arab nations. Their support was a buffer against resentment of Arab masses. With success in the war against Iraq, the United States became committed to the UN Security Council and international law. The United States found itself in a position where it would be regarded as a hypocrite if it ignored international law in the use of force.

THE SOURCES OF INTERNATIONAL LAW

International law is a body of principles, customs, and rules that are recognized as binding obligations by sovereign states and international organizations in their mutual relations. The father of international law is often said to be Hugo Grotius, whose *Concerning the Law of War and Peace* was written after the terrible Thirty Years' War, which devastated Europe at the beginning of the seventeenth century. There is a parallel today. The revival of international law under the United Nations also came after a terrible war—World War II, the worst war in history. Grotius was concerned about the disintegration of society and the need for a system of law to replace the spiritual unity of Christendom, which had been broken by war. He proposed a system derived from natural law and the Christian conscience to preserve the sovereignty of states.[2] He compiled the international customs and precedents of that day for his seminal work.

International law governs relations between states, and only states can take up cases before international tribunals. One important exception is the optional protocol of the Covenant of Economic and Cultural Rights of 1976, discussed below. This broke new ground by allowing individuals and groups to appeal to the UN Commission on Human Rights.

Individuals as a rule apply international law in domestic courts. Such cases include issues involving foreign corporations, jurisdiction over foreigners, extradition to other countries, crimes committed aboard ships, and many other cases involving suits between foreigners and citizens of a country.

The sources of international law are listed in Article 38 of the Statute of the International Court of Justice, which is part of the UN Charter, as follows: (1) Treaties. This covers international agreements, or treaties, such as treaties, conventions, pacts, and executive agreements, although in the United States treaties in a narrow sense mean only those international agreements approved by two-thirds of the Senate. Unilateral statements by presidents can be recognized as international agreements and commitments under international law. Article 102 of the UN Charter requires all treaties and other international agreements to be registered with the United Nations, and states may not invoke such an agreement unless it is registered. (2) Custom. This includes the rules that are generally accepted by states and observed in their relations with each other. The classic court case is that of the *Scotia*. The U.S. Supreme Court in 1872 ruled that the ship *Birkshire* could not collect damages from the ship *Scotia* because the *Birkshire* had not been following the custom of using different colored lights and was only displaying white lights. At that time, most ships were observing British regulations that required colored lights to show fore and aft, and white lights starboard and port. Since that time the many customs for shipping, trade, and many other international transactions have been formalized in international agreements, so that they, rather than custom, are a much more important source of international law today. (3) General principles of law. This covers principally Roman law, and ordinary law principles covering property and territorial rights. (4) Judicial and arbitral decisions of previous cases involving international law. There is, of course, a growing body of this law. (5) Writings by scholars in journals and reviews of international law. This has become much less important as norms have been formalized in international agreements.

The United Nations has been a major source for international law. Under Article 13 the General Assembly shall make recommendations for encouraging progressive development of international law and its codification. The major instruments for this are the International Law Commission and the General Assembly's sixth committee, which debates the commission's reports. The International Law Commission was established by the General Assembly in 1947 to promote the development and codification of international law. Its 34 members, who meet annually in Geneva, are experts, serving as individuals and not as representatives of governments. The commission prepares drafts of conventions for consideration by the Economic and Social Council and the General Assembly. Generally, the commission approves and calls an international conference of plenipotentiaries to approve and "sign" the agreements. Alternatively, agreements may be approved by the General Assembly. The agreements do not come into effect, however, until the specific ratifications are obtained through the countries' legal processes. In the United States this normally involves a two-thirds approval by the Senate. Other parts of the UN System also initiate international conventions and agreements in their areas of specialty, which go through a similar signature and ratification process. Resolutions and agreements approved by the General Assembly can become evidence of international law even if they are not formally ratified.

WAR AND INTERVENTION
UNDER INTERNATIONAL LAW

There is a considerable body of international agreements developed since the beginning of the century that forbids offensive war. Article 1 of the UN Charter states the major purpose of the United Nations as maintaining peace within a framework of international law:

> 1. To maintain international peace and security, and to that end: to take effective collective measures for the prevention and removal of threats to the peace, and for

the suppression of acts of aggression or other breaches of the peace, and to bring about by peaceful means, and in conformity with the principles of justice and international law, adjustment or settlement of international disputes or situations which might lead to a breach of the peace.

Paragraph 3 of Article 2 states that "All Members shall settle their international disputes by peaceful means in such a manner that international peace and security, and justice, are not endangered." Article 33 requires parties to a dispute to seek to settle it by peaceful means and if that does not succeed, the Security Council then has the power to settle it.

As noted in the introduction, the United Nations grew out of the League of Nations experience and a body of international law that opposed aggression. The League itself was designed to prevent war. Article 1 obligated League members not to resort to war, and Article 10 called on members to respect the territorial integrity of other members. Articles 15 and 16 stated that if any nation went to war in disregard of the actions of the League, it was deemed to have gone to war against all the members. Some authors have stressed that there was a loophole in these articles implying that a state could go to war if unanimous agreement in the League council did not oppose such action. However, that loophole was only a loophole, and it does not invalidate the plain language of the rest of the Covenant.

The Hague conventions of 1899 and 1907 also had committed nations to use their best efforts to settle disputes peacefully, and they set up the Permanent Court of Arbitration for this purpose. It was able to arbitrate several important disputes before World War I.

In 1928 the world nations formally renounced war and agreed to settle all disputes by peaceful means. The Kellogg-Briand Pact, or Pact of Paris, which grew out of an American initiative, was ratified by the important nations of the world. It renounced recourse to war and committed the signatories not to seek settlement of disputes except by peaceful means. This "outlawry of war" proved to be ineffective, however, against the World War II aggression of the Axis powers.

At the close of the war, Britain, France, the United States, and the Soviet Union set up the Nuremburg tribunal, which tried Nazi war criminals. The jurisdiction of the court included "crimes against peace: namely, planning, preparation, initiation or waging of a war of aggression or a war in violation of international treaties." The UN General Assembly endorsed the principles of the Nuremburg trials unanimously in a resolution on December 11, 1946.

The General Assembly in 1987 adopted without a vote resolutions calling on nations to refrain from the threat or use of force, suggesting negotiation of disputes and encouraging the secretary general to exercise his functions fully in the cause of peace and to make use of the International Court.

The point is that there is a solid body of precedent and international agreements for prohibiting war and requiring nations to settle disputes peacefully. This precedent is routinely supported in UN resolutions by the Security Council and General Assembly in dealing with aggression. This precedent, as noted in previous chapters, has played an important part over the long run in containing and discouraging aggression. "A habit of reliance on an international institution to deal with large political questions even if only in debate will increase the pressure for recourse to that institution at the crisis point."[3] However, the appeasement of aggression of the 1930s and 1940s created cynicism about the effectiveness of international law and a belief in the need to rely on military power. After World War II the philosophers of power politics were more popular among the diplomats and academics than the international lawyers, who had dominated the university courses on international affairs in the 1930s.

As indicated, the major international law issue of recent years for the United States has involved intervention. International law was founded on Grotius' aim of promoting a respect for sovereignty. Intervention is an attack on that sovereignty through "dictatorial interference by one state in the affairs of another state for the purpose of either maintaining or changing the existing order of things."[4] In December 1974, about 24 years after the General Assembly had first considered the matter, it approved by consensus a draft definition of aggression, which is the most flagrant kind of intervention. The sponsors of the resolution included the United States and the Soviet Union. The definitions of aggression, in addition to obvious aggression by military attacks, included a state allowing its territory for perpetrating an act of aggression against another state, and also the sending of armed bands of mercenaries against another state. Article 5 added that no consideration whatever may serve as a justification for aggression.[5]

International law like domestic law is frequently broken, and there have been numerous wars since the United Nations was established. The Soviet Union and the United States, although sponsors of the UN definition of aggression, had themselves committed aggression. Previous chapters also described the procedures used in the United Nations to oppose aggression. These chapters stressed that the UN Charter is a flexible instrument and showed the many ways it was used to contain and settle wars. It is even designed to take care of the problem of the "rogue cop" in which one of the permanent members supports aggression. In that case the issue can be transferred to the General Assembly by a procedural vote of the Security Council not subject to the veto. In a number of cases beginning with the Korean War, the General Assembly took charge of protecting the victim of aggression.

There are cases in which the right of intervention is recognized under international law. The right of intervention may be by right when it takes place at the explicit invitation of the lawful government of a state. Examples are the landing of American troops in Lebanon in 1958 at the invitation of that government. They were withdrawn within a few months. French forces have intervened in Chad to protect against a rebellion sponsored by Libya. Often aggressors make a false claim that they have been invited to intervene—Germany in invading Austria in 1938 and the Soviet Union in invading Afghanistan in 1979. Such intervention, of course, is a flagrant violation of international law.

There is considerable debate among international lawyers about the allowable intervention in a civil war. Article 2, paragraph 7 of the Charter states that "Nothing contained in the present Charter shall authorize the United Nations to intervene in matters which are essentially within the domestic jurisdiction of any state . . . ." This is generally interpreted to prohibit intervention in a civil war. On the other hand, when foreign assistance is given to the rebels, it is generally assumed that providing aid to the government threatened is legal.[6] However, there usually is much room for debate whether a government is legitimate, how much a rebel force is being aided from the outside, and how much the government that intervenes takes over control of the local government and thereby intervenes excessively.

The major difference between international and domestic law is that there is no governmental police or military force to enforce the former. International law still depends largely upon the willingness of world leaders to work within the United Nations to settle disputes, and that in turn depends in large part upon the public support for the United Nations. Colonel House, President Wilson's foreign policy adviser, in exploring ideas for the League of Nations in a letter to Lord Robert Cecil of Great Britain, said:

> I believe the most vital element in bringing about a worldwide reign of peace is to have the same stigma rest upon the acts of nations as upon the acts of individuals. When the people of a country are held up to the scorn and condemnation of the world because of the dishonorable acts of their representatives, they will no longer tolerate such acts.[7]

President Wilson repeated this theme in his inaugural address. John F. Kennedy in reporting on the founding of the United Nations made a similar statement. Kennedy was disappointed that the leaders did not create a stronger organization to keep the peace but added that they were not at fault—the people must insist on giving up sovereignty to the organization. He was one of the war heroes, but he added: "War will exist until the conscientious objector enjoys the same prestige as the warrior has today."

The supporters of international law call upon their governments to respect international law in dealings with other nations. They are planning for the long run and hope to create public acceptance of a system where nations respect sovereignty of other nations and do not use force or else face punishment by the world community. It is easy for a powerful president to become impatient with the slowness of diplomacy and difficulties of working through the UN Security Council or General Assembly and to take unilateral action without regard for United Nations procedures and international law. There were serious failures in the United States using power politics and some important successes in using the United Nations to settle and contain wars.

THE WORLD COURT

The International Court of Justice is the supreme court of international law, but it is outside the mainstream of settling disputes that could lead to war. None of the major disputes that led to war described in the previous chapters were submitted to the International Court. The court is situated at the Hague and its statute is a part of the UN Charter. It inherited the records and the precedents of the Permanent Court of International Justice, which functioned under the League of Nations.

Under Article 36 of the statute of the International Court, states may accept compulsory jurisdiction in all legal disputes concerning (1) interpretation of a treaty, (2) a question of international law, (3) existence of any fact that might constitute breach of international law, and (4) reparation for breach of an international obligation. This sounds much like the charge of domestic courts interpreting contracts and agreements and judging cases of breaking the law. The United Nations can also seek an advisory opinion from the International Court on issues in dispute. The United States, in approving the statute of the International Court of Justice, adopted the famous Connally amendment. Under it, the United States does not have to submit cases it considers to be within its domestic jurisdiction, and it can decide whether such cases are within its jurisdiction or not. About 100 of the 160 countries that have ratified the UN Charter and the Statute of the Court have made similar reservations.

The court consists of 15 independent judges elected by the Security Council and the General Assembly. They are elected for nine years, and the terms of five expire every three years, permitting a rotation of the membership. If there is no judge of the nationality of a party before the court, that party can choose one to take part. In the 1980s the International Court had a budget of about $6 million, with about 31 on its payroll.

Major issues of war and peace between great powers are seldom submitted to the court. A typical case is that of the United Kingdom v. Norway (Norwegian Fisheries Case) of 1951. This dispute originated when British fishing vessels operated in waters claimed by Norway. The court ruled in favor of Norway, approving the Norwegian practice of drawing the boundary for its territorial sea from straight baselines following the general directions of the coast but not the indentations of that coast. This case set a precedent used by the International Law Commission in drafting provisions on the limits of the territorial sea in the subsequent Law of the Sea conventions.

The cases involving the international status of Southwest Africa in 1950, 1962, and 1966 illustrate the limitations of the court but also the potential of the United Nations for enforcing international law. A basic issue addressed in these cases was the status of South-West Africa (now called Namibia), which had been a mandate under the League of Nations and was controlled by South Africa. Ethiopia and Liberia brought the case before the International Court objecting to South Africa's suspension of human rights there and requesting it to enforce conditions of the League mandate for Southwest Africa. In 1962 the court ruled that South Africa's obligations under the mandate continued, but in 1966 by another split decision it ruled that UN members could not invoke compulsory jurisdiction of the court on these issues. However, political pressures of the African countries in the United Nations resulted in the Security Council condemning South Africa for not giving Namibia independence and for continuing the practice of apartheid. The Council imposed sanctions against South Africa prohibiting the export to it of military goods. Similar resolutions supporting Namibia and condemning apartheid were also passed by the General Assembly, which then refused to recognize the credentials of South Africa and in effect suspended its membership in the United Nations. The United States at first voted against such actions as interference in internal affairs not authorized by the Charter, but public opposition to the South African apartheid continued to mount. By 1985 as a result of congressional acts the U.S. government joined other UN nations in invoking economic sanctions against that country. Thus, although the World Court could not directly enforce its ruling on South Africa, other organs of the UN System took strong action in line with the court's decisions to condemn South Africa for its policies of apartheid. These political organs of the UN System made South Africa feel the weight of international condemnation. By the end of 1988 South Africa had negotiated an agreement for Namibian independence, including elections supervised by the United Nations.

In April 1984 Nicaragua lodged a complaint that the United States had supported military and paramilitary action against the Sandinista government. On

May 10 the court gave an initial ruling that the United States should respect Nicaragua's sovereignty. In November in a series of rulings it ruled that the court had jurisdiction over the dispute. On January 18, 1985, the United States unilaterally withdrew from the hearing and denounced the court. As indicated above, however, the U.S. Congress ended military aid to the contras, and the international condemnation including the court's action was reflected in the congressional action.

The court also ruled against the United States in an advisory opinion of April 26, 1988, that the United States was obligated to arbitrate its demand that the PLO close its office in New York. The Manhatten Federal Court ruled against the Department of Justice's position on this case. This was a victory of sorts for the Department of State, which had openly opposed the Department of Justice on this issue on the grounds that the Justice position violated the U.S. host-country agreement with the United Nations.

On the other hand, the court gave support to the United States during the Iranian hostage crisis beginning in November 1979 by condemning Iran's action in holding as hostages about 50 American diplomatic personnel. This was a small part of the pressures exerted on Iran, which included unanimous resolutions in the Security Council and U.S. government action to freeze about $13 billion of Iranian assets in the United States. The crisis was resolved in complicated negotiations headed by Algeria after the Iranian prime minister visited the United Nations hoping to get support against Iraq in the Iraq-Iran war and finding the UN diplomats overwhelmingly condemning Iran on the hostage issue. Although the court action in itself was not at the center of the action, it, as well as UN resolutions, helped demonstrate international support for the basic principle of international law, which requires the host country to protect diplomats. Support of this principle by the diplomatic community exerted a great deal of pressure on Iran to release the hostages.

Although the International Court has not been used to settle the major issues of war and peace, it has been used to reinforce respect for international law on several major controversies affecting the United States. These include the Iran-hostage issue and U.S. use of the CIA to attack Nicaragua. In both these cases the general support of the international community for the position enunciated by the court helped bring about an eventual solution.

Over the years the World Court supported granting independence of Namibia, which helped eventually in bringing about a solution of that issue in 1988 after many years of negotiation in other forums. This demonstrates how the court can be used in major disputes. In 1988, as political solutions were negotiated for the Afghanistan war, the Iran-Iraq conflict, the Vietnam-Kampuchea war, and others, there was hope that the World Court could play a larger role in adjudicating issues, giving opinions, and reinforcing moves toward peace. It is more than a truism that international peace depends on countries developing a respect for international law.

THE LAW OF THE SEA, GENOCIDE, AND OTHER AGREEMENTS

The Law of the Sea conferences illustrate an important area where the United Nations has codified international law. On September 17, 1976, Secretary of State Kissinger stated that these negotiations were among the most important, complex, and difficult of any of this century. He explained that they were aimed at establishing a legal regime for about three-fourths of the surface of the globe. The treaty came into effect on November 16, 1994, with the 60th ratification. The ratification care after four years of consultation that resulted in an agreement approved by the General Assembly modifying a controversial provision on mining the deep seabed. Resolution of this issue led to approval by Western European countries. The U.S. Senate, however, did not act on the Clinton administration's recommendation for approval. The United States observes many of the principles of the treaty although it has not ratified it.

At its first session the International Law Commission included the law of the sea as a topic for codification. This has continued to be one of the most ambitious attempts to codify international law on an important subject. The commission appointed a special rapporteur who prepared reports for consideration of the topics involved, and articles were prepared and submitted to governments for comments. This prepared the way for the General Assembly to call the First UN Conference on the Law of the Sea in 1958, which prepared four conventions: the high seas, the continental shelf, the territorial sea and contiguous zone, and fishing. These were duly ratified by 1966 and became part of international law. The Second UN Conference on the Law of the Sea in 1958 did not accomplish any important business.

In 1967 Ambassador Arvid Pardo from Malta proposed that resources of the seabed "beyond the limits of present national jurisdiction" be declared "the common heritage of mankind" to be held in trust by a new international authority. This resolution was approved in 1970 by the General Assembly by a vote of 108 to 0 with only 14 abstentions, mostly from the Soviet bloc. (The United States voted in favor, but as indicated below, the Reagan administration later reversed the U.S. position.) The General Assembly then called, in 1973, the Third UN Conference on the Law of the Sea. It was charged to try again to set an agreed breadth for the territorial sea, involving jurisdiction over navigation, and to define the rights and duties of all states in the oceans.

Major divisions of opinion centered around the industrial states with advanced ocean technology versus the third-world states without such technology, and those states with coastlines versus those without. After extended negotiations, agreement was reached on these issues, including establishment of a regime that would administer the resources of the high seas for the benefit of all. The third conference produced a UN convention addressing this and other issues including:

—breadth of the territorial sea
—freedom of transit through straits
—jurisdiction over adjacent marine resources
—control of mining
—pollution
—scientific research
—settlement of disputes

The Intergovernmental Marine Consultative Organization (IMCO), a UN Specialized Agency, carries on work related to the law of the sea issues. IMCO has worked on technical matters, including pollution issues. Its convention on pollution as amended in 1962 and 1969 requires states not to discharge their ballast tanks or leave visible traces on the water within 50 miles of coastal zones. Photographs from aircraft are admissible as evidence of violation of this convention. A 1973 convention requires separate ballast tanks on tankers over 70,000 dead-weight tons so they do not pollute the sea with ballast tanks that hold petroleum.

The sixth committee of the General Assembly has drafted a convention providing punishment for genocide. The genocide convention was approved unanimously by the UN General Assembly in 1948, but it was not approved by the U.S. Senate until 1986. The convention provides for states to punish all persons guilty of genocide or incitement to commit it. The U.S. implementing legislation was not passed until 1988, forty years after the initial approval by the United Nations. Opponents of the treaty were afraid that it would supersede the U.S. Constitution and be used in ways detrimental to the United States. The U.S. Senate approved the convention with reservations in 1986.

On May 25, 1993, the Security Council under Chapter VII of the Charter unanimously approved setting up a tribunal to judge grave violations of international law in the former territory of Yugoslavia. The scope of the resolution included genocide and violation of the laws and customs of war. The Council decided to require all UN members to cooperate with the tribunal. The expenses of the tribunal including the special prosecutor's office would be part of the regular UN budget. Subsequently the prosecutor named Serb leaders, which complicated but did not stop the negotiation of a peace agreement in 1995.

In 1994 the Security Council, finding that genocide in Rwanda "constituted a threat to the international peace and security," set up a new "international criminal tribunal" for Rwanda. Because the Rwandan government requested the tribunal, this avoided the problem of encroaching on its domestic jurisdiction. The jurisdiction of the Rwandan tribunal is about the same as the one for the former Yugoslavia, but the Rwandan tribunal does not cover violations of laws and customs of war.

Bodies created by the General Assembly for drafting international law include the Commission on International Trade Law, which was established in 1966. It has completed many conventions on international trade including one on the sale of goods and one on international bills of exchange.

The Specialized Agencies also are in on the act. The International Labor organization has drafted numerous conventions on labor welfare. The International Bank for Reconstruction and Development has drafted an important convention on settling investment disputes. The United States is a party to well over a hundred multilateral agreements negotiated within the UN System.[8]

UN ATTEMPTS TO STOP
INTERNATIONAL TERRORISM

The United Nations has addressed international terrorism, but like its other international law activities, its actions have not been so dramatic or newsworthy as more direct action. The widespread outrage against acts of international terrorists in 1986 generated a surge of opinion demanding that the United States strike back and punish those responsible for violent crimes. The voices calling for reasoned and legal action against such crimes were lost in the public call for retribution. This section examines what has been accomplished in the United Nations through cooperation under international law and evaluates chances for success in comparison to the forceful actions that have been taken outside that framework.[9]

We first look at the general UN resolution calling for cooperation against international terrorism and then evaluate the specific conventions that cover hijacking of aircraft, taking of hostages, attacking diplomatic targets, and supporting nuclear terrorism. The UN System is not in a position to act like an international police force to arrest terrorists and punish countries that support them. The United Nations is more like a forum to promote cooperation and develop a body of international law to help countries act together. Such an international process can precipitate positive action and fix positions near a high level of cooperation.

UN Resolutions

The May 1972 massacre of 28 civilian passengers at Israel's Lod Airport by Japanese terrorists working with a Palestine group, and the September 1972 Munich massacre of 11 Israeli athletes by the Palestinian Black September group stimulated worldwide horror and determination to take action. Secretary General Waldheim asked that terrorism be placed on the agenda of the General Assembly. The Arab nations agreed, but they insisted that the agenda item also include a study of the underlying causes of terrorist acts. The Arab nations supported the Palestine Liberation Organization, whereas the Africans did not want to hamper the "freedom fighters" fighting the colonial powers in Portugal and South Africa.

The United States tabled a convention to punish acts of terrorism. The initial General Assembly action was to approve a resolution creating a 35-member *ad hoc* committee in 1972 to study the matter. The United States opposed the wording of the resolution because it appeared to limit condemnation of terrorism to acts committed by colonial, racial, and alien (Israeli) regimes and implied encouragement of violence by "freedom fighters."

During years of negotiation that followed, the West continued to condemn all acts of international terrorism, whereas communists and Arab-Africans did not want to condemn "national liberation" struggles. Certain delegates pointed out that the way to go was to conclude specific conventions, such as those against hijacking and the protection of diplomats. Finally, by December 1979 the first major antiterrorist resolution was adopted by 118 countries with 22 abstentions including the United States and Western Europe. The United States and certain Western European countries abstained because changes were made in the final resolution from what had been agreed on in the working group. However, by 1981 as the subject received its annual consideration by the General Assembly, the United States and Western Europe approved a resolution that condemned all acts of international terrorism but did not propose to give a free reign when colonial, racist, and alien regimes were involved. By December 9, 1985, in another resolution, the UN General Assembly adopted a general resolution against terrorism without a role-call vote with no objections. The compromise wording of the resolution reaffirmed the inalienable right to self-determination and independence of all peoples under colonial and racist regimes, thus meeting the problem of the Arab-African delegations.

The resolution unequivocally condemned as criminal all acts of terrorism and deplored the loss of innocent lives from such acts. It appealed to all states to become party to the existing international conventions such as those on hijacking and hostages. It called on states to fulfill their obligations under international law not to assist terrorist acts and urged them to cooperate in exchanging information and to enforce the law against persons committing acts of international terrorism.[10]

This was a major step forward, but there is little prospect that the United Nations will agree on a comprehensive convention on international terrorism. On the one hand, the Arab-African group and the communists do not want to provide legal instruments that could be used to oppose national liberation struggles; moreover, the European countries are concerned about legal safeguards to protect individuals for asylum against prosecution for political crimes. Nevertheless, the above resolution and the following agreements show that there is a growing body of international law and increasing international cooperation against terrorist crimes.

ICAO Conventions

The actions of the International Civil Aviation Organization (ICAO) against terrorism demonstrate what can be accomplished by international cooperation and respect for international law. In the late 1960s hijacking of aircraft peaked, stimulating action by national governments and the ICAO. The first important agreement was the Tokyo Convention of 1963, which defined jurisdiction for hijacking crimes and gave power to the aircraft commanders to act against hijackers. This was followed by the Hague Convention of 1970, which obligated states to punish the guilty severely or to extradite them expeditiously. Although nations under this convention could refuse to extradite prisoners if the crime were politically motivated, this loophole has not been used to a significant extent to permit hijackers to escape trial and punishment. This was followed by the Montreal Convention of 1971, which covers unlawful acts on the ground and obligates states to take measures to prevent such crimes. The above conventions were reinforced by ICAO technical manuals to strengthen precautions against skyjacking. In 1987 ICAO adopted another protocol on acts of violence at airports. In 1991 its protocol controlling plastic explosives was signed by 41 countries.

More than 110 countries cooperated under these conventions to stop skyjacking. As a result, the number of terrorist skyjackings or attempted skyjackings fell from a high of about 18 in 1969 to an average of 1.5 in 1986–87.[11]

The United States in the 1960s was particularly affected by skyjackers who forced planes to go to Cuba. Although Cuba is not a member of ICAO and did not subscribe to the above conventions, it negotiated a special agreement with the United States that provided for extradition or punishment of hijackers. It has punished them severely with sentences ranging from 2 to 50 years. Following the negotiation of this agreement, hijacking to Cuba fell drastically. It is interesting to note that the special agreement included something for Cuba, namely that the parties to the agreement would not support armed probes against the other. This reflected Cuba's concern about the CIA probes after the Bay of Pigs incident that were mounted from Florida during the Kennedy administration against Cuban targets.

Crimes Against Diplomats

The United States was the primary sponsor of measures to protect diplomats. On November 28, 1972, a General Assembly resolution formed a committee to draft articles, and a convention was approved by Resolution 3166 on December 14, 1973. In 1985 65 nations were parties, including the United States. The aim of the convention is to prosecute or extradite persons alleged to have committed serious crimes against diplomats and "internationally protected persons." This requires states to conform their legislation to the international conventions. This presented a problem for the United States, which has a tradition of leaving to local officials rather than to the national government the responsibility for protecting consuls and diplomats. This is expensive, and local governments have problems covering the cost. Under subsequent U.S. legislation, limited authority is provided for the national government to extend financial assistance to any of the 50 American states burdened with this problem.[12]

Convention on the Taking of Hostages

The Federal Republic of Germany instigated discussions in 1976 on a convention against the taking of hostages. Germany had been shocked by a siege of its embassy in Sweden by terrorists. The General Assembly passed the German proposal to the General Assembly's Sixth Committee in 1976.

The 1979 convention adopted by the General Assembly obligates states to punish offenders or to extradite them. The major problem was that Algeria and Libya wanted to exclude populations attacking racist and colonial regimes; others wanted to exclude national liberation movements from penalties for hostage taking. The Western nations, on the other hand, insisted on no exceptions for hostage-takers. The national liberation movement issue was settled by letting the Geneva Convention of 1949 on the laws of war apply to national liberation conflicts.[13] This convention does prohibit hostage taking. Another issue arose out of the Israeli attack at the Entebbe Airport of Uganda, when terrorists held a plane hostage and the Ugandan government took no effective action. Israeli commandos attacked the airport, destroyed the plane, and rescued the hostages with a few casualties among the passengers and terrorists. The convention on the taking of hostages states that nothing in this convention should be construed as justifying the violation of territorial integrity of the state. Finally, the asylum issue was settled by a similar provision that nothing in the convention would impair the right of asylum. The General Assembly adopted the hostage convention in December 1979 opening it for signature. In June 1985 it was in effect for 27 countries and was being observed by many more.[14]

In 1992 there was dramatic success by behind-the-scenes UN diplomacy in getting hostages released. Years of U.S. efforts, including trading arms for hostages in the Iran-contra scandal, had failed. Lebanon had been the source of most hostage problems. The UN secretary general and his aide, Giandomenico Picco, took over behind-the-scenes negotiations, which were aided by the decision of the Arab countries to begin face-to-face negotiations with Israel. Between August and December 1991 nine Western hostages and the remains of another were released in Lebanon, and 91 Lebanese detainees were released in South Lebanon and Israel. The secretary general kept details of negotiations secret, but he thanked groups in Lebanon and the assistance of Israel, Iran, Libya, and Syria.

In February 1992 the Security Council in a resolution urged Libya to meet U.S. and British demands to try suspects accused of bombing Pan Am flight 103 in which 270 people were killed. The International Court rejected an appeal from Libya to stop the United States from using a threat of force to coerce Libya to turn over the suspects. Libya did not meet the deadline, so on March 31, 1992, the Security Council passed a resolution imposing sanctions. There were no negative votes, although there were abstentions. The sanctions included an air embargo and an end to arms sales. The same day the International Court rejected a Libyan appeal to declare the sanctions invalid. Libya was forced to offer compromises such as offering to have the accused tried in Malta, but they were rejected by the Security Council. The Security Council's resolution was a landmark, the first time a country had been punitively isolated by that body. After the sanctions, press reports indicated 1,700 Soviet military and technical advisers left Libya, severely weakening its air defense system.[15]

International Cooperation to Recover Nuclear Materials

In the last 20 years, there were moves to control nuclear materials to prevent terrorist groups from using them. The major agreement was a treaty ratified in

1982 that had been negotiated at meetings of the International Atomic Energy Agency in its headquarters in Vienna. It sets standards for shipment and storage of sensitive nuclear materials used for peaceful purposes and includes provisions for guards. States must punish or extradite offenders and assist each other in prosecution.

In the years before the agreement there had been many incidents. In 1974, police had arrested men plotting to steal uranium in India. In 1977, undercover U.S. agents arrested persons offering two tons of nuclear material for sale. In 1979, federal officials arrested two other persons who stole thousands of pounds of semi-refined uranium ore from a New Mexico uranium mill. From 1977 to 1982, eight nuclear reactors in Germany were sabotaged. Similar incidents occurred in France. From 1970 to 1982, there were 60 threats against American cities claiming nuclear devices were involved, but all were hoaxes.[16]

A major effort was made during the breakup of the Soviet Union for Moscow to keep control of its nuclear weapons. Also, the June 1992 agreement of the United States and Russia to cut nuclear arms included provisions for a senior group to protect against limited nuclear launches. Its primary goal would be antiballistic missile defense. Such a group would also want to coordinate action on terrorist use of nuclear weapons.

The above provisions of international law against various types of terrorism leave a gap for acts not involving aircraft, diplomatic persons, nuclear terrorism, or hostages. For example, no international agreement covered the bombing of a nightclub in Berlin in which innocent people were killed. However, local law would punish criminals involved in such crimes, and many states routinely cooperate in extraditing criminals for crimes. The most dangerous gap is nuclear terrorism, a crisis in which terrorists would steal nuclear weapons, but the major nuclear powers are trying to close that gap. Moreover, when hijackings and terrorist incidents occur, there is international cooperation, including that of third-world governments to punish the culprits. This includes refusing to let hijacked planes land and refusing demands to release terrorists already imprisoned. The UN resolutions of 1979 to 1985 provide a general obligation for such cooperation.

There was a great increase in international terrorism after 1980. However, cooperation under the ICAO dramatically lessened terrorist skyjackings and attempted skyjackings from an average of about 18 in 1970 to less than 2 at the end of the 1980s.

The moderate, cooperative efforts of nations under the ICAO conventions and international law effectively reduced terrorist incidents after the early 1970s. International terrorism will probably exist as long as war does. However, the success of ICAO against skyjacking, and of the United Nations in negotiating the release of hostages from Lebanon and in mobilizing sanctions against Libyan terrorism shows what can be a done under international law and the United Nations.

HUMAN RIGHTS

The UN Charter differs from the League Covenant in affirming as a principal objective the encouraging of respect for human rights. On the other hand, Article 2, paragraph 7 states that nothing in the Charter shall authorize the United Nations to intervene in matters essentially within the domestic jurisdiction of a state. Article 1 of the Charter is also relevant in saying the purpose of the United Nations includes suppressing "breaches of the peace" and settlement of disputes that "might lead to a breach of the peace." It can be argued that gross violations of human rights such as genocide (1951 convention) and also situations that disrupt other states such as flows of refugees are breaches of the peace and can be acted on by the Security Council. As noted above the Security Council did set up tribunals for the Bosnian and Rwandan conflicts to punish gross violations of human rights. It did not refuse to intervene because of the Article 2, paragraph 7 provision on domestic jurisdiction.

In terms of "encouraging" respect for human rights, a number of conventions have been approved in the UN System in addition to the basic Universal Declaration of Human Rights approved by the General Assembly in 1948 with no negative votes. Building on this the General Assembly in 1966 adopted two covenants—one on political and the other on economic and social rights. They came into effect after 35 ratifications each.

The covenants include in great detail provisions for civil and political rights such as those included in the U.S. Bill of Rights. The covenant on economic and cultural rights is more far reaching. The first covenant includes the right to life, liberty, and security of person, freedom from slavery, freedom from arbitrary arrest and detention, the right to a fair trial and to be presumed innocent until proved guilty, inviolability of the home, freedom of movement, freedom of opinion and peaceful assembly, and the right to vote and participate in government. The second includes the right to social security, the right to work, the right to education, and the right to an adequate standard of living.

The UN Human Rights Commission has established working groups and rapporteurs for the following types of human rights violations: torture, disappearances, arbitrary execution, religious intolerance, and arbitrary detention. They take action and report to the commission after investigating and asking governments to explain thousands of alleged human rights violations. Only a small percentage of the violations are clarified, and perhaps the most effective actions are taken by the private groups such as Amnesty International. Nevertheless, the UN action reinforces actions of private groups and establishes international standards against which the actions of states can be measured. Condemnation by the international community of human rights violations can have an effect on even the most hardened regimes and rulers, and help correct at least the most blatant violations.

Obviously human rights will not be honored throughout the world until the millenium, and for this reason some writers take a cynical view toward the conventions. This causes problems of ratification by legislators who take laws seriously, particularly in the United States, although the United States is one of the leading supporters of such rights. Another problem is a fear by some U.S. politicians that the United Nations would use the UN covenants to threaten the sovereignty of the United States. Also, critics say that the covenants are not taken seriously by some states, and they, therefore, are not important. Moreover, the provision guaranteeing a job and social security causes problems for those advocating a free enterprise philosophy and opposing excessive state intervention.

Supporters of the covenants reply that these are goals that nations should seek to achieve and that the covenants give leverage to those supporting human rights as an international policy objective. As an argument they note that many domestic laws are not enforced strictly—as many as 90 percent of incidents of theft in the United States are not punished, but this does not mean it should not bother with laws against theft.

Support by the United States for the covenants on human rights reached a high point under President Carter, who supported them by speeches and actions. Reports on human rights were used in decisions on aid programs.[17] His ambassador to the United Nations, Andrew Young, a black, carried the flag on this issue including a visit to South Africa.

The General Assembly also has adopted conventions against slavery (1953, 1957), on refugees and stateless persons (1954 and 1967). In its first years the General Assembly set up the Commission on Human Rights to promote additional agreements, and in April 1994 established the post of High Commissioner for Human Rights with a broad mandate to take an activist role.

As new African members were admitted to the United Nations, it took increasingly strong action against racism, particularly apartheid policies of South Africa. The Security Council approved a voluntary arms embargo in 1963 and a mandatory one in 1977. The United States tended to lag behind in such actions, asserting that racism was a matter of domestic jurisdiction. The U.S. Congress with President Carter's encouragement supported the embargo in 1977. In 1986 Congress increased sanctions against South Africa.

From December 12 to 14, 1989, the General Assembly held a special session on apartheid and proposed specific guidelines for dismantling the system. Events accelerated in the following year under the new South African president F. W. de Klerk. He lifted the ban on political action by the African National Congress, which represented black opposition to the government, and released its leader, Nelson Mandela, from prison. The UN pressures and Mandela's moderation encouraged the South African government to repeal major pieces of discriminatory legislation, including laws that restricted movement and areas where blacks could live. The government entered into negotiations with black political groups on amendments to the constitution that would give blacks the vote and equal political rights. Elections were held in July 1994 and Nelson Mandela was installed as South Africa's president. The United Nations lifted its sanctions.

There was more success on the Namibian issue. In 1945 the United Nations had inherited the South African mandate of South-West Africa, now recognized as Namibia. For more than 40 years the United Nations in resolutions and action by the International Court tried to get South Africa to agree to Namibian independence. South Africa finally tied the issue to the presence of Cuban troops in Angola, which had intervened in South-West Africa. On December 22, 1988, two agreements, reflecting a U.S. initiative, were signed at UN headquarters providing for withdrawing Cuban troops from Angola, and for holding elections monitored by the United Nations. The elections were held with 97 percent participation, and on March 21, 1990, Namibia achieved its independence. The UN force of 7,900 military and civilian personnel was withdrawn at the end of March.

The basis of international law is for nations to respect other's sovereignty and to settle disputes peacefully. It differs from domestic law in that there is no powerful supergovernment to enforce its norms and rulings of the International Court. Enforcement of international law to maintain the peace is left to individual governments and political processes of the Security Council, which is composed of sovereign governments. The vision of the founders and supporters of the United Nations is to end wars with a UN system of collective security and respect for international law.

Leaders of the great powers have tended to rely on power politics to achieve their goals, and on many occasions have not kept their actions within international law. Other leaders, particularly of smaller nations and officials who worked in the UN System, often had a longer range view of strengthening international law to achieve world peace. However, when Iraq attacked Kuwait in 1990, the

United States was so successful in mobilizing UN support to repel the invasion, the United Nations and international law had a major revival of prestige, particularly in the United States.

Meanwhile, the United States negotiated treaties, the major instruments of international law, with drastic reductions in nuclear weapons. By 1992, the United States had committed itself to UN processes and international law, to the point where it would be an obvious hypocrite to reverse course.

The process of negotiation and international cooperation to control terrorism showed marked success in drastically reducing skyjacking as a form of international terrorism. This contrasted with the lack of success of the United States as it tried to stop terrorism by retaliation, such as bombing Libya and Lebanon, which could not be justified under international law.

CONCLUSIONS

UN support for human rights faced the dilemma of the international law principle of not interfering in matters of domestic jurisdiction. There are exceptions, however, if violations of human rights are so flagrant they threaten international peace and security. This occurred with apartheid in South Africa. Moreover, the pressure of Security Council sanctions supported by the General Assembly, which suspended South Africa's seating privileges, and rulings of the International Court helped persuade South Africa to give Namibia independence. By 1991 such pressures also had a major impact on South Africa's government and it also repealed apartheid legislation and gave blacks the vote.

The slogans of human rights played a part in the overthrow of the communist empires in Eastern Europe and of the Soviet Union. Without the human rights covenants, there would have been no agreed international standards for judging political and economic freedoms.

The above are only a few of many examples of UN activities directly and indirectly supporting international law. The entire UN System works within that framework, and the final chapter evaluates its effectiveness.

Notes to Chapter 7

1. L. Henkin et al., *Right v. Might: International Law and the Use of Force* (New York: Council of Foreign Relations Press, 1989).

2. R. Falk, F. Kratochivil, and S. Medelovitz (eds.), *International Law* (Boulder, CO: Westview Press, 1985); H. Lauterpaucht, in H. Falk et al., *The Grotian Tradition in International Law* (Boulder, CO: Westview Press, 1985).

3. A. Chayes, *The Cuban Missile Crises* (New York: Oxford University Press, 1974), p. 106.

4. G. von Glahn, *Law Among Nations* (New York: Macmillan, 1981), p. 160.

5. *UN Chronicle*, January 1975, p. 104; May 1974, p. 96.

6. B. Weston et al., *International Law and World Order* (St. Paul, MN: West, 1980), pp. 302–310.

7. C. Seymour, *The Intimate Papers of Colonel House* (Cambridge, MA: Houghton Mifflin Company, 1928), Vol. 4, Chap. 1.

8. U.S. Department of State, *Treaties in Force* (Washington, DC: U.S. Government Printing Office, 1981).

9. *Terrorism, An International Journal*, Vol. 6, No. 4, 1983.

10. A. Yoder, "United Nations' Resolutions Against International Terrorism," *Terrorism, An International Journal*, Vol. 6, No. 4, pp. 503–512.

11. U.S. Department of State, Office of the Ambassador at Large for Counterterrorism, "International Terrorist Incidents, 1986–1987."

12. K. Shamwell, "Implementing the Convention on the Prevention and Punishment of Crimes Against Internationally Protected Persons, Including Diplomatic Agents," *Terrorism, An International Journal*, Vol. 6, No. 4, 1983, pp. 529–544.

13. In the view of Abraham Sofaer, legal adviser to the Department of State, this did not create a gap in the hostage convention. He goes on to say that it did permit some states to have a rhetorical and political victory, which I translate as saving face. "Terrorism and the Law," *Foreign Affairs* (Summer 1986), pp. 901–922.

14. J. McDonald, "The UN Convention Against Hostage-Taking," *Terrorism, An International Journal*, Vol. 4, No. 4, 1983, pp. 545–560.

15. *New York Times*, June 22, 1992.

16. B. Jenkins, "International Cooperation in Locating and Recovering Stolen Nuclear Materials," *Terrorism, An International Journal*, Vol. 6, No. 4, 1983, pp. 561–576.

17. J. Carter, *Keeping Faith* (New York: Bantam, 1982), pp. 143–163.

Chapter VIII

ECONOMIC AND SOCIAL ACTIVITIES OF THE UNITED NATIONS

The General Assembly and its Economic and Social Council (ECOSOC) are the central UN organs for promoting international cooperation for economic and social problems. This is one of the principal aims of the Charter, and most of the budget of the UN System is spent for this purpose. The General Assembly determines policies for the economic and social activities of the United Nations. With 185 members and only a limited meeting time each fall, the General Assembly has come to depend on ECOSOC to do the spade work and make recommendations for approval by the Assembly.

THE ECONOMIC AND SOCIAL COUNCIL

The functions of the Economic and Social Council, which are covered in Chapter 10 of the Charter, reflect recommendations made by a League of Nations committee to establish a special organ for such work. As laid out in the Charter, ECOSOC carries out studies and reports, calls international conferences, prepares draft conventions, and sets up commissions to accomplish its aims.

ECOSOC has 54 members that rotate every three years. By custom the United States and other large powers stay on ECOSOC and do not take turns because ECOSOC resolutions would have little meaning if they were not approved by these larger nations. The Charter was amended twice to increase its size at the demand of the smaller states, which wanted an opportunity to be represented more often on this body.

ECOSOC works efficiently as a committee, considering its size. It has two major meetings a year, one in Geneva and one in New York. With a limited time to work through an ambitious agenda, it avoids long debates in its plenary sessions by passing on to the next item and letting concerned nations settle issues outside the plenary. When these issues are settled, they are brought back to the plenary.

The section on the UN Conference on Trade and Development (UNCTAD) describes the complicated compromises on multinational corporations, the international monetary reform, and trade negotiations. The negotiations for the compromises were begun first in the UNCTAD context, but they were concluded in a July 1972 ECOSOC resolution.[1] It is revealing to review other major issues considered by ECOSOC in the 1970s, and then examine major issues taken up in the 1980s and 1990s.

In the 1970s the developing countries were pressing for support for international commodity agreements. They were led and supported by the newly rich oil countries that pointed to the Organization of Petroleum Exporting Countries (OPEC) as the model for making commodity agreements and getting bargaining power vis-à-vis the developed countries. They hoped to create a "new international economic order" with such agreements and with other major reforms to the international trading system. The developing countries found, however, that this was not a panacea, because some were buyers as well as sellers of commodities, and high prices would hurt some of them and help others.

In the 1980s ECOSOC and related bodies in the UN System were concerned with the debt burden of the developing countries. Their large debts in part were caused by an increased burden of imports caused by the high oil prices and inflation. These also helped cause high interest rates, which increased the debt burden on the developing countries. Discussion of the issue in ECOSOC often caused splits between the developing countries, which called for general debt relief, and the developed countries, which in general wanted the debts considered on a case-by-case basis. By the end of the 1980s the case-by-case method seemed to be winning, and debts were being sold at a discount, or swapped for equity or other assets in local currencies.

By the 1990s the slogan of "sustainable development" was popular. This bridged a gap between developed countries, which needed foreign investments to employ their people and introduce new technology, thus relieving poverty. The developing countries hoped that the end of the Cold War would allow some of the tremendous sums used for armaments to be transferred to development.

Critics have asserted that a lot of the resolutions on such general issues are wasted effort because ECOSOC does not control the funds and organizations that carry out broad economic programs. However, this overlooks the fact that for the most part the same nations that are represented on ECOSOC are also members of governing boards of Specialized Agencies, including the powerful International Monetary Fund. Governments try to be consistent, so that compromises in general resolutions hammered out by countries in ECOSOC will normally be honored by these countries in other organizations of the UN System. Moreover, representatives of these other organizations attend ECOSOC meetings and are consulted on controversial issues.

The General Assembly and ECOSOC also give policy guidelines for the work of the various bodies of the UN proper, whereas the secretary general appoints their heads and is responsible for administering them. Most of these organs have their own governing bodies and sources of funds, and the major donor nations tend to have the most influence in their activity. In this chapter we focus on the work of the social and economic organs of the UN proper that are most active, including the UN Development Program (UNDP), the UN Children's Fund (UNICEF), the UN High Commissioner for Refugees (UNHCR), the UN Environment Program (UNEP), the population organs, UNCTAD, and those dealing with the transnational corporations. It is not a comprehensive survey, but it illustrates interactions that take place among the many UN agencies. In the previous chapter we covered social and economic activities of the United Nations in the field of international law, including civil aviation, law of the sea, and human rights.

The next chapter examines the work of the Specialized Agencies, many of which have been around longer than the United Nations and are closely associated with it. Representatives of these agencies report to ECOSOC and the General Assembly, although they take policy direction only from their governing bodies. As in the case of the bodies in the UN System, the fact that the Specialized Agencies report to the General Assembly and ECOSOC and the fact that the same governments give directions both to the United Nations and to the Specialized Agencies allows the United Nations to coordinate activities of the Specialized Agencies both at the world level and, as indicated below, at the local level through the UNDP resident representative. Appendix E lists the Specialized Agencies and other units of the UN System with their budgets.

THE REGIONAL ECONOMIC COMMISSIONS

The regional economic commissions act like regional coordinating bodies for UN activities. The first one established by the ECOSOC was the Economic Commission for Europe (ECE), designed to help in the economic reconstruction of Europe after World War II. The Marshall Plan and the Organization for European Economic Cooperation (OEEC) took over this function in Western Europe.[2] Since then the ECE has become an important center for promoting East-West trade, particularly through standardization of administrative procedures. It leaves the major initiatives to promoting trade among Western European countries to the European Economic Community. The regular membership of the ECE consists of European nations plus Canada and the United States.

The ECE's work is carried out by 10 subsidiary bodies and four working parties. Important work of the Inland Transport Committee includes reducing paperwork and restrictions. Its Senior Advisor on Environmental Problems represents countries causing about 90 percent of the world's industrial pollution, so that the ECE promotes international cooperation in this area. In recent years it has called on governments to use water resources more effectively, since irrational use of water is a major factor limiting development and causing pollution.

The Economic and Social Commission for Asia and the Pacific (ESCAP), formerly the Economic Commission for Asia and the Far East (ECAFE), points with pride to establishing the Asian Bank and promoting regional projects such as in the Mekong Valley, the Asian Telecommunications Network, and links in the Asian Highway. Four of its five nonregional members (the United States, France, the Netherlands, and the United Kingdom) have provided considerable economic and technical assistance in promoting the above projects. Contributions of the other member, the Soviet Union, have been minor. The success in helping promote the region's industrial development was reflected by the need for a 1985 ministerial meeting to deal with environment problems caused by industrial pollution.

The Economic Commission for Latin America and the Caribbean (ECLAC) has four nonregional members—France, the Netherlands, Spain, and the United Kingdom. It has concentrated on promoting economic integration and has attempted to reactivate the Central American Common Market, but this has been blocked by the political conflicts in the area. ECLAC has called for support of the Contadora peace process for Nicaragua and an end to foreign intervention against peace and economic development in the region. Its major concern has shifted from trade restrictions to the foreign debt problem in recent years.

The Economic Commission for Africa (ECA), established in 1958, initially concentrated on developing a statistical and factual base for development activities. Its substantive work concentrates on agriculture, and a joint ECA/Food and Agriculture Organization division assists livestock and food production of small farmers. ECA also tried to help meet the almost unlimited need to promote and coordinate transport and communications in Africa. As indicated above, the severe drought problem has been managed by UNDP, but ECA has carried out long-term studies of the problem.

The headquarters of the Economic and Social Commission for Western Asia was moved from Baghdad to Amman, Jordan, after the outbreak of the Gulf War in 1991. Its meetings have been highly politicized by admitting the Palestine Liberation Organization but not admitting Israel as a member.

THE UN DEVELOPMENT PROGRAM (UNDP)

The UNDP is one of the most important of the regular UN bodies, although it is not featured in the organization charts. It was formed originally as the Expanded Program of Technical Assistance by General Assembly Resolution 304 of November 16, 1949. This grew out of the inspiration of President Truman's Point 4 Program, which proposed that the United States and other nations provide technical assistance to the developing world.

The UNDP is under the UN secretary general, but it has its own governing council of 49 members—21 from developed countries and 28 from developing countries. It reports to the General Assembly through ECOSOC, which elects members of the UNDP council. It gets virtually all of its money from voluntary contributions. Its budget includes that of the UN Fund for Population Activities and other funds. Recognizing the original U.S. contribution of 25 to 30 percent of the total budget, its directors have been U.S. citizens. However, this percentage fell under the Reagan and subsequent administrations to about 10 percent.

The UNDP assists more than 6,000 projects annually in more than 150 countries and territories. Under its 1980 consensus 80 percent of its funds go to the least-developed countries (those with average per-capita gross national product less than $500). It provides technical assistance to better-off third-world countries, but it expects them to pay for it.

The annual UNDP expenditure of about $800 million a year does not give the complete picture of technical assistance. The countries benefitting from the projects also make contributions in terms of experts assigned to the projects, and in office space, transportation, and secretarial help. In 1981 these local contributions to UNDP projects amounted to more than $1 billion in addition to the $820 million by the UNDP.[3] Its annual budget, therefore, has been larger than that of the UN proper.

Most of UNDP technical assistance is oriented toward problem solving. This consists of relatively short-range projects requested by a country to solve production and other problems in agriculture, industry, and other areas. Another major category of UNDP activity covers preinvestment surveys in mineral exploration, hydraulic development, power, and similar areas. In 1991 the UNDP estimated that it generated $9 billion in private investment from its preinvestment and other studies, including investment from external sources.

The Senegal River project is an example of such follow-up investments. Mali, Mauritania, and Senegal in Africa's Sahel region have a combined population of 14 million. They have in common the 1,000-mile Senegal River with its flow rate varying as much as 200 percent in any three-to-four-year period, and with its flow dropping drastically downstream where rainfall is least. Salinization prevented food production on some 12,000 square miles of farmland. The major irrigation dam of the system is being built with the aid of the World Bank. The UNDP worked with a trigovernmental coordinating committee, which has assisted in studies and training for rural development, in surveys of natural resources, control of crop pests, animal husbandry, fish production, and relocation of people displaced by the dam. By the end of 1981 the UNDP had helped mobilize $900 million in investment for the projects. About $360 million of this was from Arab resources with the remainder from Western Europe, the United States, the African Development Bank, and the European Development Fund. Work is under way on the irrigation and hydropower dam at Mannantali, Mali, for an antisalt barrier at the river's mouth, and a harbor 500 miles upstream. The UNDP played a major role in assisting the trigovernmental committee coordinate the development efforts associated with the project.[4]

One of the innovations of the UNDP in the field of technical assistance is the TOKTEN program to reverse the brain drain. The program of *transfer of know-how through expatriate nationals* involves sending experts who have settled in other countries back to their home nations for volunteer consultation for three to five weeks. They welcome a chance to visit friends and family. With their knowledge of the language and culture, they often can make quick and meaningful contributions on technical problems. By 1982 about 350 consultancies had been completed. The consultants normally waive consulting fees and settle for per diem and economy-class fares. More often than not, the TOKTEN experts carry more weight in advising than the foreign expert, although sometimes their advice is discounted.[5]

The UNDP administrator also manages the UN Volunteer Program, which was established by the General Assembly in 1970 along the lines of the U.S. Peace Corps program. By 1991 more than 2,000 UN volunteers were serving about 100 countries with most of them serving in Africa. Sixty-four, or about 3 percent, were from the United States. About 85 percent were from developing countries. The U.S. Peace Corps worked closely helping recruit and sponsor volunteers. However, they were not typical Peace Corps volunteers; they were experienced professionals of retirement age. In the early 1980s the United States through the Peace Corps budget provided the largest contribution to this UN program and in addition spent more than $200,000 on the U.S. volunteer expenses. Often the UN volunteers were assigned to UNDP projects. In the 1990s, however, with pressure to cut the U.S. budget, the Congress drastically cut the U.S. contributions to this program.

The fellowship programs are another important part of technical assistance. The UNDP in 1991 financed about 12,000 students and trainees. Generally, the selection of students and trainees grows out of a specific project. Training is usually for three months to a year and does not involve working for a higher degree.

The UNDP Resident Representatives (Resreps) for more than 25 years have coordinated and evaluated aid programs of the United Nations and the Specialized Agencies. In 1983 the UN Joint Inspection Unit (JIU), which evaluates the management of UN organizations, recommended that the UNDP should continue evaluations of other agencies because of its special relationship with host governments and with the UN agencies that provide the technical experts. In line with JIU recommendations UNDP established a small, independent evaluation unit in UNDP to oversee that function of the UNDP field offices. While the office was being established, UNDP published evaluations on the technical assistance activities of UNIDO, WHO, UNESCO, and the International Trade Center.

In 1989 UNDP and the World Bank published a study of development strategies and concluded that African countries carrying out the conservative adjustment programs of the World Bark were showing the most success in development. These policies included balancing government budgets, privatizing enterprises, and freeing trade and exchange rates. African countries, the ECA, other UN bodies, and the Organization for African Unity took exception and pointed at devastating social consequences of the above adjustments. They blamed factors such as low levels of aid and low commodity prices for development problems.

For many years the UNDP Resreps have prepared annual reports on donor aid activities in their countries, which are useful for country planning. In Thailand and some other countries the Resrep assists the government in coordinating all external technical assistance. They have had varying degrees of success in getting other bodies of the UN System to provide information for these reports because of a natural inclination of some of the Specialized Agencies to protect their turf.

In a follow-up to the UN Conference on Least-Developed Countries held in Paris in 1981, the UNDP organized roundtables in certain countries to help the many aid agencies coordinate their aid efforts. The *1983 OECD Review* noted that although it is too early to assess the effectiveness of the UNDP roundtables for coordinating assistance, they had contributed to improved planning and setting of priorities.[6]

The UNDP is sensitive to the need for the developing countries themselves to provide the leadership in its roundtables. The annual report of the administrator for 1983 noted that government administrative structures could be overwhelmed by what could often be a hundred or more bilateral, multilateral, and nongovernmental aid organizations knocking at the door. Even with the help of the UNDP Resrep, governments coordinating the assistance of dozens of donors have an immense task.

For a number of countries the roundtables gave them their first opportunity to present their requirements to donors as a group. Isabell V. Gruhn, in her article "The U.N. Maze Confounds Development," throws up her hands as if such coordination is a hopeless task, even for an experienced and effective UNDP representative.[7] The Organization for Economic Cooperation and Development (OECD) and the UN reports agree that such coordination is difficult, but they are more optimistic about the potential for the UNDP roundtables as a useful instrument. The chairman of OECD/Development Advisory Committee notified members to request their local representatives to extend full cooperation in these consultations at the country level. UNDP noted that the approach of the resident coordinator should be to let the host government make the ultimate decision, while UNDP assists it in the process.

The leading role of the Resrep at the local level has made the Resrep a natural coordinator for the United Nations in emergency and disaster operations. The UN Disaster Relief Organization (UNDRO), rather than establishing a network of officials in various countries waiting for a disaster, relies on the local UNDP Resrep to represent it locally when a disaster occurs. In the summer of 1984 at the beginning of the severe famine in the Sahel, the UNDP administrator obtained a special allocation from the UNDP council for the volunteers to help deal with the tragic food emergency in Africa. On the average, UNDP helps provide emergency disaster assistance to about 20 countries a year, while continuing to follow up on similar assistance to numerous other countries from previous years.

The UNDP is in a unique position in the UN System to evaluate and coordinate the many UN and other multilateral and bilateral aid activities carried on in the developing world. The UNDP's control of technical assistance funds, which it contracts out to the various Specialized Agencies, gives it leverage to get their cooperation in evaluating aid activities. The fact that UNDP does not have to renew contracts leads to more efficient aid projects and works against a tendency for them to become self-perpetuating. With UNDP's extensive operational and coordinating responsibilities, one would expect a large bureaucratic organization. However, its central headquarters staff is relatively small. The overhead cost of UNDP for its projects in the 1980s was only 6.3 percent.

Developing countries obviously have a stake in continuing UNDP technical assistance projects, and they support UNDP. They do not, however, control the U.S. government's appropriations, which have been reduced in recent years. UNDP in recent years has obtained relatively less support for technical assistance than that provided to the UN Specialized Agencies. The above brief survey of its activities indicates that it is doing an essential job of coordination and a useful job of providing a major share of the technical assistance to the developing world.

THE UN CHILDREN'S FUND (UNICEF)

UNICEF is the best-known subsidiary organ of the United Nations. Children in the United States solicit contributions for it at Halloween, and many people send UNICEF Christmas cards. With its imaginative ways of obtaining contributions, it has a budget about 40 percent of the size of its parent, the United Nations.

UNICEF was created by a unanimous vote of the General Assembly, December 11, 1946, to provide emergency relief for children victimized by World War II. It took over from the UN Relief and Rehabilitation Administration (UNRRA), which was the principal relief organization for Europe after World War II. UNICEF works closely with the World Health Organization on immunization of children, AIDS and other health matters, nutrition, and education. Donor and beneficiary governments have equal voices on its executive board. Recipient governments have assumed responsibility for delivering supplies provided by UNICEF. In December 1965 UNICEF was awarded the Nobel Peace Prize for its work.

The 1990 World Summit for Children sponsored by UNICEF announced that UNICEF and the World Health Organization in 1990 were close to their goal of immunizing from diphtheria, polio, tetanus, whooping cough, tuberculosis, and measles 80 percent of the children under 1 year of age. The conference report estimated that the effort already made had saved more than 12 million young lives. The World Summit set ambitious and probably unrealistic goals for the year 2000 that included reducing under-five death rates by one-third, halving maternal mortality, developing safe water, and halving children's severe and moderate malnutrition. In the 1990s UNICEF was emphasizing AIDS prevention including saving children from prostitution. Its reports indicated as many as 1 million children are forced into prostitution every year, which may mean a death sentence from AIDS for many.[8]

REFUGEE RELIEF

The League of Nations organized international assistance to refugees in 1921 under the High Commissioner for Refugees. In 1943 the United Nations Relief and Rehabilitation Administration was set up to help the millions of displaced persons of World War II. In 1946 the International Refugee Organization took over refugee relief from UNRRA, and in 1951 the UN High Commissioner for Refugees resumed the task. The UNHCR has had its mandate renewed at five-year intervals by the General Assembly. The High Commissioner reports to that body and works under the guidance of a 41-member executive committee. The High Commissioner not only provides aid to refugees but attempts to help voluntary repatriation or permanent resettlement in an asylum country.

The legal status of refugees is defined in two international treaties, the 1951 Convention on Refugees and the 1967 Protocol on Refugees. This defines refugees as persons outside their country who have a well-founded fear of persecution on the basis of race, nationality, and political opinion. It has promoted the principle of *nonrefoulement*, which prohibits the expulsion or forcible return of a person to a country where he or she has reason to fear persecution. Almost 100 countries have agreed to be bound by these international agreements.

For many years the UNHCR has assisted more than 5 million refugees affected by severe African droughts, and it helped coordinate the major world relief effort of 1985 and the following years to assist these people. Other large UNHCR programs included assistance to the millions of refugees created by the war in Afghanistan, the hundreds of thousands of "boat people" fleeing from Vietnam, and more than 1 million refugees in Central America. In 1945 and 1981 it received the Nobel Prize for its operations.

The assistance to the 2.4 million Palestinian refugees has been carried out by the UN Relief and Works Agency for Palestine refugees in the Near East (UNRWA). It not only has provided food for the refugees created by the wars, but also has established schools and provided other assistance for their camps. The General Assembly has continued to call in vain for a solution to this problem through permitting refugees to return to their original homes in Israel and the West Bank. As indicated earlier, little progress has been made on this issue since Camp David.

THE UN ENVIRONMENT PROGRAM (UNEP)

The growing concern in the late 1960s about the environment stimulated convening the UN Conference on the Human Environment in Stockholm in 1972. The delegates formulated 109 recommendations, including a proposal to establish UNEP. This body has no operating functions, but it works through committees under a 58-member governing council. It provides an annual state-of-the-environment report and facilitates cooperation and the exchange of knowledge in this field. It actively promotes cooperation in the pollution problem of the Mediterranean and other regional seas, and works with the International Maritime Organization (IMO) to prevent pollution of the oceans. It has established the Global Environmental Monitoring System (GEMS) and a computerized information bank. It has also set up a fund for financing environmental programs. It has received donations of as much as $40 million a year for this fund.

In their 1981 session the General Assembly requested UNEP to prepare a list of products that governments consider harmful to health and the environment. The resolution was adopted by a vote of 146 to 1, with the United States in opposition because it considered the resolution ambiguous and expensive. UNEP now maintains the "International Register of Potentially Toxin Chemicals."

In March 1985 a UNEP-sponsored conference produced the Convention for the Protection of the Ozone Layer, which promotes research and an exchange of information. An annex referred to the need to limit production of chlorofluorocarbons. In 1987 another conference in Montreal agreed on protocol for restricting the uses of substances that damage the ozone layer. One of the consequences if this problem is not solved would be an increase in skin cancers. UNEP also continued work on guidelines for disposal of toxic wastes.

The Earth Summit in 1992 in Rio de Janeiro established the Commission on Sustainable Development (CSD) to follow up on the Summit recommendations. More than 100 heads of state and government as delegates from 170 nations attended. The CSD and UNEP working groups work closely with the UNDP, which is an operational agency. They also work closely with the World Bank in managing the Global Environment Facility, which funds costs of developing countries incurred for projects that provide global environmental benefits. The CSD in 1995 asked for a $2 billion replenishment of this fund as a minimal step to meet environmental goals.

POPULATION ACTIVITIES

Population activities are carried out by the Population Commission of ECOSOC and by the UN Fund for Population Activities (UNFPA). The commission provides analyses of world population trends and technical help to countries planning population programs. The UNFPA was set up as a trust fund in 1967 by the UN secretary general to assist countries to obtain basic data on population and later to help them formulate programs for research and family planning. Since 1973 it has operated under the guidance of ECOSOC and the UNDP.

The Population Commission organized the World Population Conference of 1974 in Bucharest, which laid out a plan of action that has been used as guidelines for countries developing programs for population control. Because some countries attending the conference wanted to promote population growth, the

World Population Plan of Action of the conference was not consistently against population growth. Similarly, the follow-up conferences in Mexico City (1984) and in Cairo (1994) straddled the issues on population control. Nevertheless, for countries wanting to put population control programs into effect, the conferences set goals and a plan of action that served as guidelines for the UN activities, including projects of the UNFPA. Its programs are popular with the developed countries but not countries with large Catholic and Muslim populations.

Countries are sensitive about aid in this field. Originally, the program in India, supported by the United States, ran into trouble in the 1960s because of criticisms about infections with the birth control "loops" and medical problems with "the pill." The Indian government phased out the U.S. program, and the World Bank substituted a loan program for family planning centers without political criticism.

In 1985 the United States withheld $10 million of its $46 million contribution to the UNFPA, because the United States alleged that there were abuses in the Chinese family planning program. (The China program was about 8 percent of the total UNFPA program.) The executive director of UNFPA said that these charges were in error and that they had been refuted by the U.S. Agency for International Development (USAID) itself. USAID then replied it might resume its support to the UNFPA program. The United States continued to have reservations about the Chinese program, and this has remained an irritant in U.S.-China relations.

The above demonstrates the advantage of channeling aid for family planning through UNFPA, because of the increased potential for political criticism when countries with different philosophies of family planning are directly involved in a donor-recipient relationship.

DRUG ABUSE CONTROL

The League of Nations from the beginning took responsibility for drug abuse control. The Hague Convention of 1912 came into effect under Article 295 of the Treaty of Versailles. An energetic American delegation and a group of reformers by 1925 brought reforming zeal to the League's Opium Committee and by 1925 obtained approval of the Geneva Convention of 1925, which limited manufacture of narcotic drugs to medical and scientific needs. The League's Permanent Central Opium Board and supervisory body evaluated and worked to control the quantity of drugs produced in more than 60 signatory states. Its powers were transferred to the United Nations, ECOSOC, and its International Narcotics Control Board.

There are three basic treaties negotiated under UN auspices against the drug traffic. The treaty of 1961 brought together the major provisions of previous treaties and provides for controlling legal drugs. The 1972 treaty covers artificial drugs. A 1988 treaty was negotiated by 107 countries and signed by 57. It provides for cooperation in arresting smugglers including police cooperation and access to bank records.

In 1990 UN drug control activities were integrated under the UN Drug Control Program (UNDCP). It coordinates UN efforts and in 1995 was working with an annual budget of $95 million. The other UN bodies include the UN Secretariat's Division of Narcotic Drugs, the UN Fund for Drug Abuse Control, and the International Narcotics Control Board of ECOSOC. The Board evaluates implementation of drug control treaties and then consults with governments when illicit drug activities exist.

UN CONFERENCE ON TRADE AND DEVELOPMENT (UNCTAD)

UNCTAD grew out of an idea of Raul Prebish, a prominent Latin American economist and statesman. He believed that the major problems of the developing world centered on foreign trade and that if developing countries could be given adequate access to the markets of the industrial countries and if they obtained a fair price for their commodity exports, they would not need huge amounts of aid. As a result of his influence, the General Assembly in December 1962 authorized a world conference, which was held in 1964 to establish UNCTAD. The UNCTAD conference, which is the governing body, meets every four years to consider problems of trade and development. In the interim the issues are considered by its Trade and Development Board and subsidiary committees, which meet mostly in Geneva. These bodies are supported by a large UNCTAD secretariat under a secretary general appointed by the UN secretary general.

UNCTAD and its subsidiary committees set broad policy guidelines on development and trade issues and propose action on these problems. It is dominated by the developing countries. As in the General Assembly and ECOSOC, the developed countries seriously consider the positions of the developing nations and often respond to their pressures. Considering the controversial issues involved, the spirit of the meetings is businesslike. For example, in the 1972 meeting in Santiago, Chile, during the Vietnam War, Cuba, the People's Republic of China, and certain other countries made speeches criticizing the United States and proposed a critical resolution on Vietnam; but by a vote of 50 to 26 with 67 abstentions, the conference supported a U.S. motion declaring the Vietnam issue not within UNCTAD's competence. The conference returned to trade and development issues. In recent years it has been distracted by the Palestinian issue, but the recent Geneva conference, described below, did not let that controversial issue interfere with the negotiation of trade and development issues.

UNCTAD VII took place in Geneva from July 9 to August 3, 1987, with increased concern about the debt problems of developing countries, inadequate capital flows, weak commodity prices, and stagnating world trade. The final statement was adopted by consensus among developed and developing countries. The statement asserted that a solution to the debt problem must be sought within a growth-oriented strategy that takes account of the particular circumstances of each country. It was suggested that the debt service burden be eased through lower interest and longer repayment periods, especially through arrangements with the Paris Club (described in the next chapter). This statement was consistent with the current policies of the International Monetary Fund and the World Bank (discussed in the next chapter). The statement as usual called for additional aid, particularly to the 40 least-developed countries (LDCs), whose per capita gross national product in the last eight years had declined from about $220 to $200. (Twenty-seven of the LDCs are in Africa.)

UNCTAD VIII, which met from February 8 to 25, 1991, in Cartagena, Colombia, added little to the above. It proposed that the secretary general should hold consultations about a world conference on commodities.

Little mention was made of the Common Fund established by UNCTAD to stabilize prices of major world commodities through financial intervention in the markets. The United States generally opposed such intervention in world markets. The fund faced the insoluble problem of establishing high market prices for producers and low market prices for consumers. The fund was directed to concentrate on 18 commodities—coffee, cocoa, bananas, hard fibers, cotton and cotton yarn, copper, bauxite, sugar, tea, beef, jute and jute products, rubber, tropical timber, vegetable oil and oil seeds, iron ore, manganese, phosphates, and tin. The fund's initial capital was only $250 million. Even OPEC's oil cartel has not been able to deal effectively with this problem in the case of petroleum in recent years. Observers who had watched organizations struggle with this concern for decades gave the new organization little chance of success.

The final UNCTAD statement also noted with approval the current Ecuador round of tariff negotiations. It offered technical assistance from the UNCTAD staff to developing countries participating in the negotiations.

The programs initiated in UNCTAD in the past have been regarded as radical by developed country delegates, but many get accepted by developed countries in watered-down and revised forms within five or ten years after they are first proposed. UNCTAD was used in pressing for trade preferences for developing countries, establishing arrangements to stabilize world commodity prices, and negotiating a code of conduct for multinational firms. UNCTAD has also played a leading role in demands for providing more aid to the LDCs and in giving developing countries more voice in the international monetary reform. The above issues are usually on the agenda of the UNCTAD conferences, and over the years progress has been made in other organs in implementing the above policies for trade and development. The latest UNCTAD conference demonstrated an encouraging convergence of views on the foreign debt problem and other basic issues of development.

UN MONITORING OF TRANSNATIONAL CORPORATIONS

Tracing actions on the transnational corporation issues demonstrates how the UN System works as a system and also how it can take years to produce results. Multinational corporation (MNC) issues have been at the center of North-South controversies among spokespeople for developed and developing countries. Socialists and communists attribute many of the world's problems, including war and technological backwardness in the third world, to MNCs and their influence on public policies. Spokespeople of the market economies, on the other hand, stress the contributions of MNCs to economic development. Some academic observers claim the MNCs are becoming so powerful that they are becoming independent of nation states and even limiting a state's sovereignty by creating webs of economic interdependence. Other scholars claim MNCs and U.S. leaders collaborate in their common aims of maintaining a strong U.S. position in foreign economies and access to raw materials.

Meanwhile, UN bodies are trying to bridge these gaps between North and South ideologues by studying the issues and drafting codes of conduct affecting MNCs. The aim is to harness the MNCs in the service of economic development by establishing guidelines affecting operations of these powerful firms. In assessing these efforts, it is useful to look at the background of the decisions and how they worked their way through the UN System. What were the motives of those initiating this process and what important deals were made during the negotiations? Did the powerful MNCs support these moves, or did they try to block attempts to set standards for their operations? What concrete effects would the codes and monitoring process, if approved, have on the MNC operations in developing countries?

The initial MNC resolution was tied to an important compromise for increasing the voice of developing countries in an international monetary reform and the General Agreement on Tariffs and Trade (GATT) negotiations. In this sense the resolution became a part of the developing countries' program for a "new international economic order."

The initial resolution, calling for a "group of eminent" persons to study the impact of the MNCs on development and to submit recommendations for appropriate action, was passed in the July 1972 meeting of ECOSOC just two months after the end of the third major world UN Conference on Trade Development (UNCTAD III), held in Santiago, Chile.

A close examination of the record discloses the seed of these ideas. At UNCTAD III President Allende of Chile, the host and first speaker, did not float the idea in his lengthy opening address, but his ambassador, Hernandes Santa Cruz, who was the leader of the Group of 77 (the caucus of developing countries), in his address referred to UN Undersecretary Philip de Seynes' statement that it would be unreasonable to continue to ignore a serious gap in international institutions, the lack of arrangements for supervising the activities of MNCs. Obviously, these two leaders had consulted on this idea.

At UNCTAD III Ambassador Bernard Zagorin of the United States represented the country with the most powerful MNCs in the world, whereas Ambassador Santa Cruz represented Chile. Jack Anderson of the *Washington Post* had just published U.S. documents about the scheme of the International Telephone and Telegraph Company (ITT) to give $1 million to help the CIA oppose Allende's election and later help in his overthrow. These were published throughout Latin America, and during UNCTAD III there were frequent demonstrations by Chileans against the CIA and ITT. (A subsequent Senate investigation of the CIA indicated that it did not accept the ITT money, although the CIA did support groups opposing Allende.) President Allende's police maintained good order during the conference, and its work was not disrupted. Despite the ITT controversy, Ambassador Zagorin, chairman of the U.S. delegation, established a good working relationship with Ambassador Santa Cruz of Chile that permitted agreement on a wide range of UNCTAD resolutions. This laid the basis for the agreement on the ECOSOC resolution two months later requesting the UN secretary general to establish a "group of eminent persons" to study the MNC impact on development and to recommend action.

Santa Cruz introduced the ECOSOC resolution on MNCs at the July 1972 ECOSOC meeting in Geneva with a customary flourish, making a hard-hitting attack on ITT for attempting to undermine the Allende government. His resolution, however, appeared designed for compromise. After negotiations with Zagorin and others, Santa Cruz agreed to draft changes acceptable to all delegations. The plenary ECOSOC sessions gave delegates, including those from communist countries, a chance to vent their ire on the multinationals. After procedural wrangles and beating off an amendment referring to previous controversial resolutions on the expropriation issue, the ECOSOC delegates adopted the resolution.

The deal made during the negotiation of the ECOSOC resolution is evident in its second part, which "stressed the need" for the "full, effective and continuous participation of developing countries in the forthcoming GATT multilateral trade negotiations, and in the decisionmaking process in the reform of the international monetary system." The deal also included the withdrawal by Ambassador Santa Cruz of an amendment that called for all interested states, including the Soviet Union, to participate in the above economic negotiations.

The international monetary reform part of this resolution was implemented in the same month by the establishment of the "Committee of Twenty" in the International Monetary Fund. About half of this committee were developing nations. During the next few years the committee designed a basic reform of the international monetary system that was put into effect on April 1, 1978. The GATT multilateral trade negotiations that continued during the decade accepted developing country demands for concessions of tariff preferences, and they were put into effect by the end of the decade. This demonstrates how coordination of policies can occur in the UN System because the same governments control the different international bodies.

The underlying element in achieving agreement on the 1972 ECOSOC resolution and subsequent related UN resolutions on monetary and trade matters was the need for both developed and developing countries to cooperate on financial and trade negotiations to address fundamental problems in the world economic order. In the process of carrying out the compromise on the resolution, the moderates agreed to reforms in the world's monetary and trading system and thereby preempted the attempt of the radicals to develop support for converting the market system into one of controlled government planning. Both moderates and radicals used the slogan of a new international economic order. There were extensive consultations among the governments concerned on MNC issues, but there was no evidence of important MNC pressures on the U.S. government in the negotiation of the 1972 resolution.

The UN secretary general, in line with the 1972 ECOSOC resolution, appointed a "group of eminent persons" numbering 20 to study the MNC issues. American representatives were J. Irwin Miller, chairman of the Cummins Engine Co., as vice chairman of the group, and Senator Jacob Javits of New York. The group also included Juan Somavia of Chile, a son-in-law of Ambassador Santa Cruz, and representatives from the Soviet Union and Yugoslavia. The two consultants were Raul Prebish, the father of UNCTAD, and Nat Weinberg, formerly an official of the United Automobile Workers. The group, with wide variations in opinion, held sessions in New York, Geneva, Rome, and New Delhi in a total meeting time of two to three months. At these meetings, spokesmen of MNCs testified as did communists, socialists, labor representatives, and others. With the help of the UN Secretariat, the group prepared comments on major substantive issues.

The key input into the group's hearings was the background study prepared by the UN Secretariat under the leadership of Philip de Seynes. This study was a detailed and objective assessment of the role of MNCs in world trade, and it contained three important recommendations on setting up machinery to monitor the activities of MNCs. These included forming a committee under ECOSOC for airing views and problems of MNCs and developing policies and programs for action, establishing a center in the United Nations for information on MNCs, and negotiating a code of conduct for MNCs. It is not surprising that the group included these recommendations in its final report, which was prepared with the aid of the UN Secretariat. The group envisioned the code as an instrument of moral persuasion more than a binding agreement. The recommendations, in turn, helped persuade ECOSOC to establish these bodies.

The Working Group on a Code of Conduct proceeded in a serious and deliberate way. It addressed issues such as whether the code should include public enterprises in the definition of a transnational corporation (TNC), whether or not TNCs should get preferential treatment in order to promote investment, how they should set prices, and how governments could provide consumer and environmental protection. There appeared to be no insuperable obstacles to a code of conduct, particularly because many TNCs would welcome establishing standards. One of their major problems is when the "rules of the game" are changed after they invest. The United States was a key figure in the negotiations, but negotiations slowed down with the noncooperative views of the Reagan administration and never recovered. Also, the Commission on Transnational Corporations was diverted by the apartheid issue from its major task, and for a while focused on encouraging countries to adopt measures to make effective the withdrawal of investments from South Africa.[9]

Agreement on a code of conduct could have a major political impact. It would tend to make TNC operations more respectable in certain countries where they are now attacked by prevailing ideologies. Just as the majority of developing countries cooperate in the reforms of the international monetary system and the GATT trade negotiations, they could work more closely with TNCs in industrial and commercial development. Even socialist leaders accept investments and operations of TNCs as a necessary fact of economic life, and UN acceptance of a code of conduct for them would make it harder for the ideologues of developing countries to put unnecessary obstructions in their way. The process would help these leaders to realize a new international economic order is becoming an accomplished fact.

The practical basis for compromises on a code for MNCs is the aim of developing countries to impose limits on undesirable activities on TNCs, along with the desire of developed countries and the TNCs to agree on standards that would discourage arbitrary action against TNCs by a host country after TNCs have begun operations. A final agreement on the overall code on TNCs would require leaders of the United States and developing countries to exert a strong push on the negotiations and to call a diplomatic conference to compromise the last drafting obstacles.

If the process is completed, it could clear the way for increased assistance by TNCs in development. Economic cooperation strengthened by a code would also help achieve cooperation on other economic and political problems that face the international community. However, it faces strong opposition from U.S. politicians who want to limit the role of government and international organizations in economic decisions.

UN WORLD CONFERENCES

The UN has used world conferences to stimulate and coordinate international action. These conferences are more than meetings, because they typically require years of preparation by governments and private specialists. Under Article 62 of the UN Charter, ECOSOC may call a conference, but in practice such conferences are approved by the General Assembly. The largest and most successful have been those dealing with environmental problems.

The Law of the Sea conventions originated in world conferences on the law of the sea. Also, UNEP was created as a result of the 1972 UN Conference on the Human Environment held in Stockholm. A 27-nation preparatory committee held four sessions of two weeks each in preparing for the convention and producing initial texts of documents. They were the bases of agreements on preventing marine pollution, monitoring the environment, and other conservation issues. The UN Secretariat played a key role in drafting background documents for the convention.

In 1990 the General Assembly launched the UN Conference on Environment and Development, which was held in June 1992 in Rio de Janeiro. The ways such conferences mobilize public support were demonstrated in this conference.

A total of about 35,000 officials, reporters, and others interested in environmental matters attended. The conference of 172 nations received top-of-the-news attention. Drama was provided by the initially cool attitude of the United States toward the conference. In May 1990 the head of the U.S. Environmental Protection Agency had been ordered by the White House not to attend a preparatory meeting for the conference.[10] Public support for action on the environment built up to such an extent that President Bush attended the Rio conference. This support for action had been reflected in a Lou Harris poll of May 1989 that revealed at least 75 percent of the people in every country surveyed believed that stronger government action is needed to fight pollution.

The United States was able to water down the Global Warming Convention, thus preventing the setting of definite targets for cutting back on carbon dioxide and other warming gasses. The United States did not sign the biodiversity treaty that would protect endangered species and require sharing research and profits with nations whose genetic resources were used. It also made small financial commitments in comparison with other major industrial countries. However, the United States joined in consensus with 27 broad principles for environmental policy and on an 800-page blueprint to clean up the environment and encourage development.

Many environmental activists were disappointed with the results of the conference, but others seized on the 800-page agenda and principles approved at the conference as a basis for lobbying for legislative action to protect the environment.

Other landmark conferences include the following: (1) The World Population Conference, which met in Bucharest in 1974. It adopted a World Population Plan of Action, which gave added impetus to countries with family planning programs but also, at the insistence of a few governments, included provisions for encouraging population growth. (2) The World Food Conference in 1974 called attention to malnutrition and starvation and instructed UN bodies such as the UNDP, the Food and Agriculture Organization, and the World Bank to increase their assistance to agriculture. This was more than an admonition, because the same countries making recommendations at the conference control the boards of directors of the other UN agencies. (3) The 1975 and 1995 Conferences on the Status of Women stressed the responsibility of governments to enable women to be fully integrated into society. (4) World conferences of 1978 and 1983 to combat racism added to the public pressures for sanctions against the racist government of South Africa. (5) World conferences on disarmament of 1978, 1982, and 1988 were part of the UN efforts that brought about the network of nuclear arms agreements described in Chapter 6. (6) The International Conference on Drug Abuse and Illicit Trafficking of June 1987 adopted by acclamation a declaration expressing the commitment to take vigorous action in ending drug abuse.

The United Nations provides a framework for international cooperation in the economic and social fields, including a means of delivering or coordinating a major part of the world's technical assistance and aid programs. The United Nations is an effective system because the many action agencies, including the Specialized Agencies, report to the Economic and Social Council and the General Assembly, which coordinate the programs and policies of these agencies. The agencies of the United Nations proper report to and take general guidance from the secretary general, although they have their own governing bodies and sources of funds. Many times, new programs and policies are debated and refined in several forums before being implemented in the UN System.

Administrative experts may be disturbed by the overlapping and duplication and may wish for a more rational organization. However, there is an advantage in allowing a number of bodies to exercise initiatives and search for funds. For example, operations of UNICEF could be incorporated in other bodies, but the UN System would then have about $200 million less for its programs every year, because UNICEF has developed its own imaginative appeals to the conscience of the world to help children.

The UNDP has been a unique and efficient instrument for recruiting experts from the UN System and coordinating its development and relief efforts. Many countries use the UN bodies as a channel for their aid, so the UN programs are large in comparison to total bilateral aid programs. However, as indicated in Figure 1, it takes a magnifying glass to see the total UN aid programs in comparison with the tremendous amounts spent on the defense budget of the United States or the Soviet Union. This reflects the dominance of power politics over international cooperation, a trend that was noted in previous chapters on the peacekeeping functions of the United Nations.

We now examine the activities of the World Bank and the International Monetary Fund, which are the world's bankers and the largest source of loans for economic assistance, as well as the activities of other Specialized Agencies in the UN System.

Notes to Chapter 8

1. A. Yoder, "U.N. Monitoring of Transnational Corporations," *Towson State Journal of International Affairs*, Spring 1981.

2. D. Acheson, *Present at the Creation* (New York: W.W. Norton, 1969), p. 231.

3. UNDP, 1981, p. 5.

4. UNDP, Document (DP/1984) 5/Add. 2 (New York: United Nations, 1984).

5. *UN Chronicle*, June 1982, pp. 96–98; J. Morse, "Statement Before the UNDP Governing Council," June 12, 1984.

6. Organization for Economic Cooperation and Development, *1983 OECD Review* (Paris: OECD, 1983).

7. I. Gruhn, "The U.N. Maze Confounds African Development," *International Organization*, Spring 1979.

8. *UNICEF Quarterly*, April–June 1992, p. 12.

9. Yoder, 1981.

10. *UN Chronicle*, August 1987, pp. 60–62.

11. *New York Times*, May 15, 1990.

12. *UN Chronicle*, November 1987, pp. 29–38; C. Boucher and W. Siebeck, "UNCTAD VII: New Spirit in North South Relations," *Finance and Development*, December 1987, pp. 14–16.

CHAPTER IX

THE INTERNATIONAL MONETARY FUND, THE WORLD BANK, AND OTHER SPECIALIZED AGENCIES

The General Assembly and its organs actually spend as much as 90 percent of their time and resources on economic and social problems. There are two major parts to the UN System, the UN proper and the Specialized Agencies (see Figure 1, p. 30). The General Assembly and under it the Economic and Social Council (ECOSOC) set general guidelines on economic and social issues, and form new bodies as necessary to address issues. The General Assembly with its 185 nations approves the UN budget. The budget is legally binding, although the United Nations cannot force a country to pay, other than by suspending it from the UN. However, the major part of funds for development purposes are voluntary contributions by the various countries to agencies of the UN proper and to the Specialized Agencies.

The Specialized Agencies of the United Nations have their own boards of directors and their own budgets. The heads of these organizations, therefore, are not appointed by, or under the direction of, the secretary general or the General Assembly like the UN organs of the previous chapter. The Specialized Agencies have negotiated agreements with the United Nations, so that they are closely associated in administrative practices, and they submit reports annually to ECOSOC. As we will see they closely cooperate with each other and with bodies of the United Nations proper, and the same governments direct their policies as pass resolutions in the General Assembly, ECOSOC, and other UN organs. Such resolutions, therefore, have an impact throughout the UN System.

THE INTERNATIONAL MONETARY FUND

The International Monetary Fund (IMF) and the International Bank for Reconstruction and Development (IBRD) are the two most powerful Specialized Agencies of the UN System and the two least dependent on the United Nations for policy guidance. Their articles of agreement with the United Nations specify that they do not take policy directions from it, but they do coordinate their administrative policies with the United Nations and report to it every year. They often work closely with other bodies of the UN System.

The articles of agreement of the two organizations were drafted at Bretton Woods, New Hampshire, in 1944 before the UN Charter itself was approved. The fact that these complicated agreements were approved by the U.S. Congress with little trouble is a tribute to the care with which the Secretary of the Treasury, Henry Morgenthau, prepared the Congress, foreign governments, and the public for accepting them. It also reflects the fact that major attention at that time was focused on World War II. Lord Keynes of Great Britain was a principal author of the agreements. Keynes, the famous economist, gained fame with his prediction of the disastrous consequences of the reparation and debt burdens of the Versailles Treaty, as well as with his monetary theories. Most historians and economists agree reparations and debts were largely responsible for the Great Depression. Keynes helped design the IMF and the IBRD so that the post–World War II arrangements would prevent such disorder.

Their charters and policies reflect a determination of Secretary of State Hull to support free international trade. Their conservatism has won the confidence of financial advisers and bankers of the major countries of the world. After World War I, there had been no international organization to prevent the severe international financial crisis that was triggered by the U.S. stock market crash in 1929. More than fifty years after World War II with the help of the IMF and IBRD there has been no comparable financial crisis despite the strains of post–World War II reconstruction, several major wars, the skyrocketing of oil prices, and the heavy burdens of international debt payments that had accumulated by the 1980s. By the 1980s, the IBRD and the IMF had become powerful financial institutions on the world scene with the IMF controlling more than $100 billion of foreign currencies and the World Bank lending close to $16 billion a year for development. Nevertheless, there were disturbing signs that many developing countries had accumulated more debt than they could service, and for the first time countries began to default on their debts to the IMF.

The IMF to a very limited extent performs the function of a federal reserve system of the world. The IMF uses a major part of its resources to buy and sell world currencies and to make balance-of-payment loans to alleviate temporary economic difficulties, but it does not dispense development loans, which are relatively long term. As we will see below, however, it comes close to development loans with its lending for structural adjustments, which means adjusting to a market system.

In the early 1970s the IMF foresaw the problems created by a limited supply of gold and a rapidly expanding international trade, so it created a new international reserve asset to back international transactions. This special drawing right (SDR) to some extent replaced gold as a reserve asset. In fact, the new paper gold is better than gold because countries can accumulate these SDRs above original allocations and draw interest on them, while countries that lose allocations of this asset pay interest. By 1986 countries had created and allocated almost $30 billion (SDR 21 billion) of paper gold on the basis of their level of world trade. To compensate the developing countries, which believed they should get a larger SDR allocation because they needed it more, the IMF finally sold much of its gold stock and distributed the profits on the basis of need rather than on economic strength. The IMF also gives them lower interest rates on certain types of loans, such as those for "structural adjustment."

The assets of the IMF are the pool of currencies provided by about 150 member nations. To assist in its complicated financial transactions, the IMF publishes the most current and comprehensive financial statistics in the world.

The IMF is a major repository of reserves of members, facilitating the financial transactions it undertakes. The IMF also cooperates with the World Bank in providing technical assistance, in developing financial statistics, and in dealing with financial problems. Another major function is to cooperate with the World Bank in arranging meetings of the Paris Club to help creditors and debtors adjust international debts when a default is threatened. Until recently the IMF did not have to worry about collecting debts owed to it, because its member countries are anxious to keep a good credit rating with the IMF and World Bank, which are a major source of balance-of-payments aid and development aid.

Each member of the IMF is given a quota based on a complicated formula of gross national product, reserves, and trade potential. The member pays the quotas in its own currency or with acceptable reserve assets including the SDRs. This quota determines a member's voting power, which is used in electing the board of governors and the 22 executive directors and in decisions on loans. The quota also determines a member's maximum access to the resources of the IMF, and its share in the allocation of SDRs when they are created. The total quotas and resources of the IMF amounted to about $141 billion in 1995. Normally, only about half of the currencies of the fund would be used for lending. In the 1990s the IMF lent $5–11 billion a year.

When the IMF helps a country beyond its original quota, the IMF applies "conditionalities." This means instead of requiring collateral the IMF insists on steps to correct a situation that gave rise to the borrowing. Fundamental principles for conditionality are to discourage restrictions on trade and foreign exchange transactions.

In recent years the IMF has created two funds for structural adjustment, which are loans at very low interest rates and with longer payment periods. The purpose is to allow the poorer countries to strengthen their balance of payments position and regenerate the development process. The funds available for this program in 1988 were about $12 billion.[1] Examples of conditionalities the IMF supports by this resource include liberalizing trade controls, lifting controls on domestic prices including interest rates, and tightening fiscal and monetary policies. The IMF often links these loans with a UNDP roundtable to encourage aid from other donors, or a meeting to reschedule debts. The IMF seal of approval for structural adjustment policies is often accompanied by loans from others, which is called "parallel financing." Most of the IMF's efforts have been directed at African countries, and it has provided structural adjustment loans to about half the African countries.[2] The African countries are beginning to recognize that the major responsibility for reform rests with them.[3]

IMF's rescheduling of debts is through meetings of creditors scheduled by the IMF through what is called the Paris Club. In the decade ending in 1985, the IMF and the World Bank participated in more than fifty such rescheduling arrangements, helping creditors and debtors reach agreement on new terms.

The IMF exercises a great deal of leverage on the economic policies of its developing country clients. It exercises its advice in a discreet way and is able to avoid the nationalist reaction that would occur if a country such as the United States tried to impose the same kind of conditions. The IMF as an international institution has a reputation for being unbiased, which is a reputation impossible for a great power to have. The IMF is gaining in stature and reputation as it helps the world avoid financial and economic crises arising from major shocks such as those caused by rises in oil prices and the heavy borrowing of developing countries.

The IMF and IBRD were in a unique position to encourage the Eastern European countries and the former Soviet republics to adopt market-oriented reforms after the revolutions of 1989. The newly independent governments were anxious to join the IMF and the IBRD to get access to billions of dollars of credits. The loans to the new members were tied to conditionalities, and these were endorsed on April 26, 1992, by finance ministers and central bank governors of the major industrial countries who were the major source of funds and voting power for the IMF.

The IMF and IBRD sent experts to the former Soviet republics and to Eastern European countries. The teams prepared frank economic reports on these former communist countries and provided experts for legal, banking, and public finance reforms. About two-thirds of the IMF's structural loans, or $5 billion, were to Eastern Europe in 1990–91. The IMF and IBRD also designed a $24 billion package to help Russia's economic reform; the IMF would finance $4.5 billion. In July 1992 Michel Camdessus, the managing director of IMF, reached an agreement in Moscow for Russia to hold back inflation in return for a $1 billion loan from the $24 billion package.

As indicated below, the debt burdens reached a new dimension after 1985, and new policies were considered for meeting the threat to world financial stability.

THE WORLD BANK

The World Bank is a group of three institutions: the IBRD, the International Development Association (IDA), and the International Finance Corporation (IFC). The IBRD and the IDA have the same officers and staff—about 5,000— although their operations are legally and financially separated. The IDA assistance is concentrated in the poor countries, and its loans are up to fifty years with very low or no interest. These loans amount to a small proportion of total loans of the World Bank group. The IFC is closely associated to the World Bank and the IDA, but the IFC staff and funds are different. Its purpose is to provide risk capital for private enterprise, and its commitments are a small percentage of the total commitments of the World Bank group.

The IDA was established in 1960 to provide long-term loans at low rates of interest to the poor countries that could not afford conventional loans. The IDA committed more than $3 billion to 45 countries in fiscal year 1985, and its cumulative loans amounted to $37 billion. The IFC since 1956 has mobilized resources for development in the private sector. In fiscal year 1985 the IFC channeled almost $1 billion in loans and equity capital directly to private businesses in 38 developing countries. Cumulative commitments were $5.6 billion.

The World Bank group's total of long-term development loans is more than that of any other institution. Following is a summary of major activities.

The IBRD, which is often called the World Bank, makes loans for infrastructure and development projects at low market rates of interest to developing countries. In the first decades after World War II its policies were relatively conservative. It designed most loans only to cover foreign exchange costs and only to finance specific projects. Loans were to be repaid in hard currencies, and interest costs were close to market rates. Total loans to developing countries up to June 30, 1952, amounted to only $582 million.

Originally its loans were devoted mostly to infrastructure projects such as large dams and irrigation projects. Each of these loans was guaranteed by the governments concerned. Since the era of Robert McNamara's presidency, the World Bank has greatly increased loans for project and sector assistance. This means that the World Bank makes loans to institutions in developing countries that relend the money to farmers, businessmen, and entrepreneurs in other economic sectors for types of projects specified in the original loan agreement. Such loans include loans to institutions that are helping with family planning.

In 1985 the IBRD made loan commitments of more than $11 billion to 44 countries. By 1987 it had about $90 billion in loans outstanding. In the forty years since its founding, it had approved more than $100 billion in loans. Most of its funds came from borrowing on the private capital markets, and it relent the funds at low rates of interest. Virtually all loans have been to developing countries with some countries passing into the developed country category. Although the IBRD has been the major single source of lending for development, the total development assistance by individual countries has been over three times as great.

By 1988 it was apparent that the World Bank's plans for lending for 1989 of $17 billion would exceed its resources, and it obtained an authorization to increase its capital by $74.8 billion over the statutory level of about $95 billion. This would allow it eventually to almost double its loans. However, the portion of capital actually paid in amounted to only about $5 billion, and it was borrowing about $11 billion a year to get the funds to meet its lending commitments. The excess of authorized capital over paid-up capital represented guarantees of governments to pay in their capital if required to make good on the IBRD guarantees of loans.

The World Bank conducts engineering and economic feasibility studies and helps coordinate assistance programs from many sources. It also works closely with the UN Development Program (UNDP) and with other organs of the UN System. The World Bank provides considerable technical assistance to developing countries to help them improve feasibility studies and supervise their loans. The World Bank's Economic Development Institute has trained thousands of officials from developing countries.

The World Bank's aim of recent years has been to emphasize improving access of the poor to better food, shelter, health care, and schooling as well as protecting the environment.[4]

THE WORLD DEBT CRISIS

In the late 1980s the world was still reeling from the wildly fluctuating oil prices that began in the early 1970s. The great increases of oil prices of the 1970s affected entire economies. Initially the skyrocketing oil prices caused a recession in the developed countries and also put many developing countries heavily in debt. Their debt rose from $130 billion in 1973, to $343 billion in 1978, to more than $1 trillion by 1988.[5] World oil prices more than doubled in each of these two periods, which stimulated inflation. During this period, the IBRD and the IMF played a leadership role in rescheduling debts of developing countries in more than fifty meetings of the so-called Paris Club, an organization set up to adjust debt burdens. The rescheduling was designed to spread out repayments over a period of years to prevent debt burdens from bunching up.

By 1985 the world's bankers were so alarmed with their overcommitment of loans that their credits dried up to 1 percent of the 1984 level. Somehow the creditors and debtors, including those most heavily in debt in Latin America, muddled through. It was clear, however, that some new initiatives were needed. Some relief occurred with falling oil prices and the revival of economic activity in 1985 in the industrial countries, which increased their demands for exports from the developing countries, which in turn helped them meet their debt payments. There was also some easing of the interest rates. However, late in 1985 there was a slackening of recovery and an adverse turn in the terms of trade (the relative cost developing countries pay for their imports compared to the price of their exports), which added about $40 billion to the burden of debt of the countries. Moreover, real interest rates (the margin of interest rates over inflation) were still much higher than historical levels. These developments hurt countries heavily in debt such as Argentina, Mexico, and Brazil, which were undergoing belt-tightening measures to try to pay off their foreign debt. Political groups from these countries blamed the conditionalities (conditions of new loans) of the World Bank and the IMF, and were unwilling to face up to stringent measures to cut back unnecessary spending, because such measures could cause unemployment.

In the late 1980s Mexico embarked on far-reaching economic reforms to reduce the state's role in the economy and integrate the economy into the world market system. This put pressure on the balance of payments, and investors' fears about the future of the peso caused a rapid withdrawal of funds from Mexico and the beginning of an international financial crisis. The IMF realized that Mexico's long-term prospects with its oil and other resources was sound, so they agreed with U.S. and European authorities to a $17.8 billion credit to tide Mexico over the crisis. President Clinton over objections in Congress pledged $20 billion and Europeans pledged another $13 billion. These funds were linked with IMF conditionalities and commitments of returns from future oil exports. In 1996 Mexico was succeeding in meeting its obligations under the program, which stabilized the situation.

Although the IMF refrains from making specific recommendations on social services and income distribution in addressing situations like that in Mexico and less serious crises, critics of the fund have blamed it for being too restrictive in its conditions for loans and for discouraging democratic initiatives for government spending in debtor nations.

In debates over economic policies, the IMF tended to take the conservative position and impose fairly strict conditionality provisions. The World Bank officials, on the other hand, who were oriented toward development, tended to want to make sound loans that would improve the productive base of the debtor nations at the risk of some inflation.

The efforts of the poorer countries to lobby for debt relief bore fruit at the June 21, 1988, Toronto summit of the "Group of Seven" major industrial countries (West Germany, Britain, France, Italy, Canada, Japan, and the United States). The summit's economic declaration acknowledged the work of the Paris Club, the IMF, and the IBRD's structural adjustment programs that will mobilize more than $18 billion for adjustment programs. The summit reached consensus on rescheduling official debts of the poorest countries that would include concessional interest rates and partial write-offs of the debts. The Paris Club was urged to work out the technicalities of the program by the end of 1988.

With the help of the World Bank and the IMF, financial officials are addressing the world debt problems. These institutions are committed to discouraging and preventing restrictions that would clog up world trade and encourage a vicious circle of retaliation. In the 1980s it appeared there was a good chance of continued success with these institutions, in contrast to the 1930s, when officials watched helplessly as a few *ad hoc* international meetings struggled in vain to prevent the Great Depression.

Both conservative and liberal economists are agreed that the world economy is tied together and that neither developing countries nor developed countries can prosper alone. World economic policies are not a zero-sum game in which gains on one side balance losses on the other. Rather, all tend to prosper or suffer together, and it is the job of the World Bank and the IMF to preserve a favorable climate to permit international prosperity.

There is a long list of other international organizations closely associated with the United Nations whose work has steadily expanded since the founding of the United Nations. These Specialized Agencies, which are formally associated in administrative agreements with the United Nations, do not gain much publicity, because their work generally is noncontroversial and is taken for granted. They exchange information with the UN proper, and they agree to report to the United Nations on any action taken as a result of UN recommendations.

Following is a summary of their work, noting how they relate to other parts of the UN System.[6]

FOOD AND AGRICULTURAL ORGANIZATION

The Food and Agricultural Organization (FAO) was founded in 1945, with the aim of raising the levels of nutrition and food production and bettering the conditions of rural populations. It was made a Specialized Agency in December 1946. It has 156 member nations, which elect its governing council of 49 members. Its predecessor was the International Institute of Agriculture, founded in Rome in 1905.

FAO carries out extensive research and technical assistance programs in the fields of agriculture, livestock, fisheries, and forestry. In 1986 it was assisting 2,500 projects. Its regular budget, supplemented by other sources including UNDP technical assistance funds, is larger than that of the United Nations. By 1984 it had helped channel more than $26 billion in aid to the agricultural sectors of 90 developing countries.

FAO broadened its activities in 1963 on the suggestion of the United States by establishing the World Food Program (WFP). The WFP uses budgets of over $500 million a year to provide disaster relief and to promote economic and social development.

The economics of food production invite international cooperation. On the one hand, population pressure and shortfalls of production in food deficit areas contrast with problems of excess production in other areas. Also, crises generating refugee flows of tens of millions demand attention of relief agencies. In recent years the famine in African countries caused by drought and conflicts have dominated relief work.

INTERNATIONAL FUND FOR AGRICULTURAL DEVELOPMENT

The International Fund for Agricultural Development (IFAD), which became a Specialized Agency in 1977, has the aim of providing resources to raise food production, particularly on small farms. Most of its operations consist of low-interest loans to help the rural poor. OPEC has been a major contributor to the fund.

Spurred on by the General Assembly these organizations have tried to design programs to use food aid to encourage food production. The root problems of food production have been poor weather and unwise development policies, where incentives are a key. Wealthier countries have cut back on agricultural production to keep prices up and protect farmers' incomes, whereas poorer countries suffer from food shortages, particularly in the drought areas of Africa and in

Asia. Therefore, the root problems of food aid are poverty and distribution, not just production.

WORLD HEALTH ORGANIZATION

The World Health Organization (WHO), which was founded in 1948, carried forward the work of the League of Nations Health Organization. WHO and its governing board coordinate the work of six major regional offices, each having its own governing committee. Its total staff is about 5,300.

A major aim of WHO since 1977 has been "health for all" by the year 2000, which means education, proper food, safe water, sanitation, maternal health, family planning, and immunization and treatment of diseases. One major part of this program is a UNDP/WHO/World Bank program that focuses on six major tropical diseases with the help of about 3,500 scientists. WHO has had success in eradication of smallpox in the world and in its program to try to immunize 90 percent of children for the six major diseases of childhood by the year 2000. WHO has also promoted the use of a cheap salt solution to cure children of diarrhea. It estimated this oral rehydration saved the lives of 1.1 million children in 1988. It has continued to combat the screwworm, a larval disease that affects humans and animals, by dropping sterile flies from aircraft, which mate with fertile flies to produce an increasing population of infertile flies.

WHO has major research programs for tropical disease, and in recent years it has campaigned against the tobacco industry and sought to find ways to combat AIDS. In February 1987 WHO adopted the Global AIDS Plan. It trained more than 350 laboratory workers in 100 countries on how to test and diagnose the disease. It helps governments set up national plans and coordinate assistance. In 1987 WHO reported the alarming news that 5 to 10 million people were probably infected. As many as 5 to 10 percent in some countries are infected, and women and men have the same rates of incidence of the disease. WHO is coordinating efforts by the UN Fund for Population Activities, the UN Economic, Social, and Cultural Organization, UNICEF, and the World Bank to educate people and carry out research. Nevertheless, in 1987 WHO was forced to cut $50 million of its $634 million budget because of U.S. demands for economy.

INTERNATIONAL CIVIL AVIATION ORGANIZATION

The International Civil Aviation Organization (ICAO), as already noted, has made successful efforts to contain skyjacking. Its major purpose is to set up standards to foster the development of safe air transport and promote the development of airports and air navigation facilities.

The twenty-seven-member council has adopted many standards and practices that are constantly reviewed and amended. In addition, it has promoted conventions that spell out rules and standards for air carriage. It has provided technical assistance to more than 100 developing countries.

The ICAO was thrust into a political controversy following the September 1, 1983, destruction by Soviet fighters of a Korean Airline Boeing 747. The ICAO council condemned the downing of the airliner and appointed a team to conduct an inquiry. The report concluded the aircraft deviated from its course as a result of a navigational error. A special ICAO assembly then approved an amendment to the ICAO treaty banning the use of military force against civilian aircraft.

UNIVERSAL POSTAL UNION

The Universal Postal Union, which has been in existence since 1875, has only a small budget of $10 million, but it has more members than any other Specialized Agency. Its major aim is to promote postal services, and over 170 members form a single postal territory for the reciprocal exchange of correspondence. It also assists with training programs for modernizing postal services.

INTERNATIONAL TELECOMMUNICATIONS UNION

The International Telecommunications Union (ITU), which was founded in 1865 by twenty European states, has established standards and practices to keep up with the rapidly changing telecommunications industry. It allocates radio frequencies, attempts to establish the lowest possible charges, promotes telecommunications in developing countries, promotes safety, and undertakes studies for the benefit of its members. The United States has objected to ITU's efforts to regulate U.S. telecommunications satellites. The ITU has a relatively small annual budget of about $51 million and a staff of 885.

WORLD METEOROLOGICAL ORGANIZATION

The World Meteorological Organization (WMO), established in 1978, facilitates exchanging weather information and standardizing of observations, and encourages research and training in meteorology. It works through six regional organizations that coordinate information. With a small budget it has been able to standardize weather reports of more than 8,000 weather stations and a similar number of aircraft and surface ships throughout the world. It processes and disseminates this information with the aid of high-speed computers. It also carries out extensive research on environmental pollution and provides technical assistance on developing water resources. It and the UNDP established the International Panel for Climate Change, which made authoritative reports on global warming used by international conferences taking action on the issue. WMO also supports environmental research on the oceans.

INTERNATIONAL MARINE ORGANIZATION

The aims of the International Marine Organization (IMO; formerly the Intergovernmental Maritime Consultative Organization) are to exchange information on technical matters affecting shipping, with special attention to safety of life at sea. The IMO has promoted the adoption of codes on shipping and, as already noted in Chapter 7, obtains approval of treaties and agreements to prevent pollution of the sea by oil.

GENERAL AGREEMENT ON TARIFFS AND TRADE

The General Agreement on Tariffs and Trade (GATT) was originally a stop-gap set of rules for negotiating tariff concessions that were to serve only until a Specialized Agency called the International Trade Organization (ITO) was established. Countries have continued to use the GATT arrangements for trade negotiations. It has a secretariat of about 200 that about every ten years facilitates comprehensive negotiations of tariff and trade concessions.

GATT has formulated a code based on the principles of nondiscrimination, protection only by tariffs instead of quotas and other restrictions, consultation to avoid damage to trade interests, and reduction of tariffs and trade barriers within the framework of multilateral GATT negotiations. The round of negotiations are complicated, involving about 120 members and taking place over several years. In the fall of 1986 the United States was successful in getting GATT to consider removing restrictions on banking and insurance in addition to those on commodity trade. The "Uruguay Round" of GATT negotiations, which began in 1987, was completed in 1994 and included provisions for these "invisibles." In addition to substantial tariff reductions, the Uruguay Round finally approved a World Trade Organization (in place of an International Trade Organization) to monitor members' trade policies and to provide a dispute settlement system.

WORLD INTELLECTUAL PROPERTY ORGANIZATION

The World Intellectual Property Organization, after many years, achieved the status of a Specialized Agency through approval of the General Assembly. Its mission is to promote international agreements to protect copyrights, patents, and other intellectual property. Its patent center in Vienna registers more than one million patents a year on its computer and makes data on them available to patent offices and other institutions. Many developing countries and the communist countries have accepted the idea that such protection promotes responsible trade in products and discourages irresponsible pirating of software and disrupting of normal trade channels.

UN ECONOMIC, SOCIAL, AND CULTURAL ORGANIZATION

The major purpose of the UN Economic, Social, and Cultural Organization (UNESCO), as defined in its constitution, is to "contribute to peace and security by promoting collaboration among the nations through education, science and culture" in order to promote respect for justice, the rule of law, and human rights.

The General Conference of UNESCO with representatives from each state meets every two years to formulate policies. National commissions representing both governmental and nongovernmental organizations link UNESCO with the educational, scientific, and cultural organizations in each country. It has provided funds for literacy programs, teacher training, scientific research in developing countries, cultural exchanges, and technical assistance in the news media field.

UNESCO like other UN bodies has become involved in political issues. The United States has strongly opposed UNESCO resolutions condemning Israeli policies in the occupied territories. The United States has also complained about poor management and extravagant spending. In December 1984 the United States withdrew from the organization, followed by the United Kingdom and Singapore. This forced the agency to start implementing a plan to cut back almost 600 positions in order to save about $44 million.

INTERNATIONAL LABOR ORGANIZATION

The International Labor Organization's (ILO) original constitution was part of the Treaty of Versailles. It is an intergovernmental agency, with each country having two governmental representatives, one labor representative, and one business representative. The ILO conference of all representatives elects the executive council—with both bodies having the same proportional representation of government, labor, and industry—and sets the budget.

One of the primary functions of the ILO is to raise labor standards, and to this end it has adopted more than 300 conventions and recommendations with more than 5,000 ratifications. Each convention represents a new extension of international law. After ratification the states concerned report periodically on the implementation of these agreements. In addition, the ILO provides technical assistance, usually through UNDP, on questions relating to productivity, small industries, social security, occupational safety, labor standards, and occupation training.

The annual ILO conference, which is attended by about 2,000 delegates, takes up controversial issues such as the treatment of the Polish Solidarity Union, apartheid, and the Palestine issue. There was no opposition to the conference condemning apartheid, but the Polish Solidarity and Palestine issues often generated heated debates.

The United States withdrew from the ILO for a number of years in the late 1970s because George Meany, head of the AFL/CIO labor union, objected to participation by Soviet trade unions, which he claimed were not genuine trade unions. After Meany's death, the United States resumed its membership in February 1980. In 1984 the ILO conference heard a report by a commission of inquiry into violations of workers' rights in Poland. The commission found that Poland had violated two ILO conventions regarding union and workers' rights. After the ILO accepted the report, Poland notified the ILO that it intended to withdraw.

UN INDUSTRIAL DEVELOPMENT ORGANIZATION

It took about twenty years before the General Assembly approved Specialized Agency status of the UN Industrial Development Organization (UNIDO) in 1986. UNIDO originated in the United Nations as the Committee for Industrial Development and later the Center for Industrial Development to coordinate UN activities in the field of industrial development and promote technical assistance and the exchange of information. The industrial countries have not been enthusiastic supporters of this organization, believing that industrial technology can best be promoted through private business operations. The annual budget for 1986 was $56 million.

NONGOVERNMENTAL ORGANIZATIONS

More than 1,000 private nongovernmental organizations (NGOs) are registered with the United Nations. They include religious organizations as well as private aid organizations. They have the right to attend UN meetings and world conferences without a vote. They provide private inputs to support UN programs. In recent years the United Nations has contracted with them to carry out programs involving aid and even peacekeeping for jobs such as clearing mines. Particularly with the U.S. Congress slashing budgets for UN programs, the NGOs have provided badly needed resources to assist UN programs.

CONCLUSIONS

The Specialized Agencies carry out many of the goals of solving international problems of "an economic, social, cultural, or humanitarian character" specified in Article 1 of the UN Charter. Although the United Nations proper does not directly control these organizations, they have been brought into a close relationship with the UN System. The Specialized Agencies have negotiated agreements with the UN Secretariat that provide for reciprocal representation at meetings, exchange of information, and coordination of statistical and administrative arrangements. Each Specialized Agency has agreed to consider recommendations to it by the United Nations and report back on action taken. These arrangements have been particularly effective in coordinating technical assistance under the leadership of UNDP, providing aid to alleviate wars, famines, and other disasters; attacking problems of pollution; and facilitating world commerce and transportation.

The problems of trade, development, debt burdens, AIDS, the environment, pollution, and many others demand international cooperation. The UN System has provided the framework to address them. The activities of Specialized Agencies have expanded with the growing interdependence of countries. A few of them occasionally have dabbled in politics with resolutions against Israel and actions against apartheid. Such controversies have attracted media attention, but these resolutions are of minor importance in comparison with the vast number of constructive activities carried out by the organizations. They have promoted a network of codes, treaties, and other international agreements.

The dream of the founders of the United Nations was that some day this network of agreements and operations would make the world so interdependent that war would be inconceivable. National rivalries still dominate the international system, but the technicians and experts cooperate and work together in these international bodies, and their work has expanded despite pressure in recent years by the United States and others for economies in operation.

Notes to Chapter 9

1. International Monetary Fund, *Annual Report 1995*, pp. 166, 235.

2. A. Ouattara, "Fund Is Helping to Resolve Africa's Debt Problem by Supporting Growth-Oriented Economic Reforms," *IMF Survey*, June 13, 1988.

3. J. Spero, *The Politics of International Economic Relations* (New York: St. Martin's, 1985).

4. S. Stern, "World Bank's General Capital Increase," *Finance and Development*, June 1988, pp. 20–22.

5. H. Eduard and B. Puckahticken, *Export Credit Policy* (Washington, DC: IMF, 1985).

6. For basic information on activities of the UN and Specialized Agencies see *Everyone's United Nations* (New York: United Nations, 1986); current issues of *UN Chronicle*; *A Global Agenda—Issues before the General Assembly of the United Nations*, published annually by the United Nations Association (New York); and the annual U.S. Department of State *Report to the President on the United Nations*.

Chapter X

MANAGING THE UN SYSTEM

The UN record of accomplishments in peacemaking noted in previous chapters is due largely to the ability and dedication of the secretaries general and the officials under them in the UN Secretariat. They have worked effectively in many crises despite strong nationalistic pressures opposing them. The secretaries general have grown with their job and have expanded the role of the Secretariat.

THE SECRETARY GENERAL

The secretary general does not head an executive branch in the ordinary sense. He or she does not submit detailed proposals to legislative organs, solicit public support for them, and then carry out the resulting programs within legislative guidelines. The UN Secretariat is primarily a service organization for meetings and for carrying out instructions of UN bodies. However, in a crisis and in difficult situations the secretary general can take initiatives behind the scenes and make proposals for settling issues. He or she can make informal suggestions on economic and social issues and do detailed work on them. The Security Council and other organs can assign the secretary general duties, such as peacekeeping, to enable him or her to act as a conventional executive. When members cannot reach agreement on problems, they can turn them over to the secretary general (Figure 4). As explained below, Dag Hammarskjöld extended the power of the secretary general by filling a vacuum in the Charter. However, the secretary general is still directed by UN organs, and the secretary general is not a crisis manager like a president or prime minister.

The secretary general is appointed by the General Assembly upon the recommendation of the Security Council. His appointment is subject to the veto of any one of the permanent members, and he also must be acceptable to developing nations, which could block his nomination. Candidates are questioned and inter-

Figure 4. Six secretaries general of the United Nations. (a) Trygve Lie (Norway) February 1, 1946–April 10, 1953; (b) Dag Hammarskjöld (Sweden) April 10, 1953–September 18, 1961; (c) U Thant (Burma) November 3, 1961–December 22, 1971; (d) Kurt Waldheim (Austria) December 22, 1971–December 15, 1981; (e) Javier Perez de Cuellar (Peru) December 15, 1981–January 1, 1992; (f) Boutros Boutros-Ghali (Egypt) January 1, 1992–. (*Courtesy*: UN Photos 165430 and 178980/M. Grant)

viewed by the members to elicit their views on controversial issues. Traditionally, the secretary general is selected after a number of votes in the Security Council in which one or more candidates are vetoed.

Chapter 15 of the UN Charter reflects the desire of the sponsoring governments to give adequate authority to the secretary general to perform the many duties assigned to him. There was a great deal of discussion about whether the General Assembly and the Security Council should appoint the deputies of the secretary general, but it was finally decided after much debate that this could undermine the authority of the secretary general and the international character of the Secretariat. Therefore, the secretary general was given the authority to appoint his deputies under regulations established by the General Assembly. This is desirable, because if members of the Secretariat tried to promote national views, this would rapidly bring a halt to meaningful action.[1] The oath of office of the staff commits a member of the staff "not to seek or accept instructions in regard to the performance of my duties from any government or other authority external to the Organization."

Listing the duties of the secretary general indicates the great scope of the job. The position is responsible for a tremendous number of reports requested by the General Assembly, the Economic and Social Council, and other bodies of the UN. These reports range from verbatim accounts of the Security Council meetings to a thoughtful analysis of the activities of multinational corporations. Normally the Secretariat plays a major role in helping committees draft reports on their activities and investigations. These reports should be prepared in a timely fashion in the six official languages of the United Nations.

In line with Article 98, the secretary general is responsible for administrative support of the meetings of the many commissions and committees of the United Nations. Most of these meetings take place in New York, Geneva, or the headquarters of the five regional commissions around the world. The secretary general participates in the major meetings and, in addition, when special meetings or conferences are called for other locations, the secretary general often attends them.

The secretary general also is responsible for the budget, personnel, and other administrative support for the many bodies of the UN proper. There are many unusual complications arising from the fact that he or she is assisting 185 different countries, dealing with many foreign languages and many currencies. He or she is instructed to meet quotas for hiring, so that the staff represents the countries of the United Nations. As explained below, the secretary general has to fight for his regular budget of over $19.1 billion a year, and in addition must help solicit special contributions amounting to much more than this for the budgets of the organizations such as UNDP under him or her. He or she must provide support for meetings in many countries, and that support includes interpreters in many languages. The secretary general, of course, must also delegate extensively, but will come under sharp criticism if facilities are not provided or if there is evidence of waste.

The most important function of the secretary general is to exercise quiet diplomacy in world crisis situations to help prevent catastrophic confrontations between the major power blocs of the world. Article 99 provides a little leverage in carrying out this task by permitting the secretary general to call to the attention of the Security Council any matter that may threaten the maintenance of international peace and security. The secretary general has used this power rarely. He normally is forced to rely primarily on the force of his own personality and diplomacy behind the scenes to try to settle disputes.

During the first major crisis faced by the United Nations to discuss the continued occupation of Iran by the Soviet Union, Secretary General Trygve Lie issued a memorandum on whether or not the issue should remain on the agenda of the Security Council. Although the Security Council overruled him, the secretary general with the above precedent has continued to contribute to political debates before the Council.

Lie was an activist, particularly in mediating the Arab-Israel issues. When North Korea invaded South Korea, he opened the debate by reporting that the UN Commission on Korea had reported that North Korea was invading the South and that the Security Council should act. He proposed even more authority for the United Nations than the U.S. government would agree to, since the Pentagon was anxious not to dilute its control over American forces, which were doing most of the fighting.[2]

As a result of Lie's actions on the Korean issue, the Soviets attacked him as acting illegally and as being an "abettor of aggression." Originally in 1946 for the first term, Soviet Foreign Minister Vyshinsky had said Lie was the only candidate they would support, but the Soviet Union vetoed his candidacy for a second term. After numerous meetings, the Security Council informed the General Assembly that it could not reach agreement on a candidate. The General Assembly then finessed the veto problem by passing a resolution by a vote of 46 to 5 extending his term for three years, noting that he had been recommended by Security Council in 1946. The Charter does not specify the length of his term, and the decision held. This satisfied Lie, who originally had indicated that he wanted to retire after the first term, but stubbornly stayed on to protect the position of the secretary general from the Russian attempt to weaken it.[3]

Dag Hammarskjöld was also an activist, particularly in the Suez crisis of 1956 and the Congo crisis in the 1960s. Hammarskjöld, at the General Assembly's request, organized the UN Emergency Force (UNEF) for the Sinai in 48 hours. This was the United Nation's first major peacekeeping force.

In the Lebanese crisis that followed, the secretary general announced a policy of "helping to fill a vacuum" if the General Assembly or Security Council did not give him guidance in safeguarding peace and security. The United States had moved troops into Lebanon at its request when its independence and Jordan's appeared threatened by coups. The United States indicated that it would be willing to withdraw troops if the UN Observer Group in Lebanon (UNOGIL) were expanded. The Soviets vetoed a Security Council resolution on this because it appeared to justify the United States sending troops there in the first place. At this point the secretary general indicated that he would fill the vacuum and expand UNOGIL, which he did. The United States and Russia agreed on an emergency meeting of the General Assembly, and in the debate the United States indicated willingness to withdraw its troops if the United Nations took steps to establish peace and security. The General Assembly then passed an Arab League resolution calling for an end to the crisis and a withdrawal of troops, and the crisis passed.[4] The U.S. troops were quickly withdrawn.

This set the stage for a high point of activism of the secretary general in the Congo crisis and subsequently a major challenge to the position's authority. When Belgian troops threatened to intervene in their former colony of the Congo to restore order and protect their citizens, Ralph Bunche, who was there representing the United Nations at the Congo's independence celebration, informally helped the government request the United Nations for assistance. Secretary General Hammarskjöld then invited the members of the Security Council to lunch and proposed the sending of a UN peacekeeping force as well as emergency food supplies. That evening, on July 14, 1960, he convened the Security Council and by prearrangement a resolution was introduced calling for such a peacekeeping force. The resolution passed 8 to 0 with 3 abstentions.

During the crisis Hammarskjöld used the initial grant of authority to create a military force of 20,000 and to close the airports of the Congo to oppose intervention by the Soviet Union and others. This infuriated the Soviets, and they refused to cooperate with him, but they could not withdraw the authority granted to him in the original Security Council resolution.

Khrushchev's reaction was to propose a three-person troika to replace the secretary general. It would represent the communists, the Western powers, and the third world. This would give the Soviets a veto on actions of the Secretariat. At one point Khrushchev attacked Hammarskjöld in the General Assembly as an agent of imperialist countries. Hammarskjöld's reply stating his intention to remain in his post in order to protect the position of the secretary general received a standing ovation. Strangely enough, an hour later Hammarskjöld was invited to a Soviet reception where he was received warmly by Khrushchev.[5]

Hammarskjöld's actions weakened the veto of the five permanent members. In the Congo operation, after the secretary general was authorized to intervene as commander-in-chief of the UN force, the Soviets or other permanent members of the Council could not withdraw the authorization and stop him with the veto. This was different from the Korean War case when action was shifted from the Security Council to the General Assembly to get around the veto. In the Lebanon case, the secretary general took action in a vacuum to carry out the general intent of the Security Council and the UN Charter without explicit authorization of the Security Council or General Assembly. These three cases represented a marked increase in the authority of the secretary general.

Later Hammarskjöld was killed in an airplane crash while visiting the UN forces, and Secretary General U Thant took over. The bitter civil war continued, which the United Nations tried to referee, and a government was finally established that was able to bring about peace.

U Thant was the first secretary general who had come from the third world, which gave him an advantage in dealing with the colonialism issues. He was instrumental in helping resolve the dispute between the Netherlands and Indonesia over Dutch New Guinea (West Irian), the 1962 civil conflict in Yemen, the dispute between the Philippines and Malaya over Sarawak and North Borneo, and in ending the disputes over the Congo.

Many observers criticized him unjustly over his role in the 1967 war crisis in the Sinai. He brought the matter up in its early stages before the advisory committee of members contributing to the peacekeeping force. Some of these insisted on agreeing to Egypt's demand for withdrawing the UNEF units. U Thant warned the Security Council of the dangers of the situation, but it did not act. Any one of the UN members could have brought the matter before the General Assembly, which was meeting at that time, but they did not. U Thant has been made the scapegoat for the failure of major powers, including the United States, to prevent the war, although it had been forewarned of Israel's intentions. As noted in Chapter 4, three weeks elapsed between Egypt's demand for UNEF to withdraw and the attack of Israel against the Egyptian and Syrian forces.

Legally the secretary general was on solid ground to withdraw the forces. UNEF was established by the General Assembly, which did not have the power of "enforcement" given by the Charter to the Security Council. This meant that legally UNEF was required to withdraw when requested by the host state, Egypt. UNEF withdrew and war broke out about two weeks later. As a result of the disastrous effect of the 1967 war, the peacekeeping forces since that time have been authorized by the Security Council. This did not solve the problem of financing the 1956 UNEF forces, since the Soviets did not help pay the cost. Finally in 1988 the Soviets agreed to pay assessments for peacekeeping forces. By that time there was a new financial crisis with the United States withholding more than $500 million in assessments.

The fact that the Security Council after the 1967 war was willing to authorize peacekeeping forces in the Middle East made the task easier for Secretary General Waldheim, U Thant's successor. Waldheim also took initiatives in mediating conflicts in Cyprus, between India and Pakistan, and in Vietnam. His critical comments about American bombing of North Vietnam resulted in a public denouncement by President Nixon. Waldheim, like his predecessors, decried the failure of nations to refer disputes to the United Nations in their early stages before they break out in war.

After ten years Waldheim stepped down. His successor, Javier Perez de Cuellar, helped bring an end to the Iran-Iraq war, the Afghanistan war, and the Cambodian war, monitor elections in Namibia and Nicaragua, and end the war in El Salvador. He did not succeed in mediating the Falklands war, since Britain's quick attack brought the conflict to an end after Argentina refused to negotiate. The U.S. news media began to report positively about the United Nations, a change from the UN bashing of previous years. He set a precedent by being reelected for a second term without a controversy.

On January 1, 1992, with unanimous approval of the General Assembly, the new secretary general, Boutros Boutros-Ghali, took office. A former Egyptian prime minister, he had played a major role in the Camp David breakthrough on the Arab-Israel disputes. In the 1992 Yugoslav crises his representative Cyrus Vance managed to get cease-fires in Slovenia and Croatia, after the European Community failed. In response to a Security Council request to keep the possibility of deploying a peacekeeping force in Bosnia-Herzegovina under review, Boutros-Ghali recommended that the Security Council consider "other means" to deliver aid to blockade Sarajevo, which implied the use of force. The Security Council president on June 26, 1992, after consulting with the Security Council publicly endorsed the recommendations and the blockade was broken. This was a precedent for UN peacekeeping forces intervening in a civil war.

In July 1992, in response to a request from Nelson Mandela, head of the African National Congress, and South Africa's president, the Security Council authorized Cyrus Vance to visit South Africa and report on the situation because of its concern that negotiations had broken down on ending apartheid. The secretary general also sent ten UN observers there to give an unbiased report on demonstrations. He later requested the Security Council authority for sending thirty more. Their objective was to defuse violence and help create conditions for negotiations. The above actions were another precedent for the Security Council action on human rights issues.

In sum, the secretaries general, despite lack of support and even opposition of major powers and despite attacks on the United Nations by the American news media, have been able to mediate major disputes while administering a large and complicated bureaucracy. Their peacekeeping units have performed a service that governments individually or collectively could not match. Their recent successes, including helping settle the Afghanistan and the Iran-Iraq wars, suggest that the United Nations could be much more effective in settling international disputes if it had consistent support from major powers.

THE UN DEBT CRISIS

In addition to the above duties, the secretary general has the onerous duty of obtaining financing for the budget of the UN proper. The regular UN budget has grown to $1.2 billion a year. Contributions are based on a formula that includes such factors as national income and the ability of members to obtain foreign currencies. The poorest members pay a minimum of .01 percent of this budget, whereas the ten largest members pay about three-fourths of the budget. In the early 1970s criticism mounted in the U.S. Congress that the U.S. share of the budget, about one-third, was too large. At that time the assessment was about 31 percent based on the above formula. After a tremendous lobbying effort by the United States, the General Assembly members were persuaded to reduce the U.S. assessment to 25 percent.

The Soviet Union with 10 percent, Japan with 11.4 percent, and Germany with 8 percent of the UN budget were the next largest contributors in 1990. In terms of a percentage of national income, Gambia was the largest contributor with .6 percent of its national income; the United States was close to the bottom of the list, contributing only .03 of its national income to the budget.[6]

The major debt crisis of the United Nations arose from the failure of the Soviet Union, France, and later the United States to pay their assessments for peacekeeping forces. This included the UNEF forces that replaced the British and French troops in the Sinai in 1956, and the ONUC forces that closed the airports to Soviet forces in the Congo during the 1960s. As an emergency measure, in 1961 the General Assembly authorized $200 million in UN bonds that matured in 25 years. The United States, at that time under President Kennedy, subscribed 50 percent of the UN bonds to tide it over the financial crisis. In July 1962 the World Court, in an advisory opinion by a 9 to 5 vote, declared that the assessments for peacekeeping were regular expenses of the UN within the context of Article 17 and that members would have to pay their peacekeeping assessments or lose their votes. The Soviets still refused to pay. During the 1964 session of the General Assembly, its president with support of its members, in order to avoid an open confrontation with the Soviet Union, passed resolutions without formal votes. In the following year the Soviet Union won since it was not challenged on its vote, although it continued to withhold its share of assessments for Middle East and other peacekeeping operations. Its rationale was that the crisis was caused by the "imperialist" powers and that the Soviet Union and the communist countries were not responsible for these expenses.

In the spring of 1986 a special General Assembly meeting was called to meet what the secretary general called "the most serious financial crisis in its history." He asserted that unless the 159 member governments paid what they owed the United Nations, it might go the way of the League of Nations. The secretary general pointed out that the financial problems of the UN were greatly intensified by the threat of the United States to withhold $90 to $100 million from its assessed contributions in 1985 and 1986. This threat arose out of U.S. congressional action to limit contributions to 20 percent of the total budget unless the UN voting procedures were changed to give the United States a weighted vote, taking into account its large financial contributions. Under the regular formula the United States would contribute more than 28 percent of the total, which had been cut to 25 percent by the concession noted above. Western European countries and others indicated, however, that they were not willing to change the voting procedure.

As the demands for peacekeeping and monitoring elections mounted, political support for the UN budget increased. In 1988 President Reagan's White House spokesperson announced it would request Congress to pay arrearages to the United Nations. This did not end the crisis because Senator Helms managed to hold up appropriations.[7] In 1990 President Bush got congressional support to pay arrearages over a period of five years. By that time member states owed the UN about $1 billion, with the United States in debt over $500 million. Moreover, the United States would pay its assessment at the end rather than the beginning of the UN fiscal year.

In 1991 the General Assembly approved the regular two-year budget of $2.3 billion by consensus for the first time in history. In addition there were peacekeeping costs, which skyrocketed. Permanent Security Council members are assessed for peacekeeping 20 percent above their normal share of the regular budget, which meant the U.S. share was 30 percent. The secretary general in dealing with the cash flow problem requested an increase in the working capital fund to $250 million, as well as a peacekeeping reserve fund of $50 million and an emergency humanitarian fund of $50 million. The relief of the financial crisis, however, had been brought with an agreement that U.S. or major contributors could veto the budget in committee. On April 30, 1992, the United States was in arrears $555 million for the regular budget and $308 million for peacekeeping operations.

By 1995 with a Republican Congress committed to a "contract with America" the UN budgets had been slashed in half and the United States was in debt well over $1 billion for the regular and peacekeeping UN budgets. It was true that in 1996 the United States was contributing more than its share with the large peacekeeping operation in Bosnia. However, that did not help the UN cash flow problem caused by the delinquency of the United States in paying its dues. Moreover, no private organization or government operation credits voluntary assistance for past taxes or dues.

In addition to the assessed budget and peacekeeping budgets of the United

Nations, the secretary general is responsible for financing operations such as UNDP and UNICEF. Actually contributions to specialized agencies are more than the UN regular budget itself. The total amount of voluntary contributions to the agencies under the secretary general amount to about $2 to $2.5 billion a year. It is a shame that the secretary general with his load of peacekeeping responsibilities must spend so much time worrying about the financial crisis caused by the U.S. Congress.

THE SECRETARIAT

The UN Secretariat is designated under Article 7 as one of the principal organs of the United Nations to assist the secretary general. The Secretariat's staff in 1992 consisted of about 14,700 professional and clerical staff. This included staff in Geneva and of the regional commissions as well as the technical experts who oversee field operations.

The hiring of about 3,800 professionals is affected by country quotas (desirable range), based on the member state's contribution to the budget and the size of its population. In 1990 the number of Americans in posts subject to country quotas amounted to about 13 percent, which was below the desirable range. The United States has a special office in the Department of State to recruit for the United Nations, but the Department of State has difficulty in finding qualified personnel willing to serve at the salary levels of the United Nations. This gives some perspective to the charge of critics that UN salary levels are too high. The salaries are comparable to those earned by federal employees of the U.S. government, which are used by the United Nations as a standard of the best-paid national civil service. The idea of such a civil service standard was accepted by the League of Nations in 1920.

Paragraphs 1 and 3 of Article 101 of the UN Charter read:

> 1. The staff shall be appointed by the Secretary-General under regulations established by the General Assembly.
>
> 3. The paramount consideration in the employment of the staff and in the determination of the conditions of service shall be the necessity of securing the highest standards of efficiency, competence, and integrity. Due regard shall be paid to the importance of recruiting the staff on as wide a geographical basis as possible.

The major powers, and particularly the Soviets, led the attack on these provisions at the San Francisco conference. They wanted four deputies of the secretary general to be elected by the General Assembly on recommendation of the

Security Council. Canada successfully led opposition to this proposal, insisting that the secretary general should appoint his own deputies free from the control of the political organs of the United Nations.[8]

The independence of the secretary general and the Secretariat were gravely challenged during the Congo crisis. At that time Dag Hammarskjöld, after an initial grant of authority by the Security Council, opposed the Soviets and other major powers by using his original authority as commander of the UN forces in the Congo to prevent intervention by the Soviets and others. Krushchev proposed that the UN executive should consist of a troika representing the West, the socialist states, and the nonaligned. This proposal and others to weaken the Secretariat were not approved.

The International Court of Justice has strengthened the status of the Secretariat by ruling that it has the right to bring a case before the Court. Other public international organizations and individuals cannot bring cases before the Court, only the governments can. In an advisory opinion concerning compensation for the death of Count Folk Bernadotte, who was killed by Israeli terrorists, the Court stated that the United Nations is an international person that can bring suit and receive compensation. Moreover, in 1964 the Court ruled that the General Assembly did not have the right to prevent the Secretariat from awarding compensation to an employee judged by an administrative tribunal to have been unjustly dismissed.

Both the Soviet Union and the United States have tried to compromise the independence of the Secretariat. During the "McCarthy era" of the 1950s Secretary General Lie, under pressure of U.S. congressional investigations, dismissed employees and even allowed the U.S. Federal Bureau of Investigation to set up shop in the UN building to interview American employees of the United Nations to see if they were communists. The dismissed employees were compensated, but the UN Secretariat lost face.

The Soviets' attempts to undermine the authority of the Secretariat were more effective, if less blatant. The Soviets controlled naming appointees from the Soviet Union and how long they would serve. After the Congo crisis, the Soviets failed in an attempt to have a troika of undersecretaries appointed by the Security Council and the General Assembly but they succeeded in getting second-level positions to represent communist, free-market, or neutral philosophies. Also, some countries including the United States "seconded" top officials to the Secretariat, which meant that they served in the Secretariat for a limited time and then returned to their career posts at home. This undermined their international status. Soviet officials made no secret of the fact that their officials received instructions from the Soviet ambassador in New York or from Moscow. In 1988 the Soviets agreed to limit seconding.

Thomas M. Franck, after serious study and evaluation of his own experience as head of the UN Institute for Training and Research (UNITAR), concludes that the effect of quotas and politicking by governments for positions in the Secretariat has been "profoundly negative."[9] I suggest that the record of UN accomplishments indicates it is possible for the secretary general to develop an effective personnel service subject to national quotas. The politics of the issue is that the quota system and seconding develops confidence of the great powers and also of the lesser powers.

THE PERMANENT MISSIONS

The members of the United Nations have established permanent missions close to the UN headquarters in New York City. Most of them have similar missions at Geneva, where the European headquarters are located. The United Nations inherited the League of Nations buildings in Geneva, which ironically were completed in the late 1930s as the League reached its nadir and closed out its operations. The Economic Commission for Europe and many of the Specialized Agencies have their headquarters in Geneva, and the Economic and Social Council and other UN organs hold meetings there.

The missions in New York City are governed by a 1947 agreement dealing with privileges and immunities of the UN headquarters staff and of the diplomatic missions assigned to that headquarters. The City of New York has found protection of the Israeli and certain other missions and its diplomats a serious burden, but has managed to keep terrorist activities to a minimum.

In March 1986 the Reagan administration ordered the Soviets to reduce their missions to the United Nations by more than one-third because of alleged spying activities. Most observers recognized that the Soviet missions included KGB officials. At about the same time, Zakharov, a physicist on the staff of the United Nations, was accused of trying to buy classified information about a U.S. military aircraft engine. The Soviets reacted indignantly to the arrest, but by October 1 had complied with the order to reduce their staff. The UN secretary general's press spokesman stated that the U.S. order to reduce the staff was not in accord with the 1947 agreement with the United Nations, and that the United Nations would try to settle the dispute informally before sending the issue to a three-person tribunal to be nominated by the secretary general.

The Soviets reacted by arresting Nicholas Daniloff, a *New York Times* reporter, for allegedly taking secret documents from a Soviet citizen. Many observers viewed this as a setup; the KGB in the past has set up someone like Daniloff by having one of their agents shove secret papers at the victim and then arresting him. After secret bargaining Daniloff and Zakharov were sent home. The United States and the Soviets then traded further reductions of their diplomatic staff before the incident blew over.

The UN Legal Counsel commented that the sending states did have a duty to assure that the size of their mission did not exceed what was reasonable, and that issues with the host country should be settled by consultation. The Soviets met the deadline of reducing their staff from 275 to 170 by March 1988.

In 1987 the U.S. Department of Justice, over the opposition of the U.S. Department of State, requested the Palestine Liberation Organization (PLO) to close its New York City mission to the United Nations. In 1988 the U.S. courts ruled that the Justice Department action was illegal. Nevertheless, in December 1988 Secretary of State Shultz denied permission of Yassar Arafat to speak to the United Nations. The General Assembly in a resolution condemned this as a violation of the 1947 agreement with the United Nations and arranged a special session in Geneva to hear Arafat speak. This seemed to clear the air, and the United States then agreed for the first time to open discussions with the PLO on Mideast peace issues.

CONCLUSION

Secretaries general have carried out their many responsibilities with remarkable efficiency. They delegate to subordinates a great deal of authority, and some of the UN organs are relatively autonomous. Nevertheless, their budgets and administrative data are compiled and organized by computers, which help in coordination of their activities, many of which overlap.

The great powers often carp at the extravagance of the UN operations, overlooking the fact that UN spending for peace literally is microscopic in comparison with the tremendous amounts spent on armaments, even by one country, the United States (see Figure 5). The United States joined with the Soviet bloc and Israel as the only votes against the 1986/87 budget.[10] The criticisms help restrain waste in the UN System, but they also help undermine its prestige and effectiveness.

The Secretariat was burdened by the national quota system and great power pressures in trying to create a truly independent international career service. Nevertheless, there are many dedicated employees on the UN staff. Ambassadors and other members of the missions to the United Nations take international law and diplomacy seriously and opposed, at least with resolutions, the power politics of the superpowers and governments not committed to international law and peaceful solutions of international issues. In the summer of 1988 as the

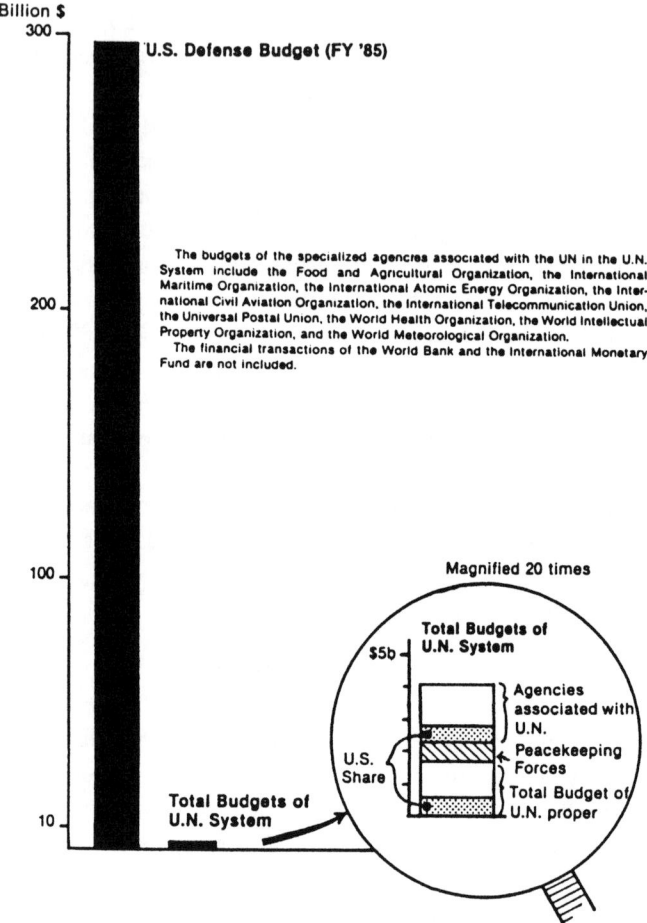

Figure 5. A Comparison of the Budgets for the UN System and the U.S. Defense Deaprtment

secretary general's efforts to achieve peace in the Afghanistan and Iran-Iraq wars bore fruit, the pendulum of popular support in the United States swung back to support the United Nations.

Secretary General Perez de Cuellar played a central role in the revival of UN prestige during the 1980s. Few realized this because he avoided controversial statements and headlines. Most of the Security Council operations that mediated and monitored conflicts were mounted during his tenure. He took initiatives despite mounting UN deficits, and somehow managed to keep it solvent despite huge U.S. arrearages.

His successor, Boutros-Ghali, was an activist. He quickly made administrative reforms by cutting the number of undersecretaries reporting to him from 14 to 8. In the Yugoslav conflicts he followed the Charter, holding back until the regional organization, the European Community, failed. His mediator, Cyrus Vance, a former U.S. secretary of state, then negotiated a truce in the two northern provinces of Croatia and Slovenia. Fighting continued in Bosnia-Herzegovina. The Security Council in August 1992, in line with the secretary general's suggestion, authorized force to deliver relief supplies to its capital, Sarajevo. This created another UN precedent of using force in a civil war, where attacks on civilians had outraged much of the world community. At his suggestion the Security Council also sent more units to Somalia to protect relief supplies. In his first year Boutros-Ghali was keeping the United Nations in the center of the international action.

Notes to Chapter 10

1. S. Bailey, *The Secretariat of the United Nations* (New York: Praeger, 1964), pp. 5–13.

2. J. Murphy, *The United Nations and the Control of International Violence* (Totowa, NJ: Towman and Allenheld, 1982), p. 30.

3. T. Lie, *In the Cause of Peace* (New York: Macmillan, 1954), Chap. xx.

4. B. Urquart, *Hammarskjold* (New York: Harper, 1972), pp. 277–299.

5. Urquart, *Hammarskjold*, Chaps. 15, 16.

6. *Everyone's United Nations* (New York: United Nations, 1988), pp. 29–30.

7. *Christian Science Monitor*, June 29, 1988; *New York Times*, July 26, 1988.

8. *Congressional Quarterly*, October 29, 1988, pp. 3142–3143; *New York Times*, October 15, 1988, p. 1; October 24, 1988, p. 4.

9. T. Franck, *Nations Against Nations* (New York: Oxford University Press, 1985), p. 113.

10. *UN Chronicle*, February 1986, p. 99.

Chapter XI

ACHIEVEMENTS, CRITICISMS, AND PROSPECTS FOR THE UNITED NATIONS

Previous chapters assess the work of the United Nations, particularly in "collective measures" for "removal of threats to the peace" (Article 1, UN Charter). For most of the period after World War II, however, the superpowers used the UN System only when it suited their purposes, while the Soviet Union committed aggressions in violation of the UN Charter. The United States at first gave strong support to the United Nations but later also violated the Charter and hindered its work by withholding its share of budgets. Beginning in 1987, however, the United States and the Soviet Union (now Russia) renewed support for the United Nations. The Clinton administration continued support despite strong opposition from Congress. Meanwhile, the myriad of UN bodies and Specialized Agencies carried on their work of "solving problems of an economic, social, cultural, or humanitarian character." This concluding chapter reviews UN accomplishments, analyzes major criticisms of the UN System, and assesses its prospects.

PEACEMAKING ACHIEVEMENTS BEFORE THE NEW ERA

Most UN military operations have been like policing actions with "peacekeeping" forces. "Peacekeeping" involves lightly armed troops with no enforcement mandate from the UN Security Council or General Assembly. They monitor cease-fires and help mediate and implement peace arrangements by the belligerents. UN officials often help mediate in conflicts before the peacekeeping units are formed.

In addition to the peacekeeping forces the UN Security Council has authorized UN coalitions for major military operations. These include the coalitions for the Korean War and the Gulf War, which were led by the United States. The Security Council gave the sanction of the United Nations and international law to these collective security actions, also called "peacemaking."

The United Nations has been criticized from many sides for its military actions. To get perspective, therefore, it is necessary to make a case-by-case review of its important actions for collective security. Details are covered in Chapters 4 and 5.

The Mideast Wars

Before the new era the peacekeeping operations were concentrated in the Middle East, where the potential for escalation was great. The 1948 war broke out when the Arab states refused to accept the General Assembly plan for Palestine. In August 1949 the Security Council established the UN Truce Supervisory Organ (UNTSO), an organ of the Security Council. It has continued to operate in the area as an observing and mediating force of up to 600 military personnel from about 17 states, including the United States. The UN mediators and UNTSO were successful in achieving a cease-fire in the 1948 war.

UNTSO with its presence helped keep the lid on until the 1956 Suez War. The war was initiated by Israel and by France and Britain, which were permanent members of the Security Council. Their aim was to regain control of the Suez Canal, which had been nationalized by President Nasser of Egypt. President Eisenhower and his Secretary of State John Foster Dulles stayed within the bounds of international law in addressing the crisis. It occurred in the middle of Dulles' attempt to negotiate a new international regime for the canal. In his memoirs Eisenhower notes that Nasser was within his rights in nationalizing the canal company since it lay in Egyptian territory. The day before the attack, Soviet forces had attacked Hungary to repress a rebellion against the communist government. Eisenhower condemned the invasion against a sovereign nation, and explained that he could not "subscribe to one law for the weak and another for the strong."

The British and French vetoed a Security Council resolution that opposed their aggression. The Council then passed the issue to the General Assembly in accordance with the Charter. By November 2 the General Assembly approved a cease-fire and established the UN Emergency Force (UNEF I) to monitor the cease-fire and the withdrawal of forces. With helpful pressure from the United States the United Nations succeeded in 1956 and continued to patrol the 145-mile border between Egypt and Israel. There were only minor incidents. The United Nations arranged for clearing the Suez Canal by the spring of 1957.

Before the 1967 war crisis, UNTSO successfully patrolled the other borders of Israel. In March 1962 fighting broke out between Syria and Israel in the Lake Tiberias area, but it was settled by direct mediation of the UN secretary general.

The 1967 war was a catastrophe that laid the basis for the 1973 war and created lasting barriers to peace in the area. In the spring of 1967 there were increased fedayeen raids against Israel encouraged by President Nasser's radio broadcasts that blanketed the Middle East. Israel retaliated with raids against Syria and Jordan. On May 22 Egypt blockaded the Strait of Tiran, Israel's outlet to the Red Sea and Asia. Anwar Sadat's memoirs note that Nasser knew this action, which was an act of war under international law, made war with Israel "100 percent certain."

On June 5 Israel attacked, first by virtually wiping out the Egyptian and Syrian air forces. Within a week the Israeli forces had taken the Sinai, the Golan Heights, Gaza, and the West Bank. By June 10 the way was open to Damascus, but the Israelis called a halt. The Security Council had called for a cease-fire, and by June 10 the fighting had stopped. The UNTSO observed a cease-fire under the instructions of the Security Council.

President Sadat was obsessed and humiliated by the 1967 war and initiated the 1973 war at the Suez Canal to get back Egyptian territory. Syrian forces joined in an attack against the Golan Heights.

On October 22 the Security Council adopted Resolution 338 calling for a cease-fire. As fighting continued President Sadat appealed for a joint Soviet-American force to be sent to the area. This precipitated a nuclear crisis when the Soviets seemed to accept Sadat's invitation despite U.S. disapproval. U.S. nuclear forces were alerted, and fortunately the Soviets backed down and did not send forces to the area. Secretary of State Kissinger shuttled back and forth among the capitals to negotiate a cease-fire. On October 23 the UN Security Council approved establishing a UN Emergency Force II (UNEF II) without soldiers from the superpowers.

The UN Commander, General Siilvasvuo from Finland, played a key role in negotiating the cease-fire arrangements in the Sinai and Golan Heights. The truce arrangements were formally approved in a Peace Conference on the Middle East on December 31, 1973, under the auspices of the United Nations. A working group chaired by the UNEF II commander then arranged for disengagement of forces from the Sinai and establishment of buffer zones between the Egyptian and Israeli forces.

On May 31, 1974, Kissinger completed an agreement for disengaging forces between Israel and Syria in the Golan Heights. The Security Council set up the UN Disengagement Observer Forces (UNDOF) to patrol a cease-fire line and neutral zone.

On September 4, 1975, Kissinger succeeded in mediating a second disengagement agreement between Egypt and Israel providing for a further withdrawal of Israeli forces in the Sinai and from the oilfields along the Red Sea. The agreement provided for a large buffer zone patrolled by UNEF II troops, and limits on military buildups in the area.

UNEF II was successful until it was terminated in 1979. Its peacekeeping mission set the stage for the Camp David peace agreements between Egypt and Israel and later for the agreements between the Palestine Liberation Organization (PLO) and Israel and between Jordan and Israel. UNDOF has been successful in preventing military incidents between Syrian and Israeli ground forces in the Golan Heights. In 1994 Syria and Israel began to explore a final settlement for this territory.

The Mideast conflicts spilled over into Lebanon after the PLO forces concentrated there. In March 1978, after Palestinian commandos killed 37 Israelis, Israel invaded southern Lebanon. The Security Council demanded Israel's withdrawal and set up a UN Interim Force in Lebanon (UNIFIL).

In 1982 Israel mounted another major attack that carried Israeli forces around the UNIFIL units into Beirut. Also, there were dogfights in the air with Syrian planes, and 88 were shot down. The Security Council again called for a cease-fire. Ambassador Habib of the United States finally was able to negotiate the PLO withdrawal from Lebanon. UNIFIL and other UN observers remained, but the major force was a non-UN force of the United States, Britain, and France. It supervised the withdrawal of the PLO. Later the force withdrew after 241 U.S. marines were killed in their Beirut headquarters by a terrorist bomb.

UNIFIL was saddled with an impossible task of making peace before agreement among the major antagonists, including internal factions in Lebanon. It was not given resources for such an immense task, and it failed to make peace. Nevertheless, no major war has broken out in the area, and it has continued to operate, in contrast with the non-UN multinational force in Lebanon that was forced to withdraw.

The peacekeeping forces in the Mideast have had limited success in helping mediate an end to wars and monitoring cease-fires. However, how can one say they were successful when during their watch five wars occurred between Israel and its neighbors and no lasting peace was achieved?

One must measure their success against the problems they faced, their missions, and the lack of support by major powers including permanent members of the Security Council. The Mideast has been one of the most explosive areas in the world with great power rivalries over its oil resources and its violent religious conflicts. A prolonged war and even a world war could have started there, as demonstrated in the 1973 nuclear-alert crisis.

The United States for the most part gave strong diplomatic support to UN efforts to mediate cease-fires, or took the lead in those efforts. However, the United States also has provided virtually no peacekeeping personnel, and it has been delinquent in paying peacekeeping dues. The UN peacekeeping units have had to improvise to carry out their assignments. The forces consist of many national units, and their resources have been limited. Their successes have been assisted by their tact and diplomacy in dealing with the nations of the area. They could not have succeeded without this cooperation. The failure to achieve a lasting peace has been due to the intractable nature of disputes between Israel and its Arab neighbors, the support of major powers for the wars in the area, and the failure of the Security Council to heed UN warnings of the 1967 war, which laid the basis for exacerbating the Palestinian problem.

Nevertheless, the peacekeeping forces of the United Nations helped limit violence and keep the conflicts from escalating out of control. Their patience and persistence paid off by setting the stage for the Camp David peace agreements between Israel and Egypt, its most powerful neighbor. Since the Camp David agreements, the chances for a major war in the area have been greatly reduced. Also, Camp David laid a foundation for the recent peace agreements between Israel with the PLO and with Jordan. The United States has taken the lead in mediating these agreements and in negotiations between Israel and Syria. In 1996 the prospects were good for a permanent peace.

The Korean War

On June 25, 1950, UN Secretary General Trygve Lie was informed by the United States ambassador and the UN military observers in Korea that North Korean forces had attacked the Republic of Korea. President Truman in his memoirs points out that in placing the issue before the Security Council he had in mind Hitler's aggression in World War II, and that there "was no suggestion from anyone that either the United Nations or the United States could back away" from this test of collective security. In view of the UN role in monitoring elections for the South Korean government and in recognizing it, North Korea's aggression challenged the United Nations. That day the UN Security Council by a vote of 9 to 0 with one abstention (Yugoslavia) and one absent (the USSR) stated that an armed attack had occurred and called for the withdrawal of North Korean forces and for assistance of UN members in carrying out the resolution. Two days later the UN Security Council by a vote of 7 to 1 adopted a UN resolution calling on all members to furnish such assistance as necessary to repel the armed attack. That same day the United States announced it had ordered its land and sea forces to repel the attack. On July 8 the Security Council in line with the secretary general's suggestion passed a resolution requesting the United States to command the UN forces and authorizing them to use the UN flag under a unified command.

General MacArthur's troops counterattacked and pressed on despite reports that the Chinese might intervene. On November 28 Chinese military units, which called themselves volunteers, mounted a mass attack on the UN coalition forces. Their calling themselves volunteers established the fiction that the government of China was not at war with the UN coalition. The continued Chinese attacks forced the UN forces back along the 38th parallel, where they dug in for a long war of attrition.

The UN secretary general transferred cease-fire negotiations to the military commanders to avoid political demands such as the admission of China into the United Nations. An Armistice Agreement was signed on July 27, 1953, establishing a cease-fire zone between the two sides and a Military Armistice Commission with representatives of the two sides to supervise the agreement. Since the armistice there have been incidents and tension along the demilitarized zone but no peace settlement. The United States continued to maintain a sizeable force in South Korea to help in its defense.

The threat of renewed war has remained with North Korea refusing to negotiate a peace agreement. Periodically it mounted terrorist attacks against the South, and there have been minor clashes along the 38th parallel. In the spring of 1994 the Security Council, the International Atomic Energy Commission, and the United States engaged North Korea about permitting inspection of its atomic weapons capability. After a visit by former President Jimmy Carter, a compromise was reached on the inspection issue that permitted North Korea to import equipment to process nuclear material for peaceful purposes.

The Congo War

The Congo crisis began on July 5, 1960, five days after the Congo (now named Zaire) achieved independence from Belgium and Belgian troops withdrew. Congolese soldiers mutinied against their officers, who were Belgians, and killed Europeans. Belgium sent back its troops to restore order despite opposition by Congo's government. It requested assistance from the United Nations against Belgian aggression. The Security Council authorized the secretary general to provide military and technical assistance to the Congolese government until its security forces could "meet fully their tasks."

The secretary general then formed the UN Operation in the Congo (ONUC), which rapidly built up to more than 14,000 troops, most of them from Africa. No troops of the permanent members of the Security Council were included in the force. Security Council resolutions authorized ONUC to use force to get

Belgian troops to withdraw, to maintain law and order, and to prevent a civil war.

Several years of confused action followed during which members of the Security Council were at odds. The major problem was that Katanga, a mineral-rich province, wanted to secede with the help of Belgian forces. Another problem was that the Soviet Union and the United States supported different factions in the Congo. Hammarskjöld continued to act on the basis of the original resolutions, when the Security Council was blocked by a veto. Hammarskjöld personally persuaded President Tshombe, head of the Katanga province, to accept UN troops. Later, fighting broke out as UN troops attempted to capture mercenaries helping the Katanga armed forces. In September 1961, Hammarskjöld was killed when his plane crashed on the way to confer with Tshombe.

The new acting secretary general, U Thant, received a stronger mandate from the Security Council. Fighting broke out again, and Tshombe finally agreed to a new federal government of all the Congo. By 1963 after a succession of leaders General Mobutu took over as president of the Congo and was able to end the civil war. The United Nations provided technical and economic assistance to the new government, which has maintained its integrity since that time.

The India-Pakistan Wars

In 1948 Great Britain granted independence to the colony of India. In the 1948 civil war that followed between Moslems and Hindus about 800,000 civilians were killed. The United Nations was not involved in this war, which was mediated by Great Britain.

After the division of the colony of India into India and Pakistan, there was a remaining dispute over Kashmir. It had a Hindu ruler and government, but most of its population was Moslem and probably wanted to join Pakistan. When Pakistani tribesmen supported by Pakistan attacked the Kashmir government, India then brought the matter to the Security Council. Pakistan entered a counter-complaint. On January 20, 1948, the UN Security Council established a three-member commission with a U.S. member to investigate and mediate. It proposed a cease-fire and withdrawal of troops, and both governments finally accepted the cease-fire line in July 1949. The United Nations also established a UN Military Observer Group (UNMOGIP), which patrolled and settled disputes over the cease-fire line. It consisted of 39 military observers.

In 1965 clashes over Kashmir triggered another war. The UN secretary general received reliable reports from UNMOGIP, and he successfully arranged a cease-fire with the Indian and Pakistani prime ministers.

In 1971 a war broke out between India and Pakistan over East Pakistan, which was situated on the other side of India from Pakistan and had demanded independence from West Pakistan. Indian forces assisted the rebels in the ensuing civil war, and West Pakistan attacked India in frustration. India quickly defeated the West Pakistan forces in East Pakistan, and it successfully broke away and formed the state of Bangladesh. The Security Council and the General Assembly demanded that India withdraw forces in East Pakistan, which India did after it became apparent that East Pakistan would win its independence. The United Nations did not establish a peacekeeping force to monitor the cease-fire between India and the new state of Bangladesh. However, UNMOGIP supervised the cease-fire in Kashmir between India and Pakistan.

The small peacekeeping force (UNMOGIP) and the diplomacy of the United Nations and the great powers have helped prevent and contain wars between India and Pakistan that could have escalated with disastrous results.

Other Conflicts

The UN Security Force in West New Guinea (UNSF) supervised a cease-fire in West Iran between Dutch and Indonesian forces in the aftermath of Indonesia gaining its independence from the Netherlands. The United Nations succeeded in its mission of administering the territory temporarily before transferring it to Indonesia.

The Cyprus crises arose out of communal conflicts in 1964 and again in 1974 between Greek and Turkish communities. The conflicts threatened to escalate to a war between Turkey and Greece, which supported their ethnic factions. The Security Council at the request of the Cyprus government and the British, who maintained a base on the island, agreed to send peacekeeping forces to separate the combatants. The UN force of 7,000 soldiers managed to stop the conflict and help mediate the issues. Despite repeated efforts, including personal intervention of the UN secretary general, the United Nations has not been able to broker a peace settlement. Nevertheless, the UN forces accomplished their mission of stopping the fighting, which at times threatened to escalate to a war between Turkey and Greece. Casualties were relatively small.

Achievements

Although the United Nations in the first forty years did not achieve the ambitious aims of its founders to remove the scourge of war, it made progress toward that goal. It worked as designed to contain and end most international wars, even when agreement was not reached in the Security Council. In this way it helped avoid the catastrophe of a world war.

Failures to settle all international wars during the first forty years were not the fault of the United Nations, which is only an instrument of its members, which are sovereign nations. The Soviets violated the UN Charter numerous times, including invading East European satellites and giving material support for North Korean aggression and for Nasser's wars against Israel. Great Britain and France engaged in aggression against Egypt in the Suez War. The United States violated the Charter by supporting covert attacks against Cuba and later against Nicaragua and against Panama to arrest a drug lord. Other UN members realized they could not effectively challenge the great powers in these crises without shattering the United Nations.

Conflicts are deterred in the international arena, just as in domestic societies, by building up a respect for law, and the great powers in the first forty years failed to build up that respect because they used power politics when it suited them. Although the United States justified its intervention in Panama, Nicaragua, and Grenada by opposing communism and the drug trade, this undermined respect for international law. The question is can enduring respect for international law be achieved in the new era of international politics.

PEACEKEEPING ACHIEVEMENTS IN THE NEW ERA

Gorbachev ended the war in Afghanistan and brought a new era of cooperation to the UN Security Council. No longer hamstrung by the veto, the United Nations in the following years embarked on more peacekeeping missions than in the previous forty years. President Bush, after he led a UN coalition to repel Iraq's invasion of Kuwait, named this a "new era" of international politics where the United Nations "could fulfill the historic vision of its founders." The key to the new era is the cooperation of all five of the permanent members of the Security Council, and particularly the Soviet Union (later Russia) and China.

The most controversial actions of the new era of peacemaking have been UN actions in Somalia and the former Yugoslavia, which were essentially civil wars. These drew much more attention than the relatively successful UN peacekeeping operations.

Soviet Aggression in Afghanistan

A local communist coup in Afghanistan in 1978 was followed by violent opposition by Islamic mujahideen, nationalist Muslims who attacked and killed Soviet military advisers to the new communist government. The Soviet invasion of Afghanistan began in December 1979. The Soviet troops moved into the capital, killing the prime minister and putting a rival, Babrak Karmal, in his place. The world was shocked by the invasion, and 52 states called for a Security Council meeting. The United States sponsored a Security Council resolution deploring the intervention and calling for the immediate withdrawal of foreign troops from Afghanistan. The vote was 12 to 2 with the Soviets vetoing the resolution and its East German satellite joining in opposition. The Council sent the issue to the General Assembly, which by a vote of 104 to 18 called for the withdrawal of foreign troops from Afghanistan.

The United States reacted by cutting back on exports of grain and ending exports of high-technology goods to the Soviets and organizing a boycott of 65 nations at the Olympic Games in Moscow the following summer. Mr. Perez de Cuellar of the UN Secretariat negotiated with the Soviets for withdrawal until he became UN secretary general on January 1, 1982. He appointed Diego Cordovez to continue that effort.

After eight years of negotiations and an exhausting war against the mujahideen guerrillas, President Gorbachev signed agreements for withdrawing Soviet forces. A plausible motive for this action was a desire to remove an impediment to opening up the Soviet Union to the West to help in reforming the communist government. The United States worked closely with the United Nations negotiators, who represented world opinion on this issue. The Afghanistan agreements provided for the UN Good Offices Mission in Afghanistan (UNGOMAP) of 50 military officers plus civilians. UNGOMAP monitored the withdrawal of Soviet troops, investigated complaints, and assisted in the voluntary return of refugees. After the Soviet withdrawal, Afghan guerilla groups continued to fight among themselves.

Iraq's Attacks Against Iran and Kuwait

The Iran-Iraq war began with an Iraq invasion in 1980 to take complete control of the Shatt al-Arab waterway. President Saddam Hussein's motive appeared also to be to establish Iraq's preeminent position in the area. The war, which was waged near the largest oilfields in the world, initially caused petroleum shortages.

The Security Council repeatedly called for a cease-fire, and the secretary general, working with the Islamic League, tried to mediate the war. The war continued in a bloody stalemate. The superpowers and nations in the area realized that as long as one side did not defeat the other decisively, the balance of power in the area would not be disrupted by the two contestants for hegemony.

In the fall of 1988, after losing battles and facing unrest, Iran announced it was ready to accept the "poison" of a cease-fire that had been repeatedly proposed by the UN secretary general. The Security Council established the Iran-Iraq Military Observer Group (UNIIMOG) to monitor the cease-fire with about 400 observers from about 30 countries, with none from the great powers.

President Bush, who had served as ambassador to the United Nations, called on the Security Council to authorize action to repel Iraq's invasion of Kuwait in 1991. Iraq not only took over the large oilfields of Kuwait, but its forces moved to threaten the major oilfields of Saudi Arabia. The United States took the lead in getting the UN Security Council to authorize forming a UN coalition to repel the invasion. The military coalition, which included Arab forces, was led by the United States. It easily defeated Saddam Hussein's forces in a brief war that liberated Kuwait. In accord with the UN Security Council resolutions the UN coalition did not press on to occupy Iraq, but it did impose strict peace terms. These included provisions for disarmament.

The subsequent action of the UN Special Commission on Disarmament (UNSCOM) to destroy weapons of mass destruction in Iraq has been one of the most important achievements related to international peacekeeping. Its actions were supported by repeated warnings of the Security Council to Iraq that its lack of cooperation would result in continued economic sanctions. These included controlling billions of dollars of Iraqi funds that were deposited abroad, establishing an embargo on exports to Iraq except for humanitarian aid, and using proceeds of Iraqi oil exports to pay for relief and compensation to victims of the war. In addition, on January 13, 1993, U.S. and British bombers attacked Iraqi military targets, and the following day the secretary general told the press that the raids were in accord with Security Council resolutions. Despite Iraqi protests, it allowed inspection teams to continue their work. The weapons destroyed by the UN teams included 2,000 Scud long-range rockets, tens of thousands of chemical weapons, the supergun, and nuclear plants for making weapons-grade materials.

Beginning in April 1991 the UN negotiated memoranda of understanding with the Iraqi ambassador to assign 300 UN guards to protect relief convoys to the Kurdish population of four million in the three northern governorates of Iraq. These convoys and the Kurdish population were also protected by daily flights of U.S., British, and French aircraft north of the 36th parallel. The memoranda also covered relief convoys to the minority populations in the south. The United States carried out periodic flights in the southern provinces to deter attacks against minority populations there.

The Security Council established an Iraq-Kuwait Boundary Demarcation Commission to demarcate the boundary coordinates agreed on by the two sides in the truce agreement. This was the first time the United Nations had drawn a border between two member states.

In February 1993, following provocative actions along the border, the Security Council transformed the Kuwait observation mission into a force that would observe violations of the demilitarized zone between Iraq and Kuwait. The Security Council authorized an increase in personnel from 350 to 3,600 for this task.

The above missions were accomplished, and the UN coalition was continuing military and economic pressure at the beginning of 1996 to ensure continued compliance with UN resolutions.

The War in Yugoslavia

The success of democratic revolutions in Eastern Europe after 1989 encouraged Yugoslavia's republics, which were dominated by non-Serbs, to break away from the Serbian-dominated, communist-oriented central government. Serious fighting broke out in the summer of 1991 as the northern republics of Slovenia and Croatia declared their independence, and the federal army, which was dominated by the Serbian Republic, fought to take over Serbian communities in those provinces.

After European Community representatives failed to achieve a truce in the conflicts, the matter was turned over to the Security Council. Cyrus Vance, former U.S. secretary of state, was named as a UN mediator. He negotiated a ceasefire, and the Security Council placed peacekeeping units, 14,000 strong, in Croatia and Slovenia. Sporadic fighting continued, with Serbian irregulars keeping control of some areas, but Slovenia and Croatia established their independence.

The focus of fighting then shifted to Bosnia-Herzegovina, which claimed independence and then was recognized by many countries. They hoped to discourage an attack by the Serbian-dominated truncated central government of the former Yugoslavia. Bosnia-Herzegovina consisted of three major ethnic groups —Moslems, 40 percent; Serbs, 33 percent; and Croats, 18 percent. In a referendum boycotted by the Serbs, an overwhelming majority voted for independence, but military units of Serbs attacked, aiming to absorb Bosnia-Herzegovina, or at least the Serbian communities in Bosnia-Herzegovina, into a greater Serbia. The Serbian military units were supported from the truncated Yugoslavia, although that government disclaimed responsibility.

Serbs used the term ethnic cleansing to describe their ruthless policy of killing civilians and forcing them to flee from homes in areas claimed by the Serbs. The Moslems and Croats, which controlled the government of Bosnia-Herzegovina, fought back.

The Security Council established the UN Protection Force (UNPROFOR) in Yugoslavia to deliver humanitarian aid to civilians, who were a major target of fighting, particularly in the capital of Sarajevo. As fighting continued the United

Nations extended the UNPROFOR mandate to deter attack against "safe areas" established by the UN negotiators, to promote withdrawal of forces, to occupy key areas, and to use all necessary measures to carry out the UN mandate.

As Serbia continued to defy UN resolutions and the cease-fire, the United Nations imposed a strict embargo on Serbia that included all but humanitarian aid. Serbia's economy was severely affected by the beginning of 1994 with runaway inflation and a severe shortage of food. Nevertheless, the Serbian prime minister continued to hold out, buttressed by an election victory in December 1993.

On April 7, 1993, the Security Council recommended Macedonia, another Yugoslavian republic, for UN membership, and on June 18 authorized deployment of troops there to reinforce the UN presence and deter a Serbian attack. Initially 300 U.S. troops participated.

Representatives of the United Nations and the European Community were frustrated as they attempted to mediate peace among the warring factions. The United Nations forces numbered only 27,000. They arranged for thousands of relief flights and hundreds of convoys of food and medical supplies to the besieged civilian populations, but they were not able to stop the killing and atrocities. The Security Council on May 25, 1993, also established an international tribunal to prosecute violations of international humanitarian law. A UN commission of experts established in 1992 continued to investigate and report on atrocities. The UN convoys prevented mass starvation, but the UN peacekeepers did not stop attacks against the civilian population, particularly in Sarajevo and other parts of Bosnia.

After a mortar shell killed about 70 people in Sarajevo's market, UN Secretary General Boutros Boutros-Ghali requested NATO to take the necessary action to respond to a UN Security Council request for air strikes. These strikes were carried out by NATO forces. With the addition of Soviet diplomatic pressure Serbia agreed to a cease-fire.

With U.S. mediation Croats and Muslims in February 1994 agreed to form a federation as part of Bosnia-Herzegovina and also agreed in principle to a confederation with the state of Croatia. The agreement was signed in Washington, DC, and provided a balance against Serbia for negotiating a peace. However, fighting continued in strategic areas until September 1995, when the United States persuaded the Yugoslav (Serb), Croat, and Bosnian governments to send top officials to Dayton, Ohio, to negotiate a peace agreement. The agreement reached at the beginning of November confirmed the existence of Bosnia-Herzegovina, which consisted of a Croat-Bosnian federation with a Serbian republic. The agreement also provided for resettlement and compensation for displaced persons, protection of human rights, and NATO Implementation Forces

(IFOR) of 60,000 authorized by a UN Security Council resolution to separate the forces and enforce the peace.

Critics could find much to criticize about how the United Nations handled the four years of conflict in the former Yugoslavia: hundreds of thousands of civilians were killed for ethnic reasons, at times UN resolutions were ignored, and UN peacekeepers were attacked. On the other hand, because of UN efforts, including economic sanctions supported by the world community, the conflict did not spread into neighboring countries, which had strong ties to various factions. Furthermore, the UN convoys prevented mass starvation and the United Nations provided an international framework for peace negotiations and agreement. UN action achieved the independence of Croatia, Slovenia, and Macedonia, and that of Bosnia embodied in the 1996 Dayton peace agreement. The alternative could have been a Vietnam-type war involving Eastern European nations and Muslim countries.

Somalia

Secretary General Boutros Boutros-Ghali in his first months in office in 1992 insisted the United Nations provide aid and assistance to Somalia. Somalia was wracked by wars between tribal factions and a severe drought, and it was estimated that hundreds of thousands had died from starvation. UN relief convoys and private relief organizations were attacked by irregular forces.

On December 3, 1992, in response to an appeal from the secretary general, the Security Council sanctioned the use of force to deliver humanitarian aid in Somalia. In the next week the United States led 20 countries in securing the airfield and port in Mogadishu and in protecting relief shipments. The operation consisted of 37,000 troops at its peak with 21,000 U.S. troops as part of the Unified Task Force (UNITAF). The forces, led by the United States, quickly established security in most of Somalia and ended the attacks on relief workers. Most of the UNITAF troops were then withdrawn, and the Security Council established UNOSOM II to take over its task.

In response to Somalia irregulars ambushing and killing 24 Pakistani peacekeepers of the remaining UNITAF forces, the Security Council on March 26, 1993, adopted a resolution authorizing the secretary general "to take all necessary measures" to establish the authority of UNOSOM throughout Somalia and to arrest, try, and punish those responsible for the attack. This was the first time a peacekeeping operation was authorized to use force under Chapter VII of the Charter.

UNITAF and UNOSOM restored order and protected relief supplies in most of Somalia, except in the part of the capital controlled by General Aidid's forces.

It is estimated that 350,000 Somalis had starved to death before UNOSOM and UNITAF intervened to protect relief convoys and stop the mass starvation.

After 18 American soldiers were killed while attacking General Aidid's head-quarters in the capital at the end of 1993, the United States announced it would withdraw troops in March 1994. Its forces assisted in the orderly evacuation of UN troops and although there are still local conflicts in Somalia, there has been no chaos or mass starvation such as had existed before the UN intervention.

Other African Conflicts

At the beginning of 1994 the United Nations was also carrying out the following African peacekeeping operations:

1. The UN Angola Verification Mission (UNAVEM) was set up by the Security Council in December 1988 to oversee withdrawal of Cuban troops from Angola. This had come about as a result of persistent negotiations led by Chester Crocker of the United States, who negotiated the withdrawal in connection with South Africa's finally agreeing to the independence of Namibia. The elections were held in Angola on September 30, 1992, with UN monitoring. UNITA President Jonas Savimbi, who had led an insurrection against the Angolan government for many years, was decisively defeated. He refused to accept the results, however, and continued to lead the insurrection. The Security Council kept UNAVEM in the country. In adopting Resolution 834 the Council expressed readiness to expand the force in the event of significant progress in the peace process. At the beginning of 1996 there was a fragile cease-fire.

2. The UN Mission for the Referendum in Western Sahara (MINURSO) was established by the Security Council on April 29, 1991, to monitor a cease-fire and to oversee a referendum to settle whether the Western Sahara would choose independence or integration with Morocco. At the beginning of 1996 the parties had not agreed on arrangements or a firm date for the referendum.

3. On June 22, 1993, the Security Council established the UN Observer Mission in Uganda-Rwanda. The civil strife had worsened there with clashes on the border of the two countries. The UN mission was to prevent military assistance from reaching Rwanda in order to dampen the civil strife and to support peace efforts. The secretary general assigned about 100 military and civilian observers to the task. The UN forces, which included an important U.S. contingent, quickly established order to permit the relief organizations to work, and helped in the formation of a new government.

4. The UN Operation in Mozambique (ONUMOZ) was established on December 16, 1992, by Security Council Resolution 797 to monitor withdrawal of foreign forces from Mozambique and to assist in elections and humanitarian efforts. Twenty-two countries contributed to the military elements. Under the Rome Peace Agreement of October 1992, government and resistance forces were to be demobilized with UN monitoring. Preparations for elections in 1994 were under way. About 3 million people had died and more than 5 million refugees had been displaced in more than a decade and a half of civil war. In 1993 Mozambique for the first time in 17 years enjoyed a combination of peace and rainfall. The UN in 1994 helped monitor efforts to establish elections, which were used to form a new government.

5. UN efforts to end civil wars that threaten the peace included a huge peacekeeping force in Cambodia that, at the beginning of 1994, had supervised free elections and established a government that could challenge remnants of the notorious Khmer Rouge. The Khmer Rouge had carried out the Cambodian holocaust after the Vietnam War.

In the aftermath of the Vietnam War a radical communist movement, the Khmer Rouge, had overthrown the military government of Cambodia and had established a repressive regime. In purging its country of "bourgeoise" elements, the Khmer Rouge caused the deaths of more than 1 million Cambodians. The regime had challenged Vietnam in border clashes, and Vietnam responded in 1979 by invading and establishing a puppet government.

The bulk of the Khmer Rouge forces eluded the Vietnamese army and began a campaign of opposition. China helped the Khmer Rouge and the Soviets aided the new government. Vietnam's aggression appeared aimed at achieving the historic aspirations of the Vietnamese Communist Party of creating a federation out of the former area of French Indochina. The UN General Assembly in a controversial decision refused to recognize the aggression and continued to accept the credentials of the old Khmer Rouge government, by then represented in the UN by a moderate delegation under Prince Sihanouk.

The Southeast Asian neighbors of Cambodia involved the United Nations in peace talks that included, in addition to the warring factions, the United States, the Soviet Union, Britain, China, and a representative of the UN secretary general. In 1991 the talks finally bridged the gap between resistance factions and the new government. The peace agreement provided for the most expensive UN peacekeeping mission (UNTAC) in previous history. In 1992 about 22,000 military and civilian personnel were assigned to the operation. After the elections UNTAC worked with the UN High Commissioner for Refugees to coordinate a major relief and reconstruction effort.

UNTAC maintained law and order, repatriated and resettled refugees, organized free elections, helped oversee a civil administration, and reconstructed infrastructure. As of the beginning of 1994 an uneasy peace had been restored, free elections held, and a new government set up under the moderate leadership of Prince Sihanouk. However, Khmer Rouge guerillas were still active. By 1995 the peacekeepers had withdrawn.

6. In 1981, President Reagan directed CIA to support the contra forces, which were trying to overthrow the Marxist government of Nicaragua. The Nicaraguan government was also supporting rebels in El Salvador. Nicaragua was able to pass a General Assembly resolution condemning U.S. support to the contras, because such support violated international law.

    Meanwhile, a Central American "Contadora" group negotiated an agreement for elections in Nicaragua to be monitored by the United Nations. The elections were held and a non-Marxist government was formed. The UN peacekeepers helped disarm the contra forces and integrate them into civilian life. Also, the United Nations mediated a truce between the rebels and the government of El Salvador and monitored elections for a new government there. The above successes reflected the end of the Cold War and the end of Soviet support to Cuba and to pro-communist elements in Central America.

So far in the new era the United Nations has succeeded in ending and deterring international wars, which was the major aim of the UN Charter. This success has escaped attention because of the many problems the United Nations has encountered when intervening in what were essentially civil wars. Normally civil wars are outside the scope of the UN Charter. The legal justification for UN intervention in some civil wars was that the Security Council could intervene if a civil war threatened to escalate or had other major international implications, such as genocide and mass starvation and migration. The UN Charter (Article 1) covers such contingencies in its "removal of threats to the peace."

The above case-by-case review of UN military operations indicates the United Nations can act effectively, even without strong U.S. support. Moreover, there are other justifications for UN military operations. The costs in casualties and money of using the United Nations to deter and contain wars are minuscule in comparison to the costs of wars and defense budgets. When a major war occurs, as in the case of the Persian Gulf War, the Security Council authorizes a coalition, because waging war is far beyond the capacity of the United Nations, which has no military units or budget for such a task. Other countries under the UN flag contribute troops and share the costs. This participation also can be of major political help as indicated by the front-line role of Arab troops in the Gulf War, which undermined the anti-West propaganda of Saddam Hussein.

Other major UN efforts for peace include the network of nuclear arms agreements, most of which reflect UN initiatives. Until 1986 the most important of these were the agreement for the International Atomic Energy Agency (IAEA) of 1956, the nuclear Nonproliferation Treaty (NPT) of 1970, the Limited Test Ban Treaty of 1961, and the nuclear-free zone in Latin America.

UN approval legitimizes the use of force to end conflicts. Some of the crises indicate support of the United States is essential if the United Nations is to accomplish its aim of creating respect for international law and ending the scourge of war. Although the United Nations has not solved some of the world's intractable security problems, the United Nations' operations deserve U.S. support.

Much depends on the leadership of U.S. presidents. Presidents Truman and Eisenhower were democratic internationalists who used the United Nations for international crises. Successors inherited involvement in successful UN operations that created a momentum to continue to work with it. However, President Johnson rejected the United Nations in the Vietnam War. There were major failures of power politics under Johnson in Vietnam and under President Reagan in conflicts in Lebanon and Central America.

President Bush introduced the new era of reliance on the United Nations in the Gulf War. However, Congressional budget cuts and attacks limited its effectiveness during the Clinton administration, which still supported UN collective security actions in Bosnia, Somalia, Haiti, and other crises. Future American policy would depend on the 1996 election where voters could chose Bob Dole and power politics or a continuation of the Clinton administration's support for the United Nations.

There were major failures of power politics under Johnson in the Vietnam War, and under Reagan in conflicts in Lebanon and Central America. This does not necessarily mean the United Nations could have solved those problems, but at least the United States would not have suffered such disastrous defeats.

ECONOMIC, SOCIAL,
AND OTHER ACHIEVEMENTS

Although the principal aim of the UN System is to maintain peace, greater than 80 percent of its funds have been devoted to the long-term goals of promoting economic development, human rights, and social progress. Also, the great majority of nations have approved the UN Covenants on Human Rights, which have become models similar to the Bill of Rights in the United States, although the UN has not tried to enforce the Covenants.

The most powerful economic institution of the UN System is the International Monetary Fund (IMF), which has supervised the world's financial system since World War II. Its loans and advice have helped prevent the type of economic crises that occurred after World War I. The IMF together with the World Bank have helped readjust the heavy debt burdens of dozens of debtor countries and thereby avoided serious defaults. With electronic transfers of investments and currencies it is important to have an international organization such as the IMF to quickly mobilize tens of billions of dollars to prevent panic. In 1995 it lent money to tide Mexico over its economic difficulties, which could have caused disaster in the international financial markets.

The World Bank is the major source of development loans and it also has lent money to debtor countries to help adjust their economic policies. The IMF and World Bank are conservative institutions that impose conditions on their loans called conditionalities. They usually require the borrowing countries to take measures to balance their budget and avoid trade restrictions. The IMF and World Bank accepted invitations of Eastern European countries and the former Soviet republics to help them design market-oriented reforms associated with support of billions of dollars of loans. Many of their programs for Eastern Europe and elsewhere have been successful, but Russia is still struggling with its reforms.

The United Nations manages the world's largest technical assistance program under the UN Development Program (UNDP). Its projects emphasize problem solving and draw on the many organs and Specialized Agencies of the UN System for expert assistance. The United States and other industrial countries of the West are major donors and prevent duplication of effort by channeling assistance through UNDP.

The UN High Commissioner for Refugees (UNHCR) also cooperates with the World Food Program, UNICEF, the World Health Organization, and many nongovernmental organizations to aid millions of refugees affected by natural disasters and conflicts. It provides aid and assists in voluntary repatriation for permanent resettlement in an asylum country.

Pollution does not recognize borders, so the UN Environment Program promotes international agreements against pollution of the oceans and the atmosphere. It maintains the Global Environmental Monitoring System (GEMS) to keep track of pollution problems such as the destruction of the ozone layer and global warming.

The UN Fund for Population Activities analyzes world population trends and provides assistance to countries for research and family planning programs. The UN Population Commission organizes World Population Conferences, which set forth goals and plans of action for countries wishing to develop programs of population control.

In 1990 UN drug control activities were integrated under the UN International Drug Control Program. It supervises programs for arresting and trying smugglers, stopping production of drugs, and preventing laundering of drug money.

In addition to the above, the following UN Specialized Agencies support economic and social programs:

1. The International Labor Organization promotes conventions for labor standards to discourage unfair competition from sweatshop labor.
2. The World Health Organization has prevented the spread of epidemics and promoted immunization programs that ended childhood diseases such as smallpox. It has carried out extensive research that has developed cures for tropical diseases. In recent years it has campaigned against the tobacco industry and promoted programs to prevent AIDS.
3. The International Civil Aviation Organization promotes safe air transport and development of airports and air navigation facilities.
4. The Universal Postal Union promotes cooperation for international postal services.
5. The International Telecommunications Union allocates frequencies and establishes standards for electronic communication.
6. The World Meteorological Organization disseminates weather information throughout the world.
7. The International Marine Organization helps control pollution of the oceans and promotes adoption of safety standards for ship construction.
8. The General Agreement on Tariffs and Trade has organized negotiations for large reductions in trade barriers.
9. The World Intellectual Property Organization has promoted agreements to protect copyrights and computer software.

The UN organs and Specialized Agencies have successfully addressed many international problems of "an economic, social, cultural, or humanitarian character" as specified in Article 1 of the UN Charter. Without these agencies the developed countries could not enjoy many of their imports, international travel, health, and clean environment, and the poor of developing countries would suffer from more disasters and chaos arising from conflicts, poverty, and disease.

SOURCES OF CRITICISM OF THE UNITED NATIONS

The UN System is recognized by most nations as indispensible for peacekeeping and addressing the world's economic and social problems. Why has there been such severe criticism in the United States?

Critics often assert the United Nations has been dominated by third-world countries. This criticism has come from the right, such as the Heritage Foundation, and from the left, such as the *New Republic*. Critics assert that although the United States contributes 25 percent of the UN budget, the United States has only one vote in the General Assembly. They point to UN resolutions passed over U.S. objections, including ones critical of the United States. It is true the General Assembly and other UN organs at times have alienated the U.S. government and powerful political groups.

Most of the UN criticisms of the U.S. government were directed against the power politics of the Nixon, Reagan, and early Bush administrations. The United States was frequently criticized in UN forums for CIA attacks against the Allende government of Chile and for CIA's alleged connections with the International Telephone and Telegraph Corporation. Latin American countries and the United Nations also criticized the United States in resolutions, for CIA attacks against Nicaragua and for the U.S. invasions of Panama and Grenada, which violated international law.

The most serious opposition arose in 1994 and 1995 in the U.S. Congress, which slashed the UN peacekeeping and regular budgets. The 1994 elections brought in a Republican majority, which pledged to cut taxes and balance the federal budget. The UN budget was an easy target because it had no immediate impact on voters. Moreover, the politicians asked why the United States should help people abroad when there are serious problems at home.

The above was part of a new isolationism. With the end of the Cold War the United States no longer faced nuclear devastation. Moreover, many in the United States were fearful that if it sent troops for peacekeeping in conflicts such as that in Bosnia, the United States would be dragged into an escalation of fighting such as occurred in the Vietnam War. Members of Congress easily won public support of UN budget cuts with statements about peace in Bosnia—where people had been fighting for centuries—not being worth even one American casualty. Latent isolationism and a powerful nationalism that rejects any foreign restraint on U.S. government actions reinforced the new isolationism.

Presidents Bush and Clinton, on the other hand, saw the end of the Cold War as a new era of opportunity to build a system of collective security, but few in Congress had such a vision. Bush and Clinton, moreover, wanted to maintain U.S. cooperation with the Soviets and other civilizations that had been so useful in the Gulf War. Working with the United Nations, they helped settle conflicts that threatened U.S. alliances and interests.

Other groups have also had conflicts with the United Nations. The UN bodies at times have appeared in the news media with a proposal for a new world information order that would be an alternative to the Western domination of the world's media. Right-to-life groups have been alienated from the U.S. Fund for Population Activities. The Jews were furious about the "Zionism is racism" and pro-Palestinian resolutions that were passed over the opposition and abstention of major powers.

Much of the criticism about the United Nations arises out of pure ignorance about its many activities. Many assume that the United States is paying more than its share, whereas the opposite is true. Most domestic taxes for services are a reflection of an ability to pay. In the United Nations the United States pays much less than its share of members' total gross national product. In terms of affording to pay its share of collective security at the end of the Cold War and for addressing world economic and social problems, Figure 6 shows the United States' tremendous emphasis on military spending. The United Nations has made remarkable accomplishments at a negligible cost.

PROSPECTS

Despite the increasing activities and successes of the UN System, the forces of nationalism still dominate international affairs. Critics have asserted the United Nations is so weak that the United States should rely on power politics to protect its interests. They tend to view the United Nations as a nuisance dominated by smaller countries. Other critics are impatient because the United Nations has not been given enough military and political power to be a super-government. Both sets of critics do not recognize the nature of governing. There have been no governments in history with the absolute power to enforce international peace for more than a short period. Moreover, many powerful governments have been wracked by civil wars, and many governments are still faced with conflicts. Great Britain has its Irish rebellion. The Soviet Union, a superpower, could not mobilize force to hold together. The United States had its civil war and internal riots, and it does not automatically move federal troops in to enforce peace, but lets local and state officials act and waits for their requests before deciding whether or not to assist them. Successful governing depends mostly on compromise and on a process of building up respect for law and for the government that provides services. In a broad sense this applies also to the United Nations.

The use of power to enforce rulings of the United Nations is delegated primarily to the Security Council, which depends on unanimity of the five permanent members plus four of the remaining ten members. Like national governments, the Security Council negotiates with the parties and only as a last resort mobilizes force to try to enforce its rulings. It has had remarkable successes when the permanent members cooperate, and there have been disasters when those members acted outside the United Nations and international law.

Although pundits have given world opinion and economic sanctions little credit in the past, such nonmilitary measures had a major impact in crises discussed here. Mussolini was hurt by the League of Nations' economic sanctions, until the diplomats outside the League ended them. Japan's attack on Pearl Harbor was triggered by the pain of a U.S. oil embargo.[1] South Africa's reforms of apartheid reflected years of trade and political sanctions by the United Nations. UN sanctions against Iraq after the war forced it to open its installations to UN inspection. Sanctions caused pain in Libya and forced it to offer compromises on releasing men for trial for terrorism. Diplomacy, sanctions, and patience are more cost-effective in terms of lives and money than the impatient use of force. The United Nations was designed for moderate approaches before applying force.

The Security Council as envisaged in the Charter has been in the center of the action in world crises, but the other organs have also played important roles. The General Assembly has proven to be much more than a debating society. It is authorized to act when the Security Council cannot make a decision. It did this in crises such as the Korean War and the 1956 Suez War. Also, it has registered overwhelming world opinion against aggression in other cases including the Soviet attacks of Hungary, Czechoslovakia, and Afghanistan. Similarly, it has opposed apartheid and U.S. intervention in Panama and Nicaragua. If the world moves into a new order where there is respect for international law, the General Assembly will continue to show the way along with the Security Council. The General Assembly also approves the UN budget, authorizes actions of the Economic and Social Council, and endorses activities of UNDP, UNICEF, UNHCR, and other organs of the UN proper that promote social and economic development.

The United Nations has been served by able and dedicated secretaries general. The last two, Perez de Cuellar and Boutros Boutros-Ghali, seized the opportunities presented by the end of the Cold War to use the UN System for peacemaking. For example, Perez de Cuellar played a key role in mobilizing the United Nations to mediate the conflicts in Nicaragua and El Salvador and monitor the peace agreements. Similarly, he reinforced the efforts of the Southeast Asian countries to end conflicts in Cambodia. Both efforts were in the midst of rivalries of great powers supporting opposing sides. Boutros-Ghali in the first months of his office took a leading role in getting the UN to contain conflicts in Yugoslavia, after the European Community representatives failed. At the same time, he stood up to the great powers by insisting they not overlook the security and starvation crises in Somalia. The above major peacekeeping and monitoring efforts were mounted despite the huge budget deficit.

As the Cold War ended, the UN System led the world in the new era of reform and international cooperation. Gorbachev and then Yeltsin accepted the international law principles of nonintervention in the countries of Eastern Europe and then allowed self-determination for the republics of the Soviet Union. These nations moved rapidly to support democratic and then free market reforms, encouraged by the IMF and World Bank. A new era of cooperation between the United States and the Soviet Union (later Russia) allowed them to use the UN Security Council as intended for ending wars. The most dramatic was the Soviet and Chinese cooperation in the Security Council resolutions authorizing a coalition to defeat Iraq's aggression in Kuwait.

There was less public attention of their cooperation in using UN units to end Vietnam's aggression in Cambodia, the local wars in Angola and Namibia, the wars in Nicaragua and El Salvador, the Afghanistan war, and the Iran-Iraq war. In 1992 the Security Council extended the scope of Security Council actions to try to end civil wars in the former Yugoslavia.

Fear of a nuclear disaster, the burdens of the arms race, and the international dimension of threats to their countries' well-being brought world leaders to the UN System to solve problems. Even power brokers were enmeshed in the United Nations because international cooperation proved to be effective in addressing critical issues.

Secretary General Perez de Cuellar as head of the UN Secretariat played a key role during this turning point in history. In his farewell recommendations he did not propose a world federal government, but practical steps for strengthening the present UN System. Few doubt that the United Nations is here to stay, but there are many calls for reform. The following proposals of Secretary General Perez de Cuellar and his successor Boutros Boutros-Ghali indicate the potential for making the United Nations more effective.[2]

(1) Preventive Diplomacy. Perez de Cuellar noted the swift response of the Security Council to repel the invasion of Kuwait. However, he added that the devastation of two states with untold loss of innocent lives and the appalling dangers to public health reflected a startling failure of collective diplomacy and demonstrated the need for preventive diplomacy. The information available to the secretary general in advance of inter-

national crises had been wholly inadequate. He had no surveillance systems and inadequate field representation. He said the Secretariat needed more political offices abroad. In his report Perez de Cuellar also asked the General Assembly to give the secretary general authority to ask the International Court of Justice for rulings on issues, such as on the Iraq-Kuwait border dispute before the Gulf War.

(2) Human Rights. Perez de Cuellar believes protection of human rights is one of the "keystones in the arch of peace." He stated that sovereignty does not include the right of mass slaughter or forced exodus of civilian populations. However, he advocated caution in modifying established principles of state sovereignty in applying new doctrines to protect human rights. The use of force should be in proportion to the violations, and it should be nondiscriminatory. A few months after Perez de Cuellar left office his successor, Boutros-Ghali, moved forward without breaking stride to expand the scope of actions of the Security Council in trying to end ethnic conflicts of the Yugoslav civil war.

(3) Arms Control. To help reduce the instability and waste arising from military spending Perez de Cuellar suggested disclosure of details of the arms trade. This "transparency" of arms sales and trade would encourage voluntary restraints.

(4) Poverty. Perez de Cuellar proposed an international conference on financing development that would include measures for safeguarding the environment. He noted the heavy burden of unnecessary arms spending and that the developing countries themselves spent close to $200 billion annually on arms. He stated before the 1992 Conference on the Environment that it would be an important test of the willingness of governments to meet the threats to the world's environment.

It is interesting that Boutros-Ghali did not call for a standing, multinational UN force, under the control of the UN Security Council, as described in Article 47, which is first on the reform list of some supporters of the United Nations. He was realistic. President Bush would not have placed U.S. forces under a UN command in an operation like the Gulf War. It would not be feasible to obtain support for a UN military budget for the transport, engineering, and combat ability of a coalition force like that for Bosnia. Instead, Boutros-Ghali noted the wide variety of tasks of UN units and how the secretary general could improvise to obtain forces for particular jobs. His budget request was for special funds for emergencies to allow the Secretariat to respond more quickly to the many new tasks assigned to it.

Secretaries general in the past have stayed on a short leash, careful to check with the Security Council each step of the way. Even with their limited scope of action they have succeeded where other diplomats have failed. Perez de Cuellar's representative Cyrus Vance had limited success in the former Yugoslavia in attempts at a cease-fire in Croatia and Slovenia, after the European Commission failed. The United Nations needs the unqualified support of world leaders in order to accomplish their demands in a world lashed by nationalist, religious, ethnic storms. A corollary of this is for the world powers to give the secretary general more authority and an adequate budget.

The world still has many unresolved conflicts and economic and social problems. With the end of the Cold War and emergence of the United States as the remaining superpower, the old power politics and balance of power concepts have become obsolete. A new world order is being built on support for the United Nations and respect for international law. The world needs leaders to speak out frankly to encourage this. For the first time there is a realistic hope for achieving the UN Charter's goals "to save succeeding generations from the scourge of war," "to maintain "obligations . . . of international law," and "to promote social progress and better standards of life in larger freedom."

Notes to Chapter 11

1. A. Yoder, *World Politics and the Causes of War* (Boston: University Press of America, 1986), Chap. IV.

2. *UN Chronicle*, September 1992, pp. 2–4. Perez de Cuellar's proposals were an extension of preventive diplomacy beyond that suggested by Secretary General Hammarskjöld, who saw it as a means of settling disputes before they were escalated by the Cold War confrontation. Brian Urquart, *Hammarskjold* (New York: Harper & Row, 1972), pp. 256–257.

A. The Covenant of the League of Nations*

The High Contracting Parties

In order to promote international co-operation and to achieve international peace and security

by the acceptance of obligations not to resort to war,
by the prescription of open, just and honourable relations between nations,
by the firm establishment of the understandings of international law as the actual rule of conduct among Governments,
and by the maintenance of justice and a scrupulous respect for all treaty obligations in the dealings of organised peoples with one another,
Agree to this Covenant of the League of Nations.

Article 1

1. The original Members of the League of Nations shall be those of the Signatories which are named in the Annex to this Covenant and also such of those other States named in the Annex as shall accede without reservation to this Covenant. Such accession shall be effected by a Declaration deposited with the Secretariat within two months of the coming into force of the Covenant. Notice thereof shall be sent to all other Members of the League.

2. Any fully self-governing State, Dominion or Colony not named in the Annex may become a Member of the League if its admission is agreed to by two-thirds of the Assembly, provided that it shall give effective guarantees of its sincere intention to observe its international obligations, and shall accept such regulations as may be prescribed by the League in regard to its military, naval and air forces and armaments.

3. Any Member of the League may, after two years' notice of its intention so to do, withdraw from the League, provided that all its international obligations and all its obligations under this Covenant shall have been fulfilled at the time of its withdrawal.

---

*The texts printed in italics indicate amendments adopted by the League.

Article 2

The action of the League under this Covenant shall be effected through the instrumentality of an Assembly and of a Council, with a permanent Secretariat.

Article 3

1. The Assembly shall consist of Representatives of the Members of the League.

2. The Assembly shall meet at stated intervals and from time to time as occasion may require at the Seat of the League or at such other place as may be decided upon.

3. The Assembly may deal at its meetings with any matter within the sphere of action of the League or affecting the peace of the world.

4. At meetings of the Assembly, each Member of the League shall have one vote, and may have not more than three Representatives.

Article 4

1. The Council shall consist of Representatives of the Principal Allied and Associated Powers, together with Representatives of four other Members of the League. These four Members of the League shall be selected by the Assembly from time to time in its discretion. Until the appointment of the Representatives of the four Members of the League first selected by the Assembly, Representatives of Belgium, Brazil, Spain and Greece shall be Members of the Council.

2. With the approval of the majority of the Assembly, the Council may name additional Members of the League whose Representatives shall always be Members of the Council; the Council with like approval may increase the number of Members of the League to be selected by the Assembly for representation on the Council.

2. *bis. The Assembly shall fix by a two-thirds majority the rules dealing with the election of the non-permanent Members of the Council, and particularly such regulations as relate to their term of office and the conditions of re-eligiblity.*

3. The Council shall meet from time to time as occasion may require, and at least once a year, at the Seat of the League, or at such other place as may be decided upon.

4. The Council may deal at its meetings with any matter within the sphere of action of the League or affecting the peace of the world.

5. Any Member of the League not represented on the Council shall be invited to send a Representative to sit as a member at any meeting of the Council during the consideration of matters specially affecting the interests of that Member of the League.

6. At meetings of the Council, each Member of the League represented on the Council shall have one vote, and may have not more than one Representative.

Article 5

1. Except where otherwise expressly provided in this Covenant or by the terms of the present Treaty, decisions at any meeting of the Assembly or of the Council shall require the agreement of all the Members of the League represented at the meeting.

2. All matters of procedure at meetings of the Assembly or of the Council, including the appointment of Committees to investigate particular matters, shall be regulated by the Assembly or by the Council and may be decided by a majority of the Members of the League represented at the meeting.

3. The first meeting of the Assembly and the first meeting of the Council shall be summoned by the President of the United States of America.

Article 6

1. The permanent Secretariat shall be established at the Seat of the League. The Secretariat shall comprise a Secretary-General and such secretaries and staff as may be required.

2. The first Secretary-General shall be the person named in the Annex; thereafter the Secretary-General shall be appointed by the Council with the approval of the majority of the Assembly.

3. The secretaries and staff of the Secretariat shall be appointed by the Secretary-General with the approval of the Council.

4. The Secretary-General shall act in that capacity at all meetings of the Assembly and of the Council.

5. *The expenses of the League shall be borne by the Members of the League in the proportion decided by the Assembly.*

Article 7

1. The Seat of the League is established at Geneva.

2. The Council may at any time decide that the Seat of the League shall be established elsewhere.

3. All positions under or in connection with the League, including the Secretariat, shall be open equally to men and women.

4. Representatives of the Members of the League and officials of the League when engaged in the business of the League shall enjoy diplomatic privileges and immunities.

5. The buildings and other property occupied by the League or its officials or by Representatives attending its meetings shall be inviolable.

Article 8

1. The Members of the League recognise that the maintenance of peace requires the reduction of national armaments to the lowest point consistent with national safety and the enforcement by common action of international obligations.

2. The Council, taking account of the geographical situation and circumstances of each State, shall formulate plans for such reduction for the consideration and action of the several Governments.

3. Such plans shall be subject to reconsideration and revision at least every ten years.

4. After these plans have been adopted by the several Governments, the limits of armaments therein fixed shall not be exceeded without the concurrence of the Council.

5. The Members of the League agree that the manufacture by private enterprise of munitions and implements of war is open to grave objections. The Council shall advise how the evil effects attendant upon such manufacture can be prevented, due regard being had to the necessities of those Members of the League which are not able to manufacture the munitions and implements of war necessary for their safety.

6. The Members of the League undertake to interchange full and frank information as to the scale of their armaments, their military, naval and air programmes and the condition of such of their industries as are adaptable to warlike purposes.

Article 9

A permanent Commission shall be constituted to advise the Council on the execution of the provisions of Articles 1 and 8 and on military, naval and air questions generally.

Article 10

The Members of the League undertake to respect and preserve as against external aggression the territorial integrity and existing political independence of all Members of the League. In case of any such aggression or in case of any threat or danger of such aggression, the Council shall advise upon the means by which this obligation shall be fulfilled.

Article 11

1. Any war or threat of war, whether immediately affecting any of the Members of the League or not, is hereby declared a matter of concern to the whole

League, and the League shall take any action that may be deemed wise and effectual to safeguard the peace of nations. In case any such emergency should arise, the Secretary-General shall, on the request of any Member of the League, forthwith summon a meeting of the Council.

2. It is also declared to be the friendly right of each Member of the League to bring to the attention of the Assembly or of the Council any circumstance whatever affecting international relations which threatens to disturb international peace or the good understanding between nations upon which peace depends.

Article 12

1. The Members of the League agree that if there should arise between them any dispute likely to lead to a rupture they will submit the matter either to arbitration *or judicial settlement* or to enquiry by the Council, and they agree in no case to resort to war until three months after the award by the arbitrators *or the judicial decision* or the report by the Council.

2. In any case under this article the award of the arbitrators *or the judicial decision* shall be made within a reasonable time, and the report of the Council shall be made within six months after the submission of the dispute.

Article 13

1. The Members of the League agree that whenever any dispute shall arise between them which they recognise to be suitable for submission to arbitration *or judicial settlement*, and which cannot be satisfactorily settled by diplomacy, they will submit the whole subject-matter to arbitration *or judicial settlement.*

2. Disputes as to the interpretation of a treaty, as to any question of international law, as to the existence of any fact which, if established, would constitute a breach of any international obligation, or as to the extent and nature of the reparation to be made for any such breach, are declared to be among those which are generally suitable for submission to arbitration *or judicial settlement.*

3. *For the consideration of any such dispute, the court to which the case is referred shall be the Permanent Court of International Justice, established in accordance with Article 14, or any tribunal agreed on by the parties to the dispute or stipulated in any Convention existing between them.*

4. The Members of the League agree that they will carry out in full good faith any award *or decision* that may be rendered, and that they will not resort to war against a Member of the League which complies therewith. In the event of any failure to carry out such an award *or decision*, the Council shall propose what steps should be taken to give effect thereto.

Article 14

The Council shall formulate and submit to the Members of the League for adoption plans for the establishment of a Permanent Court of International Justice. The Court shall be competent to hear and determine any dispute of an international character which the parties thereto submit to it. The Court may also give an advisory opinion upon any disputed or question referred to it by the Council or by the Assembly.

Article 15

1. If there should arise between Members of the League any dispute likely to lead to a rupture, which is not submitted to arbitration *or judicial settlement* in accordance with Article 13, the Members of the League agree that they will submit the matter to the Council. Any party to the dispute may effect such submission by giving notice of the existence of the dispute to the Secretary-General, who will make all necessary arrangements for a full investigation and consideration thereof.

2. For this purpose, the parties to the dispute will communicate to the Secretary-General, as promptly as possible, statements of their case with all the relevant facts and papers, and the Council may forthwith direct the publication thereof.

3. The Council shall endeavour to effect a settlement of the dispute, and if such efforts are successful, a statement shall be made public giving such facts and explanations regarding the dispute and the terms of settlement thereof as the Council may deem appropriate.

4. If the dispute is not thus settled, the Council either unanimously or by a majority vote shall make and publish a report containing a statement of the facts of the dispute and the recommendations which are deemed just and proper in regard thereto.

5. Any Member of the League represented on the Council may make public a statement of the facts of the dispute and of its conclusions regarding the same.

6. If a report by the Council is unanimously agreed to by the members thereof other than the Representatives of one or more of the parties to the dispute, the Members of the League agree that they will not go to war with any party to the dispute which complies with the recommendations of the report.

7. If the Council fails to reach a report which is unanimously agreed to by the members thereof, other than the Representatives of one or more of the parties to the dispute, the Members of the League reserve to themselves the right to take such action as they shall consider necessary for the maintenance of right and justice.

8. If the dispute between the parties is claimed by one of them, and is found by the Council, to arise out of a matter which by international law is solely

within the domestic jurisdiction of that party, the Council shall so report, and shall make no recommendation as to its settlement.

9. The Council may in any case under this article refer the dispute to the Assembly. The dispute shall be so referred at the request of either party to the dispute provided that such request be made within fourteen days after the submission of the dispute to the Council.

10. In any case referred to the Assembly, all the provisions of this article and of Article 12 relating to the action and powers of the Council shall apply to the action and powers of the Assembly, provided that a report made by the Assembly, if concurred in by the Representatives of those Members of the League represented on the Council and of a majority of the other Members of the League, exclusive in each case of the Representatives of the parties to the dispute, shall have the same force as a report by the Council concurred in by all the members thereof other than the Representatives of one or more of the parties to the dispute.

Article 16

1. Should any Member of the League resort to war in disregard of its covenants under Articles 12, 13, or 15, it shall, *ipso facto*, be deemed to have committed an act of war against all other Members of the League, which hereby undertake immediately to subject it to the severance of all trade or financial relations, the prohibition of all intercourse between their nationals and the nationals of the Covenant-breaking State, and the prevention of all financial, commercial or personal intercourse between the nationals of the Covenant-breaking State and the nationals of any other State, whether a Member of the League or not.

2. It shall be the duty of the Council in such case to recommend to the several Governments concerned what effective military, naval or air force the Members of the League shall severally contribute to the armed forces to be used to protect the covenants of the League.

3. The Members of the League agree, further, that they will mutually support one another in the financial and economic measures which are taken under this article, in order to minimise the loss and inconvenience resulting from the above measures, and that they will mutually support one another in resisting any special measures aimed at one of their number by the Covenant-breaking State, and that they will take the necessary steps to afford passage through their territory to the forces of any of the Members of the League which are co-operating to protect the covenants of the League.

4. Any member of the League which has violated any covenant of the League may be declared to be no longer a Member of the League by a vote of the Council concurred in by the Representatives of all the other Members of the League represented thereon.

Article 17

1. In the event of a dispute between a Member of the League and a State which is not a member of the League or between States not members of the League, the State or States not members of the League shall be invited to accept the obligations of membership in the League for the purposes of such dispute, upon such conditions as the Council may deem just. If such invitation is accepted, the provisions of Article 12 to 16 inclusive shall be applied with such modifications as may be deemed necessary by the Council.

2. Upon such invitation being given, the Council shall immediately institute an enquiry into the circumstances of the dispute and recommend such action as may seem best and most effectual in the circumstances.

3. If a State so invited shall refuse to accept the obligations of membership in the League for the purposes of such dispute, and shall resort to war against a Member of the League, the provisions of Article 16 shall be applicable as against the State taking such action.

4. If both parties to the dispute when so invited refuse to accept the obligations of membership in the League for the purposes of such dispute, the Council may take such measures and make such recommendations as will prevent hostilities and will result in the settlement of the dispute.

Article 18

Every treaty or international engagement entered into hereafter by any Member of the League shall be forthwith registered with the Secretariat and shall, as soon as possible, be published by it. No such treaty or international engagement shall be binding until so registered.

Article 19

The Assembly may from time to time advise the reconsideration by Members of the League of treaties which have become inapplicable and the consideration of international conditions whose continuance might endanger the peace of the world.

Article 20

1. The Members of the League severally agree that this Covenant is accepted as abrogating all obligations or understandings *inter se* which are inconsistent with the terms thereof, and solemnly undertake that they will not hereafter enter into any engagements inconsistent with the terms thereof.

2. In case any Member of the League shall, before becoming a Member of the League, have undertaken any obligations inconsistent with the terms of this

Covenant, it shall be the duty of such Member to take immediate steps to procure its release from such obligations.

Article 21

Nothing in this Covenant shall be deemed to affect the validity of international engagements, such as treaties of arbitration or regional understandings like the Monroe doctrine, for securing the maintenance of peace.

Article 22

1. To those colonies and territories which as a consequence of the late war have ceased to be under the sovereignty of the States which formerly governed them and which are inhabited by peoples not yet able to stand by themselves under the strenuous conditions of the modern world, there should be applied the principle that the well-being and development of such peoples form a sacred trust of civilisation and that securities for the performance of this trust should be embodied in this Covenant.

2. The best method of giving practical effect to this principle is that the tutelage of such peoples should be entrusted to advanced nations who, by reason of their resources, their experience or their geographical position, can best undertake this responsibility, and who are willing to accept it, and that this tutelage should be exercised by them as Mandatories on behalf of the League.

3. The character of the mandate must differ according to the stage of the development of the people, the geographical situation of the territory, its economic conditions and other similar circumstances.

4. Certain communities formerly belonging to the Turkish Empire have reached a stage of development where their existence as independent nations can be provisionally recognised subject to the rendering of administrative advice and assistance by a Mandatory until such time as they are able to stand alone. The wishes of these communities must be a principal consideration in the selection of the Mandatory.

5. Other peoples, especially those of Central Africa, are at such a stage that the Mandatory must be responsible for the administration of the territory under conditions which will guarantee freedom of conscience and religion, subject only to the maintenance of public order and morals, the prohibition of abuses such as the slave trade, the arms traffic and the liquor traffic, and the prevention of the establishment of fortifications or military and naval bases and of military training of the natives for other than police purposes and the defence of territory, and will also secure equal opportunities for the trade and commerce of other Members of the League.

6. There are territories, such as South West Africa and certain of the South

Pacific Islands, which, owing to the sparseness of their population, or their small size, or their remoteness from the centres of civilisation, or their geographical contiguity to the territory of the Mandatory, and other circumstances, can be best administered under the laws of the Mandatory as integral portions of its territory, subject to the safeguards above mentioned in the interests of the indigenous population.

7. In every case of mandate, the Mandatory shall render to the Council an annual report in reference to the territory committed to its charge.

8. The degree of authority, control or administration to be exercised by the Mandatory shall, if not previously agreed upon by the Members of the League, be explicitly defined in each case by the Council.

9. A permanent Commission shall be constituted to receive and examine the annual reports of the Mandatories and to advise the Council on all matters relating to the observance of the mandates.

Article 23

Subject to and in accordance with the provisions of international Conventions existing or hereafter to be agreed upon, the Members of the League:

(a) will endeavour to secure and maintain fair and humane conditions of labour for men, women and children, both in their own countries and in all countries to which their commercial and industrial relations extend, and for that purpose will establish and maintain the necessary international organisations;

(b) undertake to secure just treatment of the native inhabitants of territories under their control;

(c) will entrust the League with the general supervision over the execution of agreements with regard to the traffic in women and children, and the traffic in opium and other dangerous drugs;

(d) will entrust the League with the general supervision of the trade in arms and ammunition with the countries in which the control of this traffic is necessary in the common interest;

(e) will make provision to secure and maintain freedom of communications and of transit and equitable treatment for the commerce of all Members of the League. In this connection, the special necessities of the regions devastated during the war of 1914-1918 shall be borne in mind;

(f) will endeavour to take steps in matters of international concern for the prevention and control of disease.

Article 24

1. There shall be placed under the direction of the League all international bureaux already established by general treaties if the parties to such treaties

consent. All such international bureaux and all commissions for the regulation of matters of international interest hereafter constituted shall be placed under the direction of the League.

2. In all matters of international interest which are regulated by general Conventions but which are not placed under the control of international bureaux or commissions, the Secretariat of the League shall, subject to the consent of the Council and if desired by the parties, collect and distribute all relevant information and shall render any other assistance which may be necessary or desirable.

3. The Council may include as part of the expenses of the Secretariat the expenses of any bureau or commission which is placed under the direction of the League.

Article 25

The Members of the League agree to encourage and promote the establishment and co-operation of duly authorised voluntary national Red Cross organisations having as purposes the improvement of health, the prevention of disease and the mitigation of suffering throughout the world.

Article 26

1. Amendments to this Covenant will take effect when ratified by the Members of the League whose Representatives compose the Council and by a majority of the Members of the League whose Representatives compose the Assembly.

2. No such amendments shall bind any Member of the League which signifies its dissent therefrom, but in that case it shall cease to be a Member of the League.

B. The Charter of the United Nations*

We the peoples of the United Nations determined

to save succeeding generations from the scourge of war, which twice in our lifetime has brought untold sorrow to mankind, and to reaffirm faith in fundamental human rights, in the dignity and worth of the human person, in the equal rights of men and women and of nations large and small, and

to establish conditions under which justice and respect for the obligations arising from treaties and other sources of international law can be maintained, and

to promote social progress and better standards of life in larger freedom, and for these ends

to practice tolerance and live together in peace with one another as good neighbors, and

to unite our strength to maintain international peace and security, and

to ensure, by the acceptance of principles and the institution of methods, that armed force shall not be used, save in the common interest, and

to employ international machinery for the promotion of the economic and social advancement of all peoples,

have resolved to combine our efforts to accomplish these aims.

Accordingly, our respective Governments, through representatives assembled in the city of San Francisco, who have exhibited their full powers found to be in good and due form, have agreed to the present Charter of the United Nations and do hereby establish an international organization to be known as the United Nations.

CHAPTER I. PURPOSES AND PRINCIPLES

Article 1

The Purposes of the United Nations are:

1. To maintain international peace and security, and to that end: to take

---

*Articles 23, 27, and 61 were revised by amendments, proposed by the General Assembly in its Resolution 1991 A & B (XVIII) of December 17, 1963, which entered into force on August 31, 1965. Article 109 was amended by a process that began with General Assembly Resolution 2101 (XX) of December 20, 1965, and was concluded on June 12, 1968.

In these articles, portions deleted by amendment are enclosed in parentheses and new provisions are printed in italics.

effective collective measures for the prevention and removal of threats to the peace, and for the suppression of acts of aggression or other breaches of the peace, and to bring about by peaceful means, and in conformity with the principles of justice and international law, adjustment or settlement of international disputes or situations which might lead to a breach of the peace;

2. To develop friendly relations among nations based on respect for the principle of equal rights and self-determination of peoples, and to take other appropriate measures to strengthen universal peace;

3. To achieve international cooperation in solving international problems of an economic, social, cultural, or humanitarian character, and in promoting and encouraging respect for human rights and for fundamental freedoms for all without distinction as to race, sex, language, or religion; and

4. To be a center for harmonizing the actions of nations in the attainment of these common ends.

Article 2

The Organization and its Members, in pursuit of the Purposes stated in Article 1, shall act in accordance with the following Principles.

1. The Organization is based on the principle of the sovereign equality of all its Members.

2. All Members, in order to ensure to all of them the rights and benefits resulting from membership, shall fulfill in good faith the obligations assumed by them in accordance with the present Charter.

3. All Members shall settle their international disputes by peaceful means in such a manner that international peace and security, and justice, are not endangered.

4. All Members shall refrain in their international relations from the threat or use of force against the territorial integrity or political independence of any state, or in any other manner inconsistent with the Purposes of the United Nations.

5. All Members shall give the United Nations every assistance in any action it takes in accordance with the present Charter, and shall refrain from giving assistance to any state against which the United Nations is taking preventive or enforcement action.

6. The Organization shall ensure that states which are not Members of the United Nations act in accordance with these Principles so far as may be necessary for the maintenance of international peace and security.

7. Nothing contained in the present Charter shall authorize the United Nations to intervene in matters which are essentially within the domestic jurisdiction of any state or shall require the Members to submit such matters to settlement under the present Charter; but this principle shall not prejudice the application of enforcement measures under Chapter VII.

CHAPTER II. MEMBERSHIP

Article 3

The original Members of the United Nations shall be the states which, having participated in the United Nations Conference on International Organization at San Francisco, or having previously signed the Declaration by United Nations of January 1, 1942, sign the present Charter and ratify it in accordance with Article 110.

Article 4

1. Membership in the United Nations is open to all other peace-loving states which accept the obligations contained in the present Charter and, in the judgment of the Organization, are able and willing to carry out these obligations.

2. The admission of any such state to membership in the United Nations will be effected by a decision of the General Assembly upon the recommendation of the Security Council.

Article 5

A Member of the United Nations against which preventive or enforcement action has been taken by the Security Council may be suspended from the exercise of the rights and privileges of membership by the General Assembly upon the recommendation of the Security Council. The exercise of these rights and privileges may be restored by the Security Council.

Article 6

A Member of the United Nations which has persistently violated the Principles contained in the present Charter may be expelled from the Organization by the General Assembly upon the recommendation of the Security Council.

CHAPTER III. ORGANS

Article 7

1. There are established as the principal organs of the United Nations: a General Assembly, a Security Council, an Economic and Social Council, a Trusteeship Council, an International Court of Justice, and a Secretariat.

2. Such subsidiary organs as may be found necessary may be established in accordance with the present Charter.

Article 8

The United Nations shall place no restrictions on the eligibility of men and women to participate in any capacity and under conditions of equality in its principal and subsidiary organs.

CHAPTER IV. THE GENERAL ASSEMBLY

Composition

Article 9

1. The General Assembly shall consist of all the Members of the United Nations.

2. Each Member shall have not more than five representatives in the General Assembly.

Functions and Powers

Article 10

The General Assembly may discuss any questions or any matters within the scope of the present Charter or relating to the powers and functions of any organs provided for in the present Charter, and, except as provided in Article 12, may make recommendations to the Members of the United Nations or to the Security Council or to both on any such questions or matters.

Article 11

1. The General Assembly may consider the general principles of cooperation in the maintenance of international peace and security, including the principles governing disarmament and the regulation of armaments, and may make recommendations with regard to such principles to the Members or to the Security Council or to both.

2. The General Assembly may discuss any questions relating to the maintenance of international peace and security brought before it by any Member of the United Nations, or by the Security Council, or by a state which is not a Member of the United Nations in accordance with Article 35, paragraph 2, and, except as provided in Article 12, may make recommendations with regard to any such questions to the state or states concerned or to the Security Council or to both. Any such question on which action is necessary shall be referred to the Security Council by the General Assembly either before or after discussion.

3. The General Assembly may call the attention of the Security Council to situations which are likely to endanger international peace and security.

4. The powers of the General Assembly set forth in this Article shall not limit the general scope of Article 10.

Article 12

1. While the Security Council is exercising in respect of any dispute or situation the functions assigned to it in the present Charter, the General Assembly shall not make any recommendations with regard to that dispute or situation unless the Security Council so requests.

2. The Secretary-General, with the consent of the Security Council, shall notify the General Assembly at each session of any matters relative to the maintenance of international peace and security which are being dealt with by the Security Council and shall similarly notify the General Assembly, or the Members of the United Nations if the General Assembly is not in session, immediately the Security Council ceases to deal with such matters.

Article 13

1. The General Assembly shall initiate studies and make recommendations for the purpose of:

a. promoting international cooperation in the political field and encouraging the progressive development of international law and its codification;

b. promoting international cooperation in the economic, social, cultural, educational, and health fields, and assisting in the realization of human rights and fundamental freedoms for all without distinction as to race, sex, language, or religion.

2. The further responsibilities, functions, and powers of the General Assembly with respect to matters mentioned in paragraph 1 (b) above are set forth in Chapters IX and X.

Article 14

Subject to the provisions of Article 12, the General Assembly may recommend measures for the peaceful adjustment of any situation, regardless of origin, which it deems likely to impair the general welfare or friendly relations among nations, including situations resulting from a violation of the provisions of the present Charter setting forth the Purposes and Principles of the United Nations.

Article 15

1. The General Assembly shall receive and consider annual and special reports from the Security Council; these reports shall include an account of the

measures that the Security Council has decided upon or taken to maintain international peace and security.

2. The General Assembly shall receive and consider reports from the other organs of the United Nations.

Article 16

The General Assembly shall perform such functions with respect to the international trusteeship system as are assigned to it under Chapters XII and XIII, including the approval of the trusteeship agreements for areas not designated as strategic.

Article 17

1. The General Assembly shall consider and approve the budget of the Organization.

2. The expenses of the Organization shall be borne by the Members as apportioned by the General Assembly.

3. The General Assembly shall consider and approve any financial and budgetary arrangements with specialized agencies referred to in Article 57 and shall examine the administrative budgets of such specialized agencies with a view to making recommendations to the agencies concerned.

Voting

Article 18

1. Each member of the General Assembly shall have one vote.

2. Decisions of the General Assembly on important questions shall be made by a two-thirds majority of the members present and voting. These questions shall include: recommendations with respect to the maintenance of international peace and security, the election of the non-permanent members of the Security Council, the election of the members of the Economic and Social Council, the election of members of the Trusteeship Council in accordance with paragraph 1 (c) of Article 86, the admission of new Members to the United Nations, the suspension of the rights and privileges of membership, the expulsion of Members, questions relating to the operation of the trusteeship system, and budgetary questions.

3. Decisions on other questions, including the determination of additional categories of questions to be decided by a two-thirds majority, shall be made by a majority of the members present and voting.

Article 19

A Member of the United Nations which is in arrears in the payment of its financial contributions to the Organization shall have no vote in the General

Assembly if the amount of its arrears equals or exceeds the amount of the contributions due from it for the preceding two full years. The General Assembly may, nevertheless, permit such a Member to vote if it is satisfied that the failure to pay is due to conditions beyond the control of the Member.

Procedure

Article 20

The General Assembly shall meet in regular annual sessions and in such special sessions as occasion may require. Special sessions shall be convoked by the Secretary-General at the request of the Security Council or of a majority of the Members of the United Nations.

Article 21

The General Assembly shall adopt its own rules of procedure. It shall elect its President for each session.

Article 22

The General Assembly may establish such subsidiary organs as it deems necessary for the performance of its functions.

CHAPTER V. THE SECURITY COUNCIL

Composition

Article 23

1. The Security Council shall consist of (eleven) *fifteen* Members of the United Nations. The Republic of China, France, the Union of Soviet Socialist Republics, the United Kingdom of Great Britain and Northern Ireland, and the United States of America shall be permanent members of the Security Council. The General Assembly shall elect (six) *ten* other Members of the United Nations to be non-permanent members of the Security Council, due regard being specially paid, in the first instance to the contribution of Members of the United Nations to the maintenance of international peace and security and to the other purposes of the Organization, and also to equitable geographical distribution.

2. The non-permanent members of the Security Council shall be elected for a term of two years. In the first election of the non-permanent members (however, three shall be chosen for a term of one year) *after the increase of the member-*

ship of the Security Council from eleven to fifteen, two of the four additional members shall be chosen for a term of one year. A retiring member shall not be eligible for immediate re-election.

3. Each member of the Security Council shall have one representative.

Functions and Powers

Article 24

1. In order to ensure prompt and effective action by the United Nations, its Members confer on the Security Council primary responsibility for the maintenance of international peace and security, and agree that in carrying out its duties under this responsibility the Security Council acts on their behalf.

2. In discharging these duties the Security Council shall act in accordance with the Purposes and Principles of the United Nations. The specific powers granted to the Security Council for the discharge of these duties are laid down in Chapters VI, VII, VIII, and XII.

3. The Security Council shall submit annual and, when necessary, special reports to the General Assembly for its consideration.

Article 25

The Members of the United Nations agree to accept and carry out the decisions of the Security Council in accordance with the present Charter.

Article 26

In order to promote the establishment and maintenance of international peace and security with the least diversion for armaments of the world's human and economic resources, the Security Council shall be responsible for formulating, with the assistance of the Military Staff Committee referred to in Article 47, plans to be submitted to the Members of the United Nations for the establishment of a system for the regulation of armaments.

Voting

Article 27

1. Each member of the Security Council shall have one vote.

2. Decisions of the Security Council on procedural matters shall be made by an affirmative vote of (seven) *nine* members.

3. Decisions of the Security Council on all other matters shall be made by an

affirmative vote of (seven) *nine* members including the concurring votes of the permanent members; provided that, in decisions under Chapter VI, and under paragraph 3 of Article 52, a party to a dispute shall abstain from voting.

Procedure

Article 28

1. The Security Council shall be so organized as to be able to function continuously. Each member of the Security Council shall for this purpose be represented at all times at the seat of the Organization.

2. The Security Council shall hold periodic meetings at which each of its members may, if it so desires, be represented by a member of the government or by some other specially designated representative.

3. The Security Council may hold meetings at such places other than the seat of the Organization as in its judgment will best facilitate its work.

Article 29

The Security Council may establish such subsidiary organs as it deems necessary for the performance of its functions.

Article 30

The Security Council shall adopt its own rules of procedure, including the method of selecting its President.

Article 31

Any Member of the United Nations which is not a member of the Security Council may participate, without vote, in the discussion of any question brought before the Security Council whenever the latter considers that the interests of that Member are specially affected.

Article 32

Any Member of the United Nations which is not a member of the Security Council or any state which is not a Member of the United Nations, if it is a party to a dispute under consideration by the Security Council, shall be invited to participate, without vote, in the discussion relating to the dispute. The Security Council shall lay down such conditions as it deems just for the participation of a state which is not a Member of the United Nations.

CHAPTER VI. PACIFIC SETTLEMENT OF DISPUTES

Article 33

1. The parties to any dispute, the continuance of which is likely to endanger the maintenance of international peace and security, shall, first of all, seek a solution by negotiation, enquiry, mediation, conciliation, arbitration, judicial settlement, resort to regional agencies or arrangements, or other peaceful means of their own choice.

2. The Security Council shall, when it deems necessary, call upon the parties to settle their dispute by such means.

Article 34

The Security Council may investigate any dispute, or any situation which might lead to international friction or give rise to a dispute, in order to determine whether the continuance of the dispute or situation is likely to endanger the maintenance of international peace and security.

Article 35

1. Any Member of the United Nations may bring any dispute, or any situation of the nature referred to in Article 34, to the attention of the Security Council or of the General Assembly.

2. A state which is not a Member of the United Nations may bring to the attention of the Security Council or of the General Assembly any dispute to which it is a party if it accepts in advance, for the purposes of the dispute, the obligations of pacific settlement provided in the present Charter.

3. The proceedings of the General Assembly in respect of matters brought to its attention under this Article will be subject to the provisions of Articles 11 and 12.

Article 36

1. The Security Council may, at any stage of a dispute of the nature referred to in Article 33 or of a situation of like nature, recommend appropriate procedures or methods of adjustment.

2. The Security Council should take into consideration any procedures for the settlement of the dispute which have already been adopted by the parties.

3. In making recommendations under this Article the Security Council should also take into consideration that legal disputes should as a general rule be referred by the parties to the International Court of Justice in accordance with the provisions of the Statute of the Court.

Article 37

1. Should the parties to a dispute of the nature referred to in Article 33 fail to settle it by the means indicated in that Article, they shall refer it to the Security Council.

2. If the Security Council deems that the continuance of the dispute is in fact likely to endanger the maintenance of international peace and security, it shall decide whether to take action under Article 36 or to recommend such terms of settlement as it may consider appropriate.

Article 38

Without prejudice to the provisions of Articles 33 to 37, the Security Council may, if all the parties to any dispute so request, make recommendations to the parties with a view to a pacific settlement of the dispute.

CHAPTER VII. ACTION WITH RESPECT TO THREATS TO THE PEACE, BREACHES OF THE PEACE, PEACE, AND ACTS OF AGGRESSION

Article 39

The Security Council shall determine the existence of any threat to the peace, breach of the peace, or act of aggression and shall make recommendations, or decide what measures shall be taken in accordance with Articles 41 and 42, to maintain or restore international peace and security.

Article 40

In order to prevent an aggravation of the situation, the Security Council may, before making the recommendations or deciding upon the measures provided for in Article 39, call upon the parties concerned to comply with such provisional measures at it deems necessary or desirable. Such provisional measures shall be without prejudice to the rights, claims, or position of the parties concerned. The Security Council shall duly take account of failure to comply with such provisional measures.

Article 41

The Security Council may decide what measures not involving the use of armed force are to be employed to give effect to its decisions, and it may call upon the Members of the United Nations to apply such measures. These may include complete or partial interruption of economic relations and of rail, sea, air, postal, telegraphic, radio, and other means of communication, and the severance of diplomatic relations.

Article 42

Should the Security Council consider that measures provided for in Article 41 would be inadequate or have proved to be inadequate, it may take such action by air, sea, or land forces as may be necessary to maintain or restore international peace and security. Such action may include demonstrations, blockade, and other operations by air, sea, or land forces of Members of the United Nations.

Article 43

1. All Members of the United Nations, in order to contribute to the maintenance of international peace and security, undertake to make available to the Security Council, on its call and in accordance with a special agreement or agreements, armed forces, assistance, and facilities, including rights of passage, necessary for the purpose of maintaining international peace and security.

2. Such agreement or agreements shall govern the numbers and types of forces, their degree of readiness and general location, and the nature of the facilities and assistance to be provided.

3. The agreement or agreements shall be negotiated as soon as possible on the initiative of the Security Council. They shall be concluded between the Security Council and Members or between the Security Council and groups of Members and shall be subject to ratification by the signatory states in accordance with their respective constitutional processes.

Article 44

When the Security Council has decided to use force it shall, before calling upon a Member not represented on it to provide armed forces in fulfillment of the obligations assumed under Article 43, invite that Member, if the Member so desires, to participate in the decisions of the Security Council concerning the employment of contingents of that Member's armed forces.

Article 45

In order to enable the United Nations to take urgent military measures, Members shall hold immediately available national air-force contingents for combined international enforcement action. The strength and degree of readiness of these contingents and plans for their combined action shall be determined, within the limits laid down in the special agreement or agreements referred to in Article 43, by the Security Council with the assistance of the Military Staff Committee.

Article 46

Plans for the application of armed force shall be made by the Security Council with the assistance of the Military Staff Committee.

Article 47

1. There shall be established a Military Staff Committee to advise and assist the Security Council on all questions relating to the Security Council's military requirements for the maintenance of international peace and security, the employment and command of forces placed at its disposal, the regulation of armaments, and possible disarmament.

2. The Military Staff Committee shall consist of the Chiefs of Staff of the permanent members of the Security Council or their representatives. Any Member of the United Nations not permanently represented on the Committee shall be invited by the Committee to be associated with it when the efficient discharge of the Committee's responsibilities requires the participation of that Member in its work.

3. The Military Staff Committee shall be responsible under the Security Council for the strategic direction of any armed forces placed at the disposal of the Security Council. Questions relating to the command of such forces shall be worked out subsequently.

4. The Military Staff Committee, with the authorization of the Security Council and after consultation with appropriate regional agencies, may establish regional subcommittees.

Article 48

1. The action required to carry out the decisions of the Security Council for the maintenance of international peace and security shall be taken by all the Members of the United Nations or by some of them, as the Security Council may determine.

2. Such decisions shall be carried out by the Members of the United Nations directly and through their action in the appropriate international agencies of which they are members.

Article 49

The Members of the United Nations shall join in affording mutual assistance in carrying out the measures decided upon by the Security Council.

Article 50

If preventive or enforcement measures against any state are taken by the Security Council, any other state, whether a Member of the United Nations or not, which finds itself confronted with special economic problems arising from the carrying out of those measures shall have the right to consult the Security Council with regard to a solution of those problems.

Article 51

Nothing in the present Charter shall impair the inherent right of individual or collective self-defense if an armed attack occurs against a Member of the United Nations, until the Security Council has taken the measures necessary to maintain international peace and security. Measures taken by Members in the exercise of this right of self-defense shall be immediately reported to the Security Council and shall not in any way affect the authority and responsibility of the Security Council under the present Charter to take at any time such action as it deems necessary in order to maintain or restore international peace and security.

CHAPTER VIII. REGIONAL ARRANGEMENTS

Article 52

1. Nothing in the present Charter precludes the existence of regional arrangements or agencies for dealing with such matters relating to the maintenance of international peace and security as are appropriate for regional action, provided that such arrangements or agencies and their activities are consistent with the Purposes and Principles of the United Nations.

2. The Members of the United Nations entering into such arrangements or constituting such agencies shall make every effort to achieve pacific settlement of local disputes through such regional arrangements or by such regional agencies before referring them to the Security Council.

3. The Security Council shall encourage the development of pacific settlement of local disputes through such regional arrangements or by such regional agencies either on the initiative of the states concerned or by reference from the Security Council.

4. This Article in no way impairs the application of Articles 34 and 35.

Article 53

1. The Security Council shall, where appropriate, utilize such regional arrangements or agencies for enforcement action under its authority. But no enforcement action shall be taken under regional arrangements or by regional agencies without the authorization of the Security Council, with the exception of measures against any enemy state, as defined in paragraph 2 of this Article, provided for pursuant to Article 107 or in regional arrangements directed against renewal of aggressive policy on the part of any such state, until such time as the

Organization may, on request of the Governments concerned, be charged with the responsibility for preventing further aggression by such a state.

2. The term enemy state as used in paragraph 1 of this Article applies to any state which during the Second World War has been an enemy of any signatory of the present Charter.

Article 54

The Security Council shall at all times be kept fully informed of activities undertaken or in contemplation under regional arrangements or by regional agencies for the maintenance of international peace and security.

CHAPTER IX. INTERNATIONAL ECONOMIC AND SOCIAL COOPERATION

Article 55

With a view to the creation of conditions of stability and well-being which are necessary for peaceful and friendly relations among nations based on respect for the principle of equal rights and self-determination of peoples, the United Nations shall promote:

a. higher standards of living, full employment, and conditions of economic and social progress and development;

b. solutions of international economic, social health, and related problems; and international cultural and educational cooperation; and

c. universal respect for, and observance of, human rights and fundamental freedoms for all without distinction as to race, sex, language, or religion.

Article 56

All Members pledge themselves to take joint and separate action in cooperation with the Organization for the achievement of the purposes set forth in Article 55.

Article 57

1. The various specialized agencies, established by intergovernmental agreement and having wide international responsibilities, as defined in their basic instruments, in economic, social, cultural, educational, health, and related fields, shall be brought into relationship with the United Nations in accordance with the provisions of Article 63.

2. Such agencies thus brought into relationship with the United Nations are hereinafter referred to as specialized agencies.

Article 58

The Organization shall make recommendations for the coordination of the policies and activities of the specialized agencies.

Article 59

The Organization shall, where appropriate, initiate negotiations among the states concerned for the creation of any new specialized agencies required for the accomplishment of the purposes set forth in Article 55.

Article 60

Responsibility for the discharge of the functions of the Organization set forth in this Chapter shall be vested in the General Assembly and, under the authority of the General Assembly, in the Economic and Social Council, which shall have for this purpose the powers set forth in Chapter X.

CHAPTER X. THE ECONOMIC AND SOCIAL COUNCIL

Composition

Article 61

1. The Economic and Social Council shall consist of (eighteen) *fifty-four* Members of the United Nations elected by the General Assembly.

2. Subject to the provisions of paragraph 3, (six) *nine* members of the Economic and Social Council shall be elected each year for a term of three years. A retiring member shall be eligible for immediate re-election.

3. At the first election *after the increase in the membership of the Economic and Social Council from twenty-seven to fifty-four members, in addition to the members elected in place of the nine members whose term of office expires at the end of that year, twenty-seven additional members shall be elected. Of these twenty-seven additional members, the term of office of nine members so elected shall expire at the end of one year, and of nine other members at the end of two years*, in accordance with arrangements made by the General Assembly.

4. Each member of the Economic and Social Council shall have one representative.

Functions and Powers

Article 62

1. The Economic and Social Council may make or initiate studies and reports with respect to international economic, social, cultural, educational, health, and related matters and may make recommendations with respect to any such matters to the General Assembly, to the Members of the United Nations, and to the specialized agencies concerned.

2. It may make recommendations for the purpose of promoting respect for, and observance of, human rights and fundamental freedoms for all.

3. It may prepare draft conventions for submission to the General Assembly, with respect to matters falling within its competence.

4. It may call, in accordance with the rules prescribed by the United Nations, international conferences on matters falling within its competence.

Article 63

1. The Economic and Social Council may enter into agreements with any of the agencies referred to in Article 57, defining the terms on which the agency concerned shall be brought into relationship with the United Nations. Such agreements shall be subject to approval by the General Assembly.

2. It may coordinate the activities of the specialized agencies through consultation with and recommendations to such agencies and through recommendations to the General Assembly and to the Members of the United Nations.

Article 64

1. The Economic and Social Council may take appropriate steps to obtain regular reports from the specialized agencies. It may make arrangements with the Members of the United Nations and with the specialized agencies to obtain reports on the steps taken to give effect to its own recommendations and to recommendations on matters falling within its competence made by the General Assembly.

2. It may communicate its observations on these reports to the General Assembly.

Article 65

The Economic and Social Council may furnish information to the Security Council and shall assist the Security Council upon its request.

Article 66

1. The Economic and Social Council shall perform such functions as fall within its competence in connection with the carrying out of the recommendations of the General Assembly.

2. It may, with the approval of the General Assembly, perform services at the request of Members of the United Nations and at the request of specialized agencies.

3. It shall perform such other functions as are specified elsewhere in the present Charter or as may be assigned to it by the General Assembly.

Voting

Article 67

1. Each member of the Economic and Social Council shall have one vote.

2. Decisions of the Economic and Social Council shall be made by a majority of the members present and voting.

Procedure

Article 68

The Economic and Social Council shall set up commissions in economic and social fields and for the promotion of human rights, and such other commissions as may be required for the performance of its functions.

Article 69

The Economic and Social Council shall invite any Member of the United Nations to participate, without vote, in its deliberations on any matter of particular concern to that Member.

Article 70

The Economic and Social Council may make arrangements for representatives of the specialized agencies to participate, without vote, in its deliberations and in those of the commissions established by it, and for its representatives to participate in the deliberations of the specialized agencies.

Article 71

The Economic and Social Council may make suitable arrangements for consultation with non-governmental organizations which are concerned with matters within its competence. Such arrangements may be made with international organizations and, where appropriate, with national organizations after consultation with the Member of the United Nations concerned.

Article 72

1. The Economic and Social Council shall adopt its own rules of procedure, including the method of selecting its President.

2. The Economic and Social Council shall meet as required in accordance with its rules, which shall include provision for the convening of meetings on the request of a majority of its members.

CHAPTER XI. DECLARATION REGARDING NON-SELF-GOVERNING TERRITORIES

Article 73

Members of the United Nations which have or assume responsibilities for the administration of territories whose peoples have not yet attained a full measure of self-government recognize the principle that the interests of the inhabitants of these territories are paramount, and accept as a sacred trust the obligation to promote to the utmost, within the system of international peace and security established by the present Charter, the well-being of the inhabitants of these territories, and, to this end:

a. to ensure, with due respect for the culture of the peoples concerned, their political, economic, social, and educational advancement, their just treatment, and their protection against abuses;

b. to develop self-government, to take due account of the political aspirations of the peoples, and to assist them in the progressive development of their free political institutions, according to the particular circumstances of each territory and its peoples and their varying stages of advancement;

c. to further international peace and security;

d. to promote constructive measures of development, to encourage research, and to cooperate with one another, and, when and where appropriate, with specialized international bodies with a view to the practical achievement of the social, economic, and scientific purposes set forth in this Article; and

e. to transmit regularly to the Secretary-General for information purposes, subject to such limitation as security and constitutional considerations may require, statistical and other information of a technical nature relating to economic, social, and educational conditions in the territories for which they are respectively responsible other than those territories to which Chapters XII and XIII apply.

Article 74

Members of the United Nations also agree that their policy in respect of the territories to which this Chapter applies, no less than in respect of their metropolitan areas, must be based on the general principle of good-neighborliness, due account being taken of the interests and well-being of the rest of the world, in social, economic, and commercial matters.

CHAPTER XII. INTERNATIONAL TRUSTEESHIP SYSTEM

Article 75

The United Nations shall establish under its authority an international trusteeship system for the administration and supervision of such territories as may be placed thereunder by subsequent individual agreements. These territories are hereinafter referred to as trust territories.

Article 76

The basic objectives of the trusteeship system, in accordance with the Purposes of the United Nations laid down in Article 1 of the present Charter, shall be:

a. to further international peace and security;

b. to promote the political, economic, social, and educational advancement of the inhabitants of the trust territories, and their progressive development towards self-government or independence as may be appropriate to the particular circumstances of each territory and its peoples and the freely expressed wishes of the people concerned, and as may be provided by the terms of each trusteeship agreement;

c. to encourage respect for human rights and for fundamental freedoms for all without distinction as to race, sex, language, and to encourage recognition of the interdependence of the peoples of the world; and

d. to ensure equal treatment in social, economic, and commercial matters for all Members of the United Nations and their nationals, and also equal treatment for the latter in the administration of justice, without prejudice to the attainment of the foregoing objectives and subject to the provisions of Article 80.

Article 77

1. The trusteeship system shall apply to such territories in the following categories as may be placed thereunder by means of trusteeship agreements:

a. territories now held under mandate;

b. territories which may be detached from enemy states as a result of the Second World War; and

c. territories voluntarily placed under the system by states responsible for their administration.

2. It will be a matter for subsequent agreement as to which territories in the foregoing categories will be brought under the trusteeship system and upon what terms.

Article 78

The trusteeship system shall not apply to territories which have become Members of the United Nations, relationship among which shall be based on respect for the principle of sovereign equality.

Article 79

The terms of trusteeship for each territory to be placed under the trusteeship system, including any alteration or amendments, shall be agreed upon by the states directly concerned, including the mandatory power in the case of territories held under mandate by a Member of the United Nations, and shall be approved as provided for in Article 83 and 85.

Article 80

1. Except as may be agreed upon in individual trusteeship agreements, made under Articles 77, 79, and 81, placing each territory under the trusteeship system, and until such agreements have been concluded, nothing in this Chapter shall be construed in or of itself to alter in any manner the rights whatsoever of any states or any peoples or the terms of existing international instruments to which Members of the United Nations may respectively be parties.

2. Paragraph 1 of this Article shall not be interpreted as giving grounds for delay or postponement of the negotiation and conclusion of agreements for placing mandated and other territories under the trusteeship system as provided for in Article 77.

Article 81

The trusteeship agreement shall in each case include the terms under which the trust territory will be administered and designate the authority which will exercise the administration of the trust territory. Such authority, hereinafter called the administering authority, may be one or more states or the Organization itself.

Article 82

There may be designated, in any trusteeship agreement, a strategic area or areas which may include part or all of the trust territory to which the agreement applies, without prejudice to any special agreement or agreements made under Article 43.

Article 83

1. All functions of the United Nations relating to strategic areas, including the approval of the terms of the trusteeship agreement and of their alteration or amendment, shall be exercised by the Security Council.

2. The basic objectives set forth in Article 76 shall be applicable to the people of each strategic area.

3. The Security Council shall, subject to the provisions of the trusteeship agreements and without prejudice to security considerations, avail itself of the assistance of the Trusteeship Council to perform those functions of the United Nations under the trusteeship system relating to political, economic, social, and educational matters in the strategic areas.

Article 84

It shall be the duty of the administering authority to ensure that the trust territory shall play its part in the maintenance of international peace and security. To this end the administering authority may make use of volunteer forces, facilities, and assistance from the trust territory in carrying out the obligations towards the Security Council undertaken in this regard by the administering authority, as well as for local defense and the maintenance of law and order within the trust territory.

Article 85

1. The functions of the United Nations with regard to trusteeship agreements for all areas not designated as strategic, including the approval of the terms of the trusteeship agreements and of their alteration or amendment, shall be exercised by the General Assembly.

2. The Trusteeship Council, operating under the authority of the General Assembly, shall assist the General Assembly in carrying out these functions.

CHAPTER XIII. THE TRUSTEESHIP COUNCIL

Composition

Article 86

1. The Trusteeship Council shall consist of the following Members of the United Nations:

a. those Members administering trust territories;

b. such of those Members mentioned by name in Article 23 as are not administering trusts territories; and

c. as many other Members elected for three-year terms by the General Assembly as may be necessary to ensure that the total number of members of the Trusteeship Council is equally divided between those Members of the United Nations which administer trust territories and those which do not.

2. Each member of the Trusteeship Council shall designate one specially qualified person to represent it therein.

Functions and Powers

Article 87

The General Assembly and, under its authority, the Trusteeship Council, in carrying out their functions, may:

a. consider reports submitted by the administering authority;

b. accept petitions and examine them in consultation with the administering authority;

c. provide for periodic visits to the respective trust territories at times agreed upon with the administering authority; and

d. take these and other actions in conformity with the terms of the trusteeship agreements.

Article 88

The Trusteeship Council shall formulate a questionnaire on the political, economic, social, and educational advancement of the inhabitants of each trust territory, and the administering authority for each trust territory within the competence of the General Assembly shall make an annual report to the General Assembly upon the basis of such questionnaire.

Voting

Article 89

1. Each member of the Trusteeship Council shall have one vote.

2. Decisions of the Trusteeship Council shall be made by a majority of the members present and voting.

Procedure

Article 90

1. The Trusteeship Council shall adopt its own rules of procedure, including the method of selecting its President.

2. The Trusteeship Council shall meet as required in accordance with its rules, which shall include provision for the convening of meetings on the request of a majority of its members.

Article 91

The Trusteeship Council shall, when appropriate, avail itself of the assistance of the Economic and Social Council and of the specialized agencies in regard to matters with which they are respectively concerned.

CHAPTER XIV. THE INTERNATIONAL COURT OF JUSTICE

Article 92

The International Court of Justice shall be the principal judicial organ of the United Nations. It shall function in accordance with the annexed Statute, which is based upon the Statute of the Permanent Court of International Justice and forms an integral part of the present Charter.

Article 93

1. All Members of the United Nations are *ipso facto* parties to the Statute of the International Court of Justice.
2. A state which is not a Member of the United Nations may become a party to the Statute of the International Court of Justice on conditions to be determined in each case by the General Assembly upon the recommendation of the Security Council.

Article 94

1. Each Member of the United Nations undertakes to comply with the decision of the International Court of Justice in any case to which it is a party.
2. If any party to a case fails to perform the obligations incumbent upon it under a judgment rendered by the Court, the other party may have recourse to the Security Council, which may, if it deems necessary, make recommendations or decide upon measures to be taken to give effect to the judgment.

Article 95

Nothing in the present Charter shall prevent Members of the United Nations from entrusting the solution of their differences to other tribunals by virtue of agreements already in existence or which may be concluded in the future.

Article 96

1. The General Assembly or the Security Council may request the International Court of Justice to give an advisory opinion on any legal question.

2. Other organs of the United Nations and specialized agencies, which may at any time be so authorized by the General Assembly, may also request advisory opinions of the Court on legal questions arising within the scope of their activities.

CHAPTER XV. THE SECRETARIAT

Article 97

The Secretariat shall comprise a Secretary-General and such staff as the Organization may require. The Secretary-General shall be appointed by the General Assembly upon the recommendation of the Security Council. He shall be the chief administrative officer of the Organization.

Article 98

The Secretary-General shall act in that capacity in all meetings of the General Assembly, of the Security Council, of the Economic and Social Council and of the Trusteeship Council, and shall perform such other functions as are entrusted to him by these organs. The Secretary-General shall make an annual report to the General Assembly on the work of the Organization.

Article 99

The Secretary-General may bring to the attention of the Security Council any matter which in his opinion may threaten the maintenance of international peace and security.

Article 100

1. In the performance of their duties the Secretary-General and the staff shall not seek or receive instructions from any government or from any other authority external to the Organization. They shall refrain from any action which might reflect on their position as international officials responsible only to the Organization.

2. Each Member of the United Nations undertakes to respect the exclusively

international character of the responsibilities of the Secretary-General and the staff and not to seek to influence them in the discharge of their responsibilities.

Article 101

1. The staff shall be appointed by the Secretary-General under regulations established by the General Assembly.

2. Appropriate staffs shall be permanently assigned to the Economic and Social Council, the Trusteeship Council, and, as required, to other organs of the United Nations. These staffs shall form a part of the Secretariat.

3. The paramount consideration in the employment of the staff and in the determination of the conditions of service shall be the necessity of securing the highest standards of efficiency, competence, and integrity. Due regard shall be paid to the importance of recruiting the staff on as wide a geographical basis as possible.

CHAPTER XVI. MISCELLANEOUS PROVISIONS

Article 102

1. Every treaty and every international agreement entered into by any Member of the United Nations after the present Charter comes into force shall as soon as possible be registered with the Secretariat and published by it.

2. No party to any such treaty or international agreement which has not been registered in accordance with the provisions of paragraph 1 of this Article may invoke that treaty or agreement before any organ of the United Nations.

Article 103

In the event of a conflict between the obligations of the Members of the United Nations under the present Charter and their obligations under any other international agreement, their obligations under the present Charter shall prevail.

Article 104

The Organization shall enjoy in the territory of each of its Members such legal capacity as may be necessary for the exercise of its functions and the fulfillment of its purposes.

Article 105

1. The Organization shall enjoy in the territory of each of its Members such privileges and immunities as are necessary for the fulfillment of its purposes.

2. Representatives of the Members of the United Nations and officials of the Organization shall similarly enjoy such privileges and immunities as are necessary for the independent exercise of their functions in connection with the Organization.

3. The General Assembly may make recommendations with a view to determining the details of the application of paragraphs 1 and 2 of this Article or may propose conventions to the Members of the United Nations for this purpose.

CHAPTER XVII. TRANSITIONAL SECURITY ARRANGEMENTS

Article 106

Pending the coming into force of such special agreements referred to in Article 43 as in the opinion of the Security Council enable it to begin the exercise of its responsibilities under Article 42, the parties to the Four-Nation Declaration, signed at Moscow, October 30, 1943, and France, shall, in accordance with the provisions of paragraph 5 of that Declaration, consult with one another and as occasion requires with other Members of the United Nations with a view to such joint action on behalf of the Organization as may be necessary for the purpose of maintaining international peace and security.

Article 107

Nothing in the present Charter shall invalidate or preclude action, in relation to any state which during the Second World War has been an enemy of any signatory to the present Charter, taken or authorized as a result of that war by the Governments having responsibility for such action.

CHAPTER XVIII. AMENDMENTS

Article 108

Amendments to the present Charter shall come into force for all Members of the United Nations when they have been adopted by a vote of two-thirds of the members of the General Assembly and ratified in accordance with their respective constitutional processes by two-thirds of the Members of the United Nations, including all the permanent members of the Security Council.

Article 109

1. A General Conference of the Members of the United Nations for the purpose of reviewing the present Charter may be held at a date and place to be fixed by a two thirds vote of the members of the General Assembly and by a vote of any (seven) *nine* members of the Security Council. Each Member of the United Nations shall have one vote in the conference.

2. Any alteration of the present Charter recommended by a two-thirds vote of the conference shall take effect when ratified in accordance with their respective constitutional processes by two-thirds of the Members of the United Nations including all the permanent members of the Security Council.

3. If such a conference has not been held before the tenth annual session of the General Assembly following the coming into force of the present Charter, the proposal to call such a conference shall be placed on the agenda of that session of the General Assembly, and the conference shall be held if so decided by a majority vote of the members of the General Assembly and by a vote of any seven members of the Security Council.

CHAPTER XIX. RATIFICATION AND SIGNATURE

Article 110

1. The present Charter shall be ratified by the signatory states in accordance with their respective constitutional processes.

2. The ratifications shall be deposited with the Government of the United States of America, which shall notify all the signatory states of each deposit as well as the Secretary-General of the Organization when he has been appointed.

3. The present Charter shall come into force upon the deposit of ratifications by the Republic of China, France, the Union of Soviet Socialist Republics, the United Kingdom of Great Britain and Northern Ireland, and the United States of America, and by a majority of the other signatory states. A protocol of the ratifications deposited shall thereupon be drawn up by the Government of the United States of America which shall communicate copies thereof to all the signatory states.

4. The states signatory to the present Charter which ratify it after it has

come into force will become original Members of the United Nations on the date of the deposit of their respective ratifications.

Article 111

The present Charter, of which the Chinese, French, Russian, English, and Spanish texts are equally authentic, shall remain deposited in the archives of the Government of the United States of America. Duly certified copies thereof shall be transmitted by that Government to the Governments of the other signatory states.

IN FAITH WHEREOF the representatives of the Governments of the United Nations have signed the present Charter.

DONE at the city of San Francisco the twenty-sixth day of June, one thousand nine hundred and forty-five.

C. Resolution 242*

The Security Council,

Expressing its continuing concern with the grave situation in the Middle East,

Emphasizing the inadmissibility of the acquisition of territory by war and the need to work for a just and lasting peace in which every State in the area can live in security.

Emphasizing further that all Member States in their acceptance of the Charter of the United Nations have undertaken a commitment to act in accordance with Article 2 of the Charter,

1. *Affirms* that the fulfillment of Charter principles requires the establishment of a just and lasting peace in the Middle East which should include the application of both the following principles:

(i) Withdrawal of Israeli armed forces from territories occupied in the recent conflict;

(ii) Termination of all claims or states of belligerency and respect for and acknowledgement of the sovereignty, territorial integrity and political independence of every State in the area and their right to live in peace within secure and recognized boundaries free from threats or acts of force;

2. *Affirms further* the necessity

(a) For guaranteeing freedom of navigation through international waterways in the area;

(b) For achieving a just settlement of the refugee problem;

(c) For guaranteeing the territorial inviolability and political independence of every State in the area, through measures including the establishment of demilitarized zones;

3. *Requests* the Secretary-General to designate a Special Representative to proceed to the Middle East to establish and maintain contacts with the States concerned in order to promote agreement and assist efforts to achieve a peaceful and accepted settlement in accordance with the provisions and principles in this resolution;

4. *Requests* the Secretary-General to report to the Security Council on the progress of the efforts of the Special Representative as soon as possible.

---

*Adopted by the Security Council at its 1382d Meeting on November 22, 1967.

D. An UN Security Council Exercise—Bosnia

Permanent members: China, France, the Russian Federation, the United Kingdom, and the United States
Nonpermanent members: Botswana, Chile, Egypt, Germany, Guinea-Bissau, Honduras, Indonesia, Italy, Poland, Republic of Korea

The major aim of the UN Charter is to remove threats to the peace and suppress aggression. At the end of 1994 the Charter had been accepted by 185 countries. The Charter gives 15 countries on the Security Council responsibility for acting for the 185 UN members and commits them to give their support. Security Council decisions require nine votes. Any one of the five permanent Security Council members (China, France, the USSR, the United Kingdom, and the United States) can veto actions but not discussions of issues.

The purpose of this exercise is to teach students how the Security Council works. Students pretend they are ambassadors at the Security Council making decisions on a realistic world crisis. The major task of the model UN meeting is to approve a resolution for action. It helps to have more than one meeting and to have proposed resolutions already drafted with sponsors before the meeting. Much can be accomplished in getting support for a draft resolution in informal caucuses either before a meeting or in a limited recess.

In view of the sensitive political nature of the hypothetical Bosnian crisis, the U.S. delegation might include the president and secretary of state. In an informal meeting students can discuss the politics involved in their decision; President Clinton had sent U.S. troops to Bosnia despite strong congressional opposition, while Senator Dole, who may become president, had opposed sending U.S. troops and had cut UN budgets.

To create interest in the Security Council meeting it may help to have students sit at tables arranged in the shape of a rectangle open at one end. The secretary general and the president of the Security Council, who chairs the meeting, should be at the head of the table. Members take turns being president. The teacher may act as the secretary general. It is also desirable to have a sign in front of each delegate with the name of the country the delegate represents.

The president may open the meeting by calling on the secretary general to make a report. The secretary general should summarize the information in the hypothetical scenario set forth below. In addition, a written report by the secretary general can be distributed in advance. The exercise is designed to be as realistic as possible, so if there has been a change in the real world, or if the exercise is dragging, the secretary general may ask for permission to speak to the Council in order to change the scenario.

In the Security Council session students should attempt to represent their country's position rather than their own. The positions of Security Council members can be implied if they have sent personnel for peacekeeping (see Table 1). Note also the Council had approved unanimously UN Resolution 1010 summarized below. It would be desirable to obtain minutes of the UN Security Council meetings on the Bosnian question or for students to write missions statements about their positions on the Bosnian issue.

The best sources of general background information on Bosnia or other issues for a Security Council exercise are the United Nations Association of the United States of America, *A Global Agenda—Issues Before the 50th General Assembly of the United Nations* (1994–1995 edition) (New York: University Press of America), and the *New York Times*. Also, *Everyone's United Nations* has a comprehensive history of United Nations activities. The U.S. Department of State *Dispatch* gives texts of UN resolutions.

The secretary general may need help in keeping track of proposed resolutions and amendments. If there is more than one session, it is desirable to have summary minutes prepared. To provide more authenticity, a meeting room rather than a regular classroom should be used.

Note in Resolution 1010 that the format of UN resolutions is to start with phrases such as "disturbed by, recalling, reaffirming, noting, welcoming," etc. Then the resolutions conclude with action paragraphs beginning with words such as "condemns, requests, demands, decides, approves, recognizes," etc.

The teacher sets forth in a report from the UN secretary general the scenario and the times reserved for the meeting. It would not be difficult to design a similar exercise on Haiti. Generally five or six sessions are appropriate.

SCENARIO FOR BOSNIA EXERCISE (HYPOTHETICAL)

The time is a month in 1996. The UN secretary general has convened a special meeting of the Security Council to act on the deteriorating situation in Bosnia and on the plans of the United States to begin withdrawing troops from the Implementation Force (IFOR). The American president states that U.S. units of the 20,000 peacekeeping force have become particular targets of terrorist attacks. The U.S. Congress is threatening to cut off all UN peacekeeping funds unless UN units are withdrawn, in line with the one-year commitments made in December 1995. The American president has requested the secretary general to ask other countries to replace the U.S. units with their peacekeeping units.

Security Council delegates should take a new look at the situation and per-

Table 1

Contributors to the UN Mission in the Former Yugoslavia (UNPROFOR)

Bangladesh	1,265	Netherlands	973
Belgium	110	New Zealand	263
Brazil	15	Nigeria	11
Canada	842	Norway	729
Czech Republic	9	Pakistan	2,739
Denmark	304	Poland	10
Egypt	346	Portugal	7
Finland	8	Russia	445
France	6,086	Spain	1,436
Germany	540	Sweden	1,076
Ghana	12	Switzerland	6
Indonesia	9	Turkey	1,488
Ireland	7	Ukraine	585
Jordan	110	U.K.	9,779
Kenya	14	U.S.	2*
Malaysia	1,559		
Nepal	4	Total	30,869

Note. This force preceded the Implementation Force (IFOR).

*This does not include about 900 U.S. peacekeepers in Macedonia.

haps try to decide whether to add U.S. troops because the multinational force is having trouble maintaining law and order. The delegates' job in the UN exercise will be to try to represent the positions of the fifteen members of the UN Security Council. Other participants could be the delegate from Bosnia, who would be asked to speak, and possibly other interested governments not members of the Security Council.

In the present exercise UN members would probably be asked by the secretary general to contribute forces to Bosnia. The secretary general may try to persuade the United States to at least delay withdrawal of its troops. European countries would probably be reluctant to volunteer additional forces, because the United States did not contribute forces to the original peacekeeping units in Bosnia. IFOR is a peace enforcement force not a "peacekeeping" force. On the other hand, the United States did contribute a small number of troops to peacekeeping in Macedonia. Moreover, the United States is already $1 billion in arrears for UN and peacekeeping dues. After speeches are given, the job would be to approve a resolution.

The ideal number of students for a UN exercise is about 20 to 30. If there are more, students might volunteer to represent a country not on the Security Council. Those contributing peacekeepers might wish to speak before the Council.

SUMMARY OF RULES
FOR THE UN SECURITY COUNCIL

1. Decisions on procedural matters are by affirmative vote of nine members. Procedural matters cover decisions on peaceful settlement of disputes up to authorizing an investigation. All other matters require the vote of nine members including concurring votes of the permanent members, except an abstention by a permanent member cannot prevent action by the Security Council.
2. Any country can participate without vote in discussions if it considers its interests are affected, but this requires a procedural vote of the Council, which routinely approves such requests (Article 31). Any member can bring a dispute to the attention of the Security Council (Article 35).
3. Parties shall first try to solve disputes by negotiation. Security Council action under Chapter VI does not involve force.
4. Actions including blockade and military operations are taken under Chapter VII.
5. The presidency rotates monthly in alphabetical order.
6. The president calls upon delegates in the order they signify a desire to speak.
7. Challenges on a point of order are submitted to a vote of the Security Council.
8. It is not necessary for a resolution to be seconded. It can be withdrawn if there has been no vote.
9. The amendments to a resolution that are furthest removed in substance from the original proposal are the first to be voted on.

EXCERPTS FROM RESOLUTION 1010 ON BOSNIA
(8/10/95)

The Security Council

Reaffirming all its earlier relevant resolutions, . . .

Reiterating the unacceptableness of the violations of the safe areas of Srebrenica and Zepa by Bosnian Serb forces, . . .

Reaffirming its commitment to the sovereignty, territorial integrity and independence of the Republic of Bosnia and Herzegovina, . . .

Affirming its commitment to the search for an overall negotiated settlement of the conflicts in the former Yugoslavia ensuring the sovereignty and territorial integrity of all the States there within their internationally recognized borders, and stressing the importance it attaches to the mutual recognition thereof,

Deeply concerned at reports of grave violations of international humanitarian law in and around Srebrenica and at the fact that many of the former inhabitants of Srebrenica cannot be accounted for, . . .

1. Demands that the Bosnian Serb party give immediate access for representatives of the United Nations High Commissioner for Refugees, the ICRC and other international agencies to persons displaced from Srebrenica and Zepa who are within the areas of the Republic of Bosnia and Herzegovina under the control of Bosnian Serb forces. . . .

3. Reiterates that all those who commit violations of international humanitarian law will be held individually responsible in respect of such acts . . .

VOTE: Unanimous (15–0)

E. U.S. Contributions to the United Nations and Specialized Agencies

Calender Years 1949–1990
(Thousands of Dollars)

	Estimate 1990		1949–1990 Cumulative total
	Contribution	Percent	
United Nations, Specialized Agencies, and the International Atomic Energy Agency (assessed budgets)			
United Nations[1]	266,600	25.00	3,281,290
Food and Agriculture Organization	69,950	25.00	658,494
International Maritime Organization	1,243	5.38	9,982
International Atomic Energy Agency	46,032	25.13	405,702
International Civil Aviation Organization	7,933	25.00	129,275
Joint Financing Program	—	—	49,867
International Labor Organization	61,898	25.00	522,666
International Telecommunications Union	5,435	7.95	60,957
United Nations Educational, Scientific and Cultural Organization[2]	—	—	546,454
United Nations Industrial Development Organization	25,913	25.00	70,192
Universal Postal Union	859	5.27	9,705
World Health Organization	83,129	25.00	1,180,826
World Intellectual Property Organization	1,057	5.72	8,882
World Meteorological Organization	8,966	24.65	79,220
United Nations, Specialized Agencies, and the International Atomic Energy Agency	579,015	—	7,013,512
United Nations Peacekeeping Forces			
United Nations Emergency Force/ United Nations Disengagement Observer Force/United Nations Interim Force in Lebanon Assessed	40,751	29.39	715,301
United Nations Force in Cyprus[3]	8,837	32.61	212,329
United Nations Iran-Iraq Military Observer Group (UNIIMOG)	12,489	31.24	12,489

| | Estimate 1990 | | 1949–1990 |
	Contribution	Percent	Cumulative total
United Nations Peacekeeping Forces (Cont.)			
United Nations Observer Group in Central			
America (ONUCA)	17,730	48.41	17,730
Inactive Peacekeeping Organizations	—	—	231,851
Peacekeeping Forces	79,807	—	1,189,700
Special Voluntary Programs			
Fund for the Protection of the World Cultural			
and Natural Heritage (World Heritage Fund)	206	8.80	2,534
International Atomic Energy Agency Technical			
Assistance Fund[4]	21,546	26.29	228,847
International Fund for Agricultural Development	34,400	14.57	504,320
United Nations Afghanistan Emergency Trust			
Fund (UNOCA)	13,283	12.43	23,283
United Nations Children's Fund	63,950	16.46	1,014,474
United Nations Development Program	105,000	10.26	3,040,305
United Nations Capital Development Fund	1,476	3.77	21,666
United Nations Center for Human Settlements			
(HABITAT)	393	5.37	1,976
United Nations Educational and Training			
Program for Southern Africa	788	16.53	12,172
United Nations Environment Program	11,805	23.90	153,130
United Nations Industrial Development			
Organization (UNIDO-IPS Voluntary)	492	100.00	1,142
United Nations Trust Fund for South Africa	492	13.67	3,859
UN/FAO World Food Program	163,000	19.73	2,411,572
United Nations Fund for Drug Abuse Control	4,000	7.64	56,872
United Nations Institute for Namibia	—	—	3,987
United Nations Fund for Population Activities	—	—	410,291
UN High Commissioner for Refugees Program:			
Regular Programs	74,318	21.24	1,063,974
Special Programs	52,668	23.00	600,269
United Nations Relief and Works Agency	57,000	23.18	1,542,883
UNRWA Special Projects	—	—	23,070
United Nations Development Fund for Women	787	9.63	10,163
United Nations Institute for Training and			
Research	—	—	7,966
United Nations Voluntary Fund for Victims			
of Torture	—	—	272
United Nations Volunteers Program	100	13.94	2,838
Voluntary Fund for United Nations World			
Assembly on Aging	—	—	400

	Estimate 1990		1949–1990 Cumulative total
	Contribution	Percent	
Special Voluntary Programs (Cont.)			
WHO Special Programs	40,000	22.22	239,307
WIPO Voluntary Programs	—	—	922
WMO Voluntary Cooperation Program	1,986	26.62	37,400
Inactive Special Voluntary Programs	—	—	679,496
Special Voluntary Programs	647,690	—	12,100,390
Total U.S. Contributions	1,306,512	—	20,303,602

Source: U.S. Department of State, *United States Contributions to International Organizations, Report to the Congress for Fiscal Year 1990.* Department of State Publication 9912.

[1]The amounts shown do not reflect the amounts received in repayment of principal and interest on UN bonds.

[2]The United States withdrew its membership from UNESCO effective December 31, 1984.

[3]UNFICYP was established in March 1964. The amounts include cash contributions and airlift services of $1,254,107 for which the United States did not charge the United Nations. The U.S. pledges have been based on the initial cost estimates of the Force with the qualification that the amount ultimately contributed will depend upon the contributions made by other governments and confirmation of the cost estimates.

[4]Amounts shown include contributions in cash, services, equipment, and fellowship training. Percentage refers to cash only. This amount also includes contributions for the Safeguards Program.

References

Acheson, D. 1969. *Present at the Creation*. New York: W.W. Norton.

Akehurst, M. 1984. *A Modern Introduction to International Law*. London: George Allen and Unwin.

Alexander, Y. and Nanes, A. 1980. *The United States and Iran: A Documental History*. Frederick, MD: University Press of America.

Baer, G. W. 1976. *Test Case: Italy, Ethiopia and the League of Nations*. Stanford: Hoover Institution Press.

Bailey, S. 1964. *The Secretariat of the United Nations*. New York: Frederick Praeger.

Bailey, S. D. 1971. *Voting in the Security Council*. Bloomington: Indiana University Press.

Bailey, T. A. 1945. *A Diplomatic History of the American People*. New York: F. Crofts.

Baker, R. 1927. *Woodrow Wilson: Life and Letters*. New York: Doubleday.

Bassett, J. 1930. *The League of Nations*. New York: Longmans, Green.

Berdiner, E. 1975. *A Time for Angels*. New York: Alfred A. Knopf.

Boucher, C. and Siebeck, W. 1987. "UNCTAD VII: New Spirit in North South Relations." *Finance and Development*.

Campbell, A. 1901. *The Rights of War and Peace*. Washington, DC: M. Walt Dunne.

Campbell, T. M. and Herring, G. C. 1975. *The Diaries of Edward R. Stettinius J.* New York: New Viewpoints.

Carter, J. 1982. *Keeping Faith*. New York: Bantam.

Chandazorkur, A. 1984. *The International Monetary Fund: Its Financial Organization and Activities*. Washington, DC: IMF.

Chayes, A. 1974. *The Cuban Missile Crisis*. New York: Oxford University Press.

Churchill, W. 1948. *The Gathering Storm*. Cambridge: Houghton-Mifflin.

Claude, Inez, Jr. 1991. *Swords Into Plowshares*. New York: Random House.

Collins, L. and Lapierre, D. 1973. *O Jerusalem*. New York: Pocket Books.

Cordier, A. 1977. *Public Papers of the Secretaries General of the United Nations*. New York: Columbia University Press, 8 vols. Trygve Lie through U Thant.

Current History. Published monthly.

Dawisha, A. 1981. "Iraq: The West's Opportunity." *Foreign Policy*, Winter.

Dayan, M. 1966. *The Story of My Life*. New York: Werner Books.

de Cuellar, Javier Perez. 1991. "Report of the Secretary-General on the Work of the Organization 1991." New York: United Nations.

Devine, R. 1981. *The Cuban Missile Crisis.* Chicago: Quadrangle.

de Vries, M. 1986. *The IMF in a Changing World—1945–85.* Washington, DC: IMF.

Dillon, K. B. 1985. *Recent Developments and External Debt Restructuring.* Washington, DC: IMF, August.

Driscoll, David. *What is the International Monetary Fund.* Washington, DC: International Monetary Fund.

Economist (London). July 26, 1986.

Eduard, H. and Puckahtickom, B. 1985. *Export Credit Policy.* Washington, DC: IMF, August.

Eisenhower, D. 1963. *Mandate for Change.* New York: Doubleday.

_____. 1965. *Waging Peace.* New York: Doubleday.

Falk, R., Kratochivil, F., and Mendlovitz, S. (eds). 1985. *International Law.* Boulder: Westview Press.

Feld, W. 1980. *Multinational Corporations and U.N. Politics.* New York: Pergamon.

Foreign Affairs. 1992. *America and the World 1992.* Published annually.

Franck, T. 1985. *Nations Against Nation.* New York: Oxford University Press.

Garthoff, R. 1987. *Reflections on the Cuban Missile Crisis.* Washington, DC: Brookings.

Gelb, L. and Betts, R. 1979. *The Irony of Vietnam: The System Worked.* Washington, DC: Brookings.

Goodrich, L. and Hambro E. 1946. *Charter of the United Nations: Commentary and Documents.* Boston: World Peace Foundation.

Gravel, M. 1971. *The Pentagon Papers.* Boston: Bacon Press.

Gruhn, I. 1979. "The U.N. Maze Compounds Development." *International Organization,* Spring.

Haig, A. 1984. *Caveat—Realism, Reagan and Foreign Policy.* New York: Macmillan.

Halberstam, D. 1969. *The Best and the Brightest.* New York: Random House.

Hardie, F. 1976. *The Abyssinian Crisis.* Hamdon, TN: Archon.

Harriman, W. and Abel, E. 1979. *Special Envoy to Churchill.* New York: Random House.

Heiberg, H. and Holst, J. 1986. "Peacekeeping in Lebanon—Comparing UNIFIL and the MNF." *Survival.* London: September/October.

Henkin, L. et al. 1989. *Right v. Might.* New York: Council on Foreign Relations.

Herring, G. 1979. *America's Longest War.* New York: John Wiley.

Hoopes, T. 1973. *The Devil and John Foster Dulles.* Boston: Little, Brown.

Hull, C. 1948. *The Memoirs of Cordell Hull.* New York: Macmillan (2 vols.).

International Labor Office Geneva. 1992. *World Labor Report 1992.* Geneva: International Labor Office.

International Monetary Fund. 1992. *Annual Report 1991.* Washington, DC: IMF. Published annually.

International Monetary Fund. *IMF Survey*. Published biweekly.

International Monetary Fund. *World Economic Outlook: May 1992*. Published biannually.

Janis, M. 1988. *An Introduction to International Law*. Boston: Little, Brown.

Jenkins, B. 1983. "International Cooperation in Locating and Recovering Stolen Nuclear Materials." *Terrorism*, Vol. 6, no. 4, pp. 561–576.

Johnson, L. 1971. *The Vantage Point*. New York: Popular Library.

Khalilzad, Z. July/August 1980. "Afghanistan and the Crisis in American Foreign Policy." *Survival*.

Khomeini, A. 1979. "Issues Related to the Struggle of Muslim People of Iran." San Francisco: Consulate General of the Islam Republic of Iran.

Khrushchev, N. 1970. *Khrushchev Remembers*. Boston: Little, Brown.

———. 1976. *Khrushchev Remembers, the Last Testament*. Boston: Little, Brown.

Kissinger, H. 1979. *White House Years*. Boston: Little, Brown.

———. 1982. *Years of Upheaval*. Boston: Little, Brown.

Lall, A. 1970. *The U.N. and the Middle East Crisis—1967*. New York: Columbia University Press.

Lauterpaucht, H. "The Grotian Tradition in International Law." In H. Falk et al., *International Law*. Boulder: Westview Press.

League of Nations, Information Section. 1926 to 1938. *The League from Year to Year*. Annual volumes. Geneva.

League of Nations. *League of Nations—A Survey 1920–26*. Geneva.

League of Nations. *Official Journal, 1922–24*. Geneva.

League of Nations. *Report of the Work of the League*. Annual reports. Geneva.

League of Nations Secretariat. 1930. *Ten Years of World Cooperation*. Geneva.

Lie, T. 1954. *In the Cause of Peace*. New York: Macmillan.

Link, A. 1965. *Wilson: Campaign for Progressivism and Peace 1916–1919*. Princeton: Princeton University Press.

Lowenthal, A. 1972. *The Dominican Intervention*. Cambridge: Harvard University Press.

McDonald, J. 1983. "The U.N. Convention Against Hostage-Taking." *Terrorism*, Vol. 6, no. 4, pp. 545–560.

McKenna, M. 1961. *Borah*. Ann Arbor: University of Michigan Press.

Mitrany, D. 1966. *A Working Peace System*. Chicago: Quadrangle Books.

Modelski, G., ed. 1979. *Transnational Corporations and World Order*. San Francisco: Freeman.

Morse, B. June 12, 1984. "Statement Before the UNDP Governing Council." United Nations, New York.

Murphy, J. M. 1982. *The United Nations and the Control of International Violence*. Totowa, NJ: Towman and Allenheld.

Newhouse, J. 1973. *Cold Dawn, The Story of SALT*. New York: Holt, Rinehart.

Nixon, R. 1979. *The Memoirs of Richard Nixon*. New York: Grosset & Dunlap (2 vols.).

Northedge, F. S. 1986. *The League of Nations*. New York: Holms and Meier.

Organization for Economic Cooperation and Development. 1983. *1983 Review*. Paris: OECD.

Organization for Economic Cooperation and Development. 1984. Paris: OECD. DP/ 1984/5/Ad. 2.

Ouattara, A. 1988. "Fund is Helping to Resolve Africa's Debt Problem by Supporting Growth-Oriented Economic Reforms." *IMF Survey*, June 13.

Pachter, H. M. 1963. *Collision Course*. New York: Praeger.

Pasha, G. 1957. *A Soldier with the Arabs*. London: Hoddar and Slaughton.

Pentagon Papers. 1976. New York Times Edition.

Peterson, M. 1986. *The General Assembly in World Politics*. Boston: Allen and Unwin.

Phillips, D. 1977. *The Night Watch*. New York: Ballantine.

Poole, P. 1973. *The United States and Indochina from FDR to Nixon*. Hinsdale, IL: Dryden.

Porter, G. 1978. "The Sino-Soviet Conflict in Southeast Asia." *Current History*, December.

Romulo, C. 1986. *Forty Years: A Third World Soldier at the UN*. New York: Greenwood Press.

Russell, R. 1958. *A History of the United Nations' Charter*. Washington, DC: Brookings.

Sadat, A. 1977. *In Search of Identity*. New York: Harper & Row.

Schlesinger, A. 1975. *A Thousand Days*. New York: Fawcett Crest.

Scott, G. 1973. *The Rise and Fall of the United Nations*. New York: Macmillan.

Seabury, P. and McDougall, W. 1984. *The Grenada Papers*. San Francisco: Institute of Contemporary Studies.

Seymour, C. 1938. *The Intimate Papers of Colonel House*. Boston: Houghton-Mifflin.

Shamwell, K. 1983. "Implementing the Convention on the Prevention and Punishment of Crimes Against Internationally Protected Persons, Including Diplomatic Agents," *Terrorism*, Vol. 6, no. 4, pp. 529–544.

Sherwood, R. 1948. *Roosevelt and Hopkins*. New York: Harper.

Siekmann, R. 1985. *Basic Documents on United Nations and Related Peacekeeping Forces*. Boston: Martinus Nijhoff.

Simon, S. 1979. "Kampuchea: Vietnam's Vietnam." *Current History*. December.

Sisco, J. "Middle East: Progress or Lost Opportunity." *America and the World—1982*. New York: Council on Foreign Relations.

Smith, G. 1962. *Dean Acheson*. New York: Cooper Square.

Sofaer, A. 1986. "Terrorism and the Law." *Foreign Affairs*, Spring.

Sorensen, T. 1966. *Kennedy*. London: Pan Books.

Spero, J. 1985. *The Politics of International Economic Relations*. New York: St. Martins.

Stalin, J. 1945. *The Great Patriotic War*. Moscow.

Stanley Foundation. July 17–22, 1988. *International Agenda for the 1990s*. Muscatine, IA.

Stern, S. 1988. "World Bank General Capital Increase." *Finance and Development.* June.

Stimson, H. 1936. *The Far Eastern Crisis.* New York: Harper.

Stimson, H. and Bundy, M. 1948. *On Active Service in Peace and War.* New York: Harper.

Stoessinger, J. 1974. *Why Nations Go to War.* New York: St. Martins.

_____. 1977. *The United Nations and the Superpowers: China, Russia and America.* New York: Random House.

Takeuchi, T. 1938. *Amerasia.* July.

Talbott, S. 1984. *Deadly Gambit.* New York: Alfred A. Knopf.

Terrorism, An International Journal. 1983. Vol. 6, no. 4.

Tessitore, J., and Woolfson, S. (eds.). 1992. *A Global Agenda: Issues Before the 47th General Assembly of the United Nations.* Lanham, MD: University Press of America. An annual publication of the United Nations Association of the United States of America.

Truman, H. 1956. *Years of Decision.* New York: Double day (2 vols.).

UN Chronicle. New York: United Nations.

U.N. Commission on Transnational Corporations. 1979. Document E/C. 10/45, 11 April. New York: United Nations.

UNDP. 1984. Annual Report of the Administrator for 1983. DP/1984/5/Add. 3. New York: United Nations.

UNDP. 1984. Document (DP/1984/5/Add. 12). New York: United Nations.

UNDP. 1981. *Promises to Keep.* New York: United Nations.

United Nations. 1970. *Basic Problems of Disarmament.* New York: United Nations.

United Nations. 1972. *Multinational Corporations in World Development.* New York. Document St/ECA/190.

United Nations. 1986. *Everyone's United Nations.* New York: United Nations.

United Nations. 1987. *Annotated Preliminary List of Items to be Included in the Provisional Agenda.* New York: United Nations. Printed annually.

United Nations. From 1946. *United Nations Security Council—Resolutions and Decisions.* New York: United Nations.

United Nations. *United Nations Security Council, Official Records.* New York: United Nations. From first meeting in January, 1946. Later issues do not give verbatim record of proceedings.

United Nations Association of the United States of America. 1991. *A Global Agenda: Issues Before the 46th General Assembly of the United Nations.* New York: University Press of America. Printed annually.

United Nations Association of the United States of America. *Interdependent.* Published monthly.

United Nations Department for Disarmament Affairs. 1991. *Nuclear Weapons: A Comprehensive Study.* New York: United Nations.

United Nations Environment Program. 1989. *Environmental Data Report.* Cambridge, MA: Basil Blackwell.

Urquart, B. 1972. *Hammarskjold.* New York: Harpers.

U.S. Arms Control and Disarmament Agency. 1980. *Arms Control and Disarmament Agreements.* Washington, DC: GPO.

U.S. Congress, Senate, Select Committee. 1975. *Alleged Assassination Plots Involving Foreign Leaders.* Washington, DC: GPO.

U.S. Department of State. 1991. *United States Contributions to International Organizations: Report to the Congress for Fiscal Year 1990.* Washington, DC: U.S. Department of State.

U.S. Department of State. 1991. *United States Participation in the UN: Report by the President to the Congress for the Year 1990.* Washington, DC: U.S. Department of State.

U.S. Department of State, Bureau of Public Affairs. *Dispatch.* Washington, DC: GPO. Published weekly.

U.S. Department of State. 1954. *Foreign Relations of the United States: East Asia and the Pacific.* Washington, DC: GPO.

U.S. Department of State. 1980. "Soviet Invasion of Afghanistan." Special Report. April. Washington, DC: GPO.

U.S. Department of State. 1981. *Treaties in Force—1981.* Washington, DC: GPO.

U.S. Department of State. 1984. *Foreign Relations of the United States: Korea 1950.* Washington, DC: GPO.

U.S. Department of State. 1986. *Terrorist Attacks on U.S. Business Abroad.* March. Washington, DC: GPO.

U.S. Department of State. 1987. Office of the Ambassador at Large for Counterterrorism. "International Terrorist Incidents, 1968–1987." Washington, DC: GPO.

Von Glahn, G. 1981. *Law Among Nations.* New York: Macmillan.

Wainhouse, D. 1966. *International Peace Observation.* Baltimore: Johns Hopkins Press.

Walp, P. 1931. *Constitutional Development of the League of Nations.* Lexington: University of Kentucky.

Walters, E. 1952. *A History of the League of Nations.* London: Oxford University Press.

Weston, B., Folk, R., and D'Amoto, A. 1980. *International Law and World Order.* St. Paul: West Publishing Co.

World Bank. 1992. *World Development Report—1992.* New York: Oxford University Press. Published annually.

Yoder, A. 1981. "UN Monitoring the Transnational Corporations." *Towson State Journal of International Affairs.* Spring.

_____. 1983. "United Nation's Resolutions Against International Terrorism." *Terrorism,* Vol. 6, no. 4.

_____. 1986. *World Politics and the Causes of War Since 1914.* Lanham, MD: University Press of America.

Yoshihashi, T. 1963. *Conspiracy at Mukden.* New Haven: Yale University Press.

Index

Aaland Islands, 14
ABC Agreements, 103
ABM Treaty (*see* Antiballistic
　　Missile Treaty)
Abyssinia (*see* Ethiopia)
Afghanistan, 37, 81–82, 96, 203–
　　204, 218
Africa, 90–93, 136, 147
Aggression, 120–124
Aidid, General, 89
AIDS, 149
Albania, 14, 46
Allende, President, 156
Angola, 90, 208
Antiballistic Missile Treaty (ABM),
　　108–109
Anti-Comintern Pact, 21
Apartheid, 136–137, 217
Arab-Israeli Wars, 48–69, 96–99,
　　197–199
　　1948 War, 49–52, 196
　　1956 War, 52–56
　　1967 War, 56–59, 196–197, 199
　　1973 War, 60–62, 197
Arafat, Yasser, 191
Aristide, President, 95
Armenians, 15
Asian Development Bank (Asian
　　Bank), 144
Aswan Dam, 52
Atlantic Charter, 25–26, 41
Atomic energy, 102
　　(*See also* International Atomic
　　　　Energy Agency)

Austria, 13,21
Austria–Hungary, 7
Awami League, 70–72
Axis Powers, 21
Azerbaijan, 40

Bacteriological weapons, 101
Baker, James, 63–64, 83–84, 113, 118
Balfour Declaration, 49
Bangladesh, 71
Baruch Plan, 104
Belarus, 28,36, 50
Belgium, 9, 14, 64–65, 103
Bengali, 69–72
Bernadotte, Count, 52
Biodiversity Treaty, 21
Biological weapons, 101
Birkshire case, 119
Bismarck, Otto von, 4
Borah, William, 121, 123
Bosnian-Croatian Federation, 207
Bosnian War, 86–88, 208
Boutros-Ghali, Boutros, 88, 185,
　　192–193, 217, 219
Brzezinski, Zbigniew, 21
Bunche, Ralph, 52, 64
Bush, George, 81, 86, 113, 215
Byleorussia, 27
　　(*See also* Belarus)

Cambodia, 77–79, 93, 210–211
Camp David, 61, 199
Canada, 47

Carter, Jimmy, 118, 136
Castro, Fidel, 66–67
Cecil, Sir Robert, 8, 123
Central Intelligence Agency, 66, 93–94, 156
Chad, 123
Chayes, Abram, 67
Chamberlain, Neville, 20
Chamorro, Violetta, 94
Charter, UN, 1, 2, 5, 11–12, 26, 29–33, 34, 35, 39, 42–43, 81
Chemical weapons, 114
Chemical Weapons Convention, 114
Chile, 153–154, 156–159
China, 9, 16–18, 26
    (See also China, People's Republic of; Taiwan)
China, People's Republic of, 35, 42, 43, 45, 46–47, 77–78, 200
Christopher, Warren, 64
Churchill, Winston, 25
CIA (see Central Intelligence Agency)
Civil aviation (see International Civil Aviation Organization)
Clemenceau, Georges, 8
Clinton, William Jefferson, 64, 97, 195, 212, 215
Coalitions (see UN coalitions)
Code of conduct (transnational corporations), 158–159
Cold War, 39, 82, 86, 99, 112
Collective Measures Committee, 46–47
Collective security, 212
    (See also UN collective security)
Commodity agreements, 154–155
Common Fund, 154
Communism and communists, 39–41, 66–68, 72–73
Communist bloc, 75
Concert of Europe, 4, 6
Conditionalities, 165–166

Conferences on the Status of Women, 160
Conflict of laws, 117
Congo, UN Operation in (ONUC), 64–66
Congo War, 64–66, 200–201
Congress, 8, 27, 97, 187
Connally, Tom, 26
Contadora group, 94, 211
Contras, 93–94
    (See also Nicaragua)
Convention on Protection of the Ozone Layer, 151
Convention on Refugees, 136
Convention on Slavery, 136
Convention on Stateless Persons, 136
Cordovez, Diego, 82
Corfu, 14
Costa Rica, 94
    (See also Contadora Group)
Covenant of Economic and Cultural Rights, 119
Criticisms, 215–217
Croatia, 206–207
Croatian Confederation, 86, 88
Cuba, 66–68, 96
Cuban Missile Crisis, 66–68, 79
de Cuellar, Perez, 82, 185, 192–193, 217–218
Cyprus wars, 73–75, 79
Czechoslovakia, 9, 14, 72–73

Danube Commission, 3
Danzig, 15
Dayan, Moshe, 61
Debt crisis (UN), 1, 142, 154, 168, 186–188
Debt crisis (world), 168–170
Democratic internationalists, ix, 5, 6n, 7, 212
Diem, Ngo Dinh, 75
Diplomats (see Internationally Protected Persons)

Disarmament (*see* specific weapons treaties)
Drug abuse control, 152–153
Dulles, John Foster, 54
Dumbarton Oaks, 26

East Germany, 204
East Pakistan, 71
Eastern Europe, 72–73, 113, 138, 206
Economic Commission for Africa, 144
Economic Commission for Europe, 143–144
Economic Commission for Latin America and the Caribbean, 144
Economic and Social Commission for Asia and the Pacific (ESCAP), 144
Economic and Social Council (ECOSOC), 141–143
Economic and Social Council for Western Asia, 144
Eden, Anthony, 26
Eisenhower, Dwight, 5, 54, 66, 104, 118, 196
El Salvador, 93–94
England, 8
(*See also* United Kingdom)
Environment, 160
Ethiopia, 18–21
European Community, 86, 206

Falkland Islands, 185
Fascism, 18
Federal Bureau of Investigation, 189
Food and Agricultural Organization (FAO), 171
Fourteen points, 8–9
France, 7, 8, 14, 15, 18, 20, 27, 54, 66, 75, 96, 196

Franck, Thomas, 190
Functionalism, 1–2

Galilee, 60
Gandhi, Indira, 71
GATT (General Agreement on Tariffs and Trade), 156, 174
Gaza, 63
General Assembly, 31, 35, 46–47, 52, 65, 72, 73, 76, 78, 93, 94, 102, 104, 107, 120, 121, 122, 124, 127, 128, 130, 133, 136, 149, 163, 179, 190, 196, 217
Geneva Agreement on Indo–China, 75
Geneva Convention of 1925, 101
Geneva Convention of 1949, 132–133
Geneva Protocol of 1925, 101
(*See also* Geneva Convention of 1925)
Genocide, 128, 129
George, Lloyd, 7, 8
Georgia, 95
Germany, 7, 14, 15–16, 20–22, 40, 101, 103
Gidi-Mitla Passes, 61
Global Environmental Monitoring System (GEMS), 151, 213
Global Warming Convention, 160
Golan Heights, 56–62
Gorbachev, Mikhail, 81, 100, 111, 113
Great Depression, 15, 16, 19, 164
Greece, 14, 40–41, 73–75
Grey, Edward, 4, 7
"Group of eminent" persons, 156–157
Group of Seven, 170
Gulf War (*see* Iraq-Kuwait War)

Hague Conferences (First, 1899 and Second, 1907), 3, 8, 100

Hague Convention of 1912, 152
Hague Convention of 1970, 131
Haiti, 94–95, 96
Hammarskjöld, Dag, 65–66, 182–
    183, 189
Hijacking, 131–132
Hitler, Adolf, 15–20
Hoare, British Foreign Secretary, 20
Honduras, 94
Hostages Convention, 132–133
House, Colonel, 10
Hull, Cordell, 5, 25
Human rights, 12, 135–138
Hungary, 54
Hussein, Saddam, 82, 83

India, 68–72
India-Pakistan conflicts, 68–72
Indochina (*see* Vietnam War)
INF (*see* Intermediate Nuclear Force
    Agreement)
Intergovernmental Marine Consul-
    tative Organization (IMCO),
    128
Intermediate Nuclear Force Agree-
    ment (INF), 105, 111–112
International Atomic Energy Agency
    (IAEA), 102,104,106
International Bank for Reconstruction
    and Development (IBRD), 163–
    164
International Civil Aviation Organiza-
    tion, 172–173
International Court of Justice, 119–
    120, 124–127
International Development Associa-
    tion, 167
International Drug Control Program,
    152–153
International Finance Corporation,
    167
International Fund For Agricultural
    Development, 171–172

International Labor Organization,
    175–176
International law, 2, 8, 117–139
International Law Association, 3
International Law Commission, 120,
    127
International Marine Organization,
    174
International Monetary Fund, 163–
    170, 213
International Narcotics Control
    Board, 153
International Refugee Organization,
    150
International Telegraphic Union, 3,
    173
International Trade Organization (*see*
    World Trade Organization)
Internationalists (*see* Democratic
    internationalists)
Internationally protected persons, 132
Iran, 39–40
Iran-Iraq War, 1, 82–83
Iraq, 14
Iraq-Kuwait War, 1, 83–86, 137–138,
    195–196, 204–206
Israel, 49–64
    (*See also* Arab–Israeli wars)
Italy, 14, 18–21

Japan, 15, 16–18, 101
Jerusalem, 50–51
Jews, 49–50
    (*See also* Israel)
Johnson, Lyndon B, 57, 76
Jordan, 49–50

Kampuchea (*see* Cambodia)
Karmal, Babrak, 81
Kashmir, 68–70
Katanga, 65
Kellogg-Briand Pact, 17, 121

Kennan, George, 21
Kennedy, Bobby, 67–68
Kennedy, John, 66–68, 123, 186
Keynes, John Maynard, 164
Khan, Yahya, 70–71
Khmer Rouge, 77–78, 93, 210–211
Khomeini, Ayatollah, 83
Khrushchev, Nikita, 43, 65–68, 106, 183
Kim Il Sung, 43
Kissinger, Henry, 61, 108–109
Korean War, 41–48, 182, 195–196, 199–200
Kurds, 85, 205
Kuwait (*see* Iraq–Kuwait War)

Land mines, 114
Latin America, 169–171
Latin American nuclear weapon–free zone, 104
Latvia, 36
Law of the Sea, 127
League Covenant, 221–231
League of Nations, 4, 5, 7, 12–16, 101, 121, 152, 187
    accomplishments, 21
    assembly, 16–18
    coordinating committee, 9
    Covenant, 10–12
    epidemic commission, 13
    Italy attacks Ethiopia, 18–21
    Manchurian incident, 16–18
    Permanent Central Opium Board, 152
    Secretariat, 10–11
League to Enforce Peace, 8
Least-developed countries, 147, 154–155
Lebanon, 62–64, 182–183, 198
Libya, 133
Lie, Trgve, 43
Limited Test Ban Treaty, 106
Lithuania, 14, 36

Locarno Pacts, 14
Lodge, Henry Cabot, 8–10
Lumumba, Patrice, 65
Luxumburg, 103
Lytton, Lord, 17

MacArthur, Douglas, 42–43, 46-7
Macedonia, 207
Makarios, Archbishop, 74
Malta, 127
Manchukuo (*see* Manchuria)
Manchuria, 16–18
Mandates, 11
Mao Zedong, 43
Membership issues, 29, 34–38
Middle East (*see* Middle East wars)
Middle East wars, 48–63, 184, 196–199
Military Armistice Commission, 48
Mitrany, David, 2
    (*See also* Functionalism)
Molotov, V. M., 26
Morgenthau, Hans, 21
Multilateral corporations (MNCs), 155–159
Mussolini, Benito, 18–21
Mutual Assured Destruction (MAD), 108–109

Nasser, Gamal, 52, 54, 57, 60
Nicaragua, 93–94
Nixon, Richard, 60, 76, 107–108
Nonproliferation Treaty, 107
North Korea, 35–36, 41–48, 79, 182, 199–200
Nuclear arms agreements, 99–115

Pakistan, 68–72
Peace Ballot, 21
Peaceful Nuclear Explosion Treaty, 105, 106

Reagan, Ronald, 99–100, 109–110, 111, 112
Russia, 95, 113, 114
(*See also* Soviet Union)

Sandinistas, 94
San Francisco Conference, 27
Santa Cruz, Hernando, 156
Sarajevo, 87–88
Saudi Arabia, 84
Scotia, 119
Secretary general, 179–186
Self-determination, 12
Senegal River, 145–146
Serbia, 86–88, 206
Sihanouk, Prince, 78
Skyjacking, 134
Slovenia, 86, 88
Somalia, 88–90, 208–209
South Africa, 125
South Korea, 35–36, 41–48, 182, 199–200
South-West Africa court case, 125
Soviet Union, 26, 39–40, 42, 43–44, 48, 52, 65–68, 72–73, 81–82, 84, 99, 102–104, 106, 108–113, 114, 121–122, 157, 186, 189, 197, 201
START Treaty, 112, 113, 114
Stimson Doctrine, 17
Suez War, 52–54, 182
Sweden, 50
Syria, 61, 62, 63

Taiwan, 35, 43, 46
Terrorism, 63, 129–133
Thailand, 78
Transnational corporations (TNCs), 155–159
Truman, Harry, 5, 27, 28, 40, 45, 46, 51, 79
Trusteeship Council, 11

Tshombe, President, 65, 201
Turkey, 14–15, 67–68

Ukraine, 27, 36
UN Angola Verification Mission, 90, 209
UN Assistance Mission Rwanda, 91
UN Charter (*see* Charter, UN)
UN Children's Fund (UNICEF), 148
UN coalitions, 41, 81, 84
(*See also* Bosnian War; Korean War; Haiti; and Somalia)
UN collective security, 202–203, 211, 219
UN Commission for India/Pakistan, 69
UN Commission for the Unification and Rehabilitation of Korea, 46
UN Commission on Human Rights, 119
UN Conference on Law of the Sea, 127
UN Conference on Trade and Development, 142, 154–155
UN Covenant of Economic and Cultural Rights, 119
UN Disengagement Observer Forces (UNDOF), 61
UN Eighteen-Nation Conference on Disarmament, 108
UN Emergency Force I, 55–56
UN Emergency Force II, 61
UN Good Offices Mission for Afghanistan and Pakistan (UNGOMAP), 204
UN Haiti Observation Mission, 94–95
UN High Commissioner for Refugees (UNHCR), 150
UN Human Rights Commission, 135
UN Industrial Development Organization (UNIDO), 176

UN Military Observer Group in India and Pakistan (UNMOGIP), 69, 71
UN Mission for the Referendum in Western Sahara (MINURSO), 90
UN Mission for the Verification of Elections (Nicaragua), 94
UN Operation in El Salvador (ONUSAL), 94
UN Operation in Mozambique (ONUMOZ), 92
UN Operation in Somalia (UNOSOM), 89
UN peacekeeping force in Cyprus (UNFICYP), 74–75
UN Relief and Rehabilitation Administration (UNRRA), 149
UN Security Force in West New Guinea, 202
UN Special Commission on Disarmament, 205
UN Volunteer Program, 146
United Kingdom, 18–26, 40–41, 49–50, 54–55, 68, 74, 85, 96, 101, 196
United States, 17, 18, 21, 39, 40, 51, 52, 63, 85, 96, 97, 102–104, 106, 108, 110–113, 121–122, 152, 186
Universal Declaration of Human Rights, 135
Universal Postal Union, 173

Veto, 26–27
Vietnam War, 75–78

Waldheim, Kurt, 184–185
Washington Naval Conference, 101
West Bank, 63
West Pakistan (*see* Pakistan)
Western Sahara, 209
Wilson, Woodrow, 5, 7, 8, 10, 25–26, 118
World Bank, 164, 165, 166, 167–168
World Court, 124–127
World Health Organization (WHO), 13, 149, 172
World Meteorological Organization, 173–174
World Trade Organization, 174 (*See also* General Agreement on Tariffs and Trade)
World War I, 1, 7, 101
World War II, 22, 26

Yalta, 27
Yugoslavia's War, 86–88, 206–208
Yeltsin, Boris, 36, 113
Young, Andrew, 136

Zagorin, Bernard, 156
Zionists, 49–50